the Unofficial Guide™ to Collecting Antiques

Sonia Weiss

IDG Books Worldwide, Inc.
An International Data Group Company
Foster City, CA • Chicago, IL • Indianapolis, IN
• New York, NY

IDG Books Worldwide, Inc.
An International Data Group Company
919 E. Hillsdale Boulevard
Suite 400
Foster City, CA 94404

For general information on IDG Books Worldwide's books in the U.S., please call our Consumer Customer Service department at 1-800-762-2974. For reseller information, including discounts and previous sales, please call our Reseller Customer Service department at 1-800-434-3422.

ISBN: 0-02-862922-1

Manufactured in the United States of America

10 9 8 7 6 5 4 3

First edition

For all the lovers of fine things and those who are just beginning their journeys. May your eyes and your hearts always be filled with the beauty derived from the fruit of your labors.

Acknowledgments

A huge amount of appreciation goes first and foremost to my assistant on this book. Jim Nearen never lagged in his enthusiasm for this project and was able to endure the rocky parts on more than one occasion. Many thanks go to development editor Kris Fehr for her support and enthusiasm as well.

Without the early direction of the indomitable Harry L. Rinker, this book would be very different from what it is. I am among the many who can credit Harry for influencing their approach to collecting, often in ways that we would never have expected. Antiques lover, attorney, and friend H. Christopher Clark lent his extensive library on American furniture to this project and spent a fair amount of time talking about his experiences as a collector and as a bankruptcy court trustee who was regularly called upon to discern the value of old things.

I owe a supreme debt of gratitude to the collectors and experts in the industry who graciously responded to our requests for information and assistance. They include: Roger Allen, Taylor Baird, private art dealer Gene Barth, auctioneer Ray Demonia, David Demonia, Sherry Heller, interior designer Julie Ann Johnson, Carol Kaplan, Leanne Stella of Stella Shows, and Gail Skelly of Sotheby's.

The *Unofficial Guide* Reader's Bill of Rights

We Give You More Than the Official Line

Welcome to the *Unofficial Guide* series of Lifestyles titles—books that deliver critical, unbiased information that other books can't or won't reveal—*the inside scoop.* Our goal is to provide you with the *most accessible, useful* information and advice possible. The recommendations we offer in these pages are not influenced by the corporate line of any organization or industry; we give you the hard facts, whether those institutions like them or not. If something is ill-advised or will cause a loss of time and/or money, we'll give you ample warning. And if it is a worthwhile option, we'll let you know that, too.

Armed and Ready

Our hand-picked authors confidently and critically report on a wide range of topics that matter to smart readers like you. Our authors are passionate about their subjects, but have distanced themselves enough from them to help you be armed and protected, and help you make educated decisions as you go through the process. It is our intent that, from having read this book, you will avoid the pitfalls everyone else falls into and get it right the first time.

Don't be fooled by cheap imitations; this is the genuine article *Unofficial Guide* series from IDG Books. You may be familiar with our proven track record of the travel *Unofficial Guides*, which have more than three million copies in print. Each year thousands of travelers—new and old—are armed with a brand new, fully updated edition of the flagship *Unofficial Guide to Walt Disney World*, by Bob Sehlinger. It is our intention here to provide you with the same level of objective authority that Mr. Sehlinger does in his brainchild.

The Unofficial Panel of Experts

Every word in the Lifestyle *Unofficial Guides* is intensively inspected by a team of three top professionals in their fields. These experts review the manuscript for factual accuracy, comprehensiveness, and an insider's determination as to whether the manuscript fulfills the credo in this Reader's Bill of Rights. In other words, our Panel ensures that you are, in fact, getting "the inside scoop."

Our Pledge

The authors, the editorial staff, and the Unofficial Panel of Experts assembled for *Unofficial Guides* are determined to lay out the most valuable alternatives available for our readers. This dictum means that our writers must be explicit, prescriptive, and above all, direct. We strive to be thorough and complete, but our goal is not necessarily to have the "most" or "all" of the information on a topic; this is not, after all, an encyclopedia. Our objective is to help you narrow down your options to the best of what is available, unbiased by affiliation with any industry or organization.

In each *Unofficial Guide* we give you:

- Comprehensive coverage of necessary and vital information
- Authoritative, rigidly fact-checked data
- The most up-to-date insights into trends
- Savvy, sophisticated writing that's also readable
- Sensible, applicable facts and secrets that only an insider knows

Special Features

Every book in our series offers the following six special sidebars in the margins that were devised to help you get things done cheaply, efficiently, and smartly.

1. **Timesaver**—tips and shortcuts that save you time

2. **Moneysaver**—tips and shortcuts that save you money

3. **Watch Out!**—more serious cautions and warnings

4. **Bright Idea**—general tips and shortcuts to help you find and easier or smarter way to do something

5. **Quote**—statements from real people that are intended to be prescriptive and valuable to you

6. **Unofficially...**—an insider's fact or anecdote

We also recognize your need to have quick information at your fingertips, and have thus provided the following comprehensive sections at the back of the book:

1. **Glossary**—definitions of complicated terminology and jargon
2. **Resource Lists**—lists of relevant agencies, associations, and institutions
3. **Recommended Reading List**—suggested titles that can help you get more in-depth information on related topics
4. **Index**

Letters, Comments, Questions from Readers

We strive to continually improve the *Unofficial* series, and input from our readers is a valuable way for us to do that.

Many of those who have used the *Unofficial Guide* travel books write to the authors to ask questions, make comments, or share their own discoveries and lessons. For Lifestyle *Unofficial Guides*, we would also appreciate all such correspondence—both positive and critical—and we will make best efforts to incorporate appropriate readers' feedback and comments in revised editions of this work.

How to write to us:
Unofficial Guides
Lifestyle Guides
IDG Books
1633 Broadway
New York, NY 10019
Attention: Reader's Comments

About the Author

Sonia Weiss can tell you everything you need to know about collecting antiques. A reporter and writer for more than 20 years, she was raised around porcelains, glass, and contemporary art, all passionately collected by her parents. As a young adult, Sonia collected antique cameras and Depression glass. She is still an avid collector of items from the Arts and Crafts and Art Nouveau periods, including art glass, pottery, beaded purses, and boxes in various media. Sonia has written many articles on collectibles for *Joy of Collecting* magazine in addition to a number of feature stories on antiques and the people who collect them. In addition to *The Unofficial Guide to Collecting Antiques,* her books include *The Complete Idiot's Guide to Baby Names, The Pocket Idiot's Guide to Baby Names,* and *The Complete Idiot's Guide to Affair-Proof Love,* all for Alpha Books; *The Cigar Enthusiast* (Berkley); and *The Metro Denver Relocation Guide* (Heritage Media Corp.). She contributed to *For the Love of Dogs* and *Hope, Faith & Healing* (Publications International, Ltd.), and the *Jones Encyclopedia of the Information Infrastructure.*

The *Unofficial Guide* Panel of Experts

The *Unofficial* editorial team recognizes that you've purchased this book with the expectation of getting the most authoritative, carefully inspected information currently available. Toward that end, on each and every title in this series, we have selected a minimum of two "official" experts comprising the Unofficial Panel who painstakingly review the manuscripts to ensure the following: factual accuracy of all data; inclusion of the most up-to-date and relevant information; and that, from an insider's perspective, the authors have armed you with all the necessary facts you need—but that the institutions don't want you to know.

For *The Unofficial Guide to Collecting Antiques*, we are proud to introduce the following panel of experts:

Art Maier—Mr. Maier has spent over 30 years appraising, restoring, lecturing on, writing about, and collecting antiques. He has taught at New York University and is the author of the *House of Collectibles Official Guide to Antiques and*

Collectibles. He is a consultant to various auction houses in the United States and Europe.

John Coker—Mr. Coker has operated a 10,000 square foot antique shop in Eastern Tennessee for the past 29 years. His business includes appraisals, estate auctions, buying, selling, and private brokering. He exhibits at major national antiques shows and on his Web site, www.antiquesonline.com, where he features over 3,000 items in stock. Mr. Coker can be seen appraising antiques on PBS's "Treasures In Your Attic," currently shown on 112 PBS Stations.

James Kettlewell—Mr. Kettlewell is a consultant and lecturer with Kettlewell Fine Arts. A graduate of Harvard University, where he received his A.B. degree in art history and his A.M. degree from the Fine Arts Department, Mr. Kettlewell continued in Harvard's museum studies program and was a Fulbright scholar in the history of art at the Courtauld Institute of the University of London.

Mr. Kettlewell has taught at Harvard, the University of Toronto, and Skidmore College, where he continues to teach a museum course, even though he is technically retired. He has vast experience in museum work, including serving as the founding curator of the Museum of Art in Ogunquit, Maine, and curator of the Hyde Collection in Glens Falls, N.Y. For eight years he was the director of the Gallery Association of New York State, an organization of all the museums in the state. He is a passionate collector of art and antiques from all over the world and from every culture.

Introduction

For a country that is often chastised for creating a "throwaway culture," the United States is actually filled with people who are also passionate collectors. Be it primitive fishing lures, Star Wars figurines, or nineteenth century Gothic furniture, there are few among us who can't lay claim to having some cherished objects in our possession that we have either gladly inherited or actively sought.

If you are very new to the world of antiques, there's a good chance that you were lured to it by the overwhelming popularity of *Antiques Roadshow*, the top-rated PBS series that entered its third year of production in 1999, or by published reports of other amazing finds. After all, it's hard not to be taken with stories like Claire Beckman, the schoolteacher from Secausus, N.J., who paid $25 for a rickety old table at an estate sale and ended up with a rare antique worth between $250,000 to $300,000; or the fellow who brought in an old sword that a neighbor gave him, only to have it identified as a Confederate army blade worth $60,000.

A pickle bottle from the early 1800s, found in a Massachusetts tag sale in April, 1999, for $3, brought more than $44,000 through a sale conducted by the online auction house eBay. The Maine Antique Digest, an antiques industry newspaper that reported on this sale, quoted the bottle's discoverer, former dealer Richard Rushton-Clem, as saying he knew nothing about bottles, but "when you recognize something of quality, you buy it." It's enough to send one off on a search through Granny's attic, or to make you regret that such a thing no longer exists in your life.

While the search for a truly remarkable piece can be a viable motivation for becoming a collector, we believe that it's one that will cause you more heartache than give you pleasure in the long run. Despite what you see on television or read in the papers, your chances of finding a high-priced, undiscovered treasure are decidedly slim.

A far better motivation, in our estimation, is to be an astute collector of items that you love. Should you happen to stumble across the Holy Grail along the way, it will come as the icing on the cake rather than the sum total of your efforts. The idea when collecting antiques is to enjoy the journey—that is, the process of collecting should be as enjoyable as the end results. Focus too strongly on the brass ring and you'll miss out on the fun along the way.

Something Old, Something New

It may come as a surprise to you, however, that the boom in collecting older items is a somewhat recent phenomenon. For a number of years, our "throw-away" reputation was a better fit than not. Although many people respected the value in old items and preferred them over new, many more were just as glad to exchange dated styles and seemingly fussy patterns for newer, more up-to-date objects.

Anyone born during the baby boom years following World War II (today the largest segment of the American population) is likely to have been raised without a great appreciation of old furniture, china, paintings, jewelry, and other items, for the simple reason that his or her parents probably didn't place much importance on them. The boom economy that followed World War II created a society that could buy new things after many years of denial, and Americans did so in droves. As they acquired new belongings, the old ones were often relegated to a less-favored status and stored, sold, or even given away.

Like all passions, the desire for everything new didn't last forever. Today, more and more of us are seeking out the objects that our parents and grandparents were only too happy to be rid of, scouring antiques shows, auctions, tag sales, and thrift shops for items that recall what came before us rather than those that reflect where we are today. So great is our desire to connect to our past that we even snap up pieces that are new but made to look old—sometimes knowingly, other times not.

There also are more opportunities to explore when it comes to finding and buying the objects of your desire, which you'll read about in Chapter 7, "Antiques on the Internet," and Chapter 10, "Buying Online." While there will always be antiques malls and galleries, shows, and auctions, the antiques industry is erasing its physical boundaries through high technology, especially the Internet. If you don't care for browsing antiques shops and malls, you can do it online. If you don't have access to the top shows and auctions, they can literally come to you instead.

The World Wide Web has been a tremendous boon to the antiques arena, opening it to new markets and new groups of collectors, and, frankly, revitalizing the industry as a whole. Not so long ago, collectors found themselves shut out of certain markets or auctions if they didn't have ready access to them or have someone who could represent their interests. Those days are quickly fading, thanks to eBay and the other online auction sites that have sprung up in the past several years.

So great is the potential represented by buying and selling antiques on the Internet that even the top auction houses have Web sites for e-trading or are in the process of establishing them. Others, like Butterfield & Butterfield, are entering into strategic alliances with companies that already have established presences on the 'Net. Doing so gives them a leg up on their competition and a chance to capture this particular audience before the others do.

While some may decry the Internet's influence on the antiques industry, we think it is more positive than negative. Yes, there are unscrupulous sellers lurking online, but you're just as likely to find them on solid ground as well. There's an air of caveat emptor to Internet transactions, but it exists (or should exist) in face-to-face dealings as well. These are inevitable, inescapable facets of the antiques business (and many others, we should add), and the best way to handle them is to be as knowledgeable and as savvy about what you're doing as you can be.

Why You Need This Book

For everything that is so alluring about collecting antiques, there is the dark side to the equation as well. For every story of an incredible find, there's one of stunning hoax. The excited buyer of a rare Tiffany lamp later finds out that the deal of the century she thought she was getting is an inspired fake. The buyer of a rare set of porcelain candlesticks through an online auction ends up with objects made of paste that are clearly cheap reproductions.

No one is immune to this—even the experts can tell stories of times when they've crashed and burned on pieces that they could have sworn were the real thing. Most *Roadshow* attendees end up with possessions that appraise out at about what they paid, or that are worth far less than they thought. While it's true that one person's junk may be another's treasure, it's just as true that one person's junk is exactly that—junk—regardless of who owns it. What is believed to be gold can often turn to dross, and routinely does in the hands of a skilled appraiser.

The focus of this book is to help you learn how to collect antiques if you are new to this particular pursuit, to help you become a better collector if you're already firmly entrenched in it, and to help you avoid the missteps that can make the collecting experience less than what it should be. Drawing from our own experiences, we know the thrill of the chase and the joy of acquiring really fine, highly desired pieces. We also know how mysterious and off-putting the antiques industry can seem, especially if you're new to the game or if you're venturing into an arena—such as an online auction—that is unfamiliar to you. It is our goal to help you leapfrog the awkward learner state, regardless of your individual situation, and be a proficient collector at all stages of your collecting career.

These are truly wonderful times to be a collector, especially a collector of antiques. The industry itself is far more comprehensive and inclusive than ever before, with many of the old stigmas about what it takes to classify an item as an antique having fallen by the wayside. Although there are still the purists who believe that anything manufactured after the early 1800s is of the modern era and not worthy of antique designation, they are by far the minority. Because of this, many more items are considered antique today, with more antiques categories and more pieces available for acquisition. Chapter 1, "The Allure of Antiques," will introduce you to the major categories and give you a good idea of what's most desirable to today's collectors.

Collecting antiques is popular for many reasons, and it can truly become a lifelong passion. Because there are so many facets to explore and avenues to travel in the antiques arena as a whole, collecting is something that you can grow into and that will grow with you. It can begin as a singular pursuit mounted by one family member and become a favorite pastime for all. It can be shared by a husband and wife, brother and sister, mother and daughter, father and son. The fruits of such labors can result in a wonderful collection that can—and should—be enjoyed now, and you'll find specific tips on how to do this in Chapter 14, "Decorating with Antiques." Throughout the book you'll find tips on creating a special legacy to hand down to future generations if you so choose. In Chapter 12, "Becoming a Seller," and Chapter 13, "Selling Options," you'll also learn how to tell when it's the right time to sell and how you can decide the selling option that's right for you.

In addition to the pure sense of satisfaction that can be gained by amassing a thorough, carefully planned collection, there are innumerable lessons to be learned along the way. While there is no way to predict the results of your particular pursuits in the antiques arena, we have no doubts that your experiences as a collector will significantly enrich your life.

Being an astute collector takes a variety of strong skills and will have you exercising little-used abilities or gaining proficiency in completely new areas. It's not uncommon to see a timid soul become a skilled, aggressive negotiator after a few years of interacting with dealers. Auctions may be daunting, especially if you don't consider yourself much of a gambler, but attending a few might reveal nerves of steel that you never before thought you possessed.

There's a good chance that you'll meet some interesting people along the way, and that you'll be able to tell more than one interesting story about how you acquired some of your most prized pieces. Over time, some of your most cherished memories may surround your collecting pursuits, which enhances the value of your experiences even further.

Few collectors have regrets when it comes to their efforts. Of course, mistakes are sometimes made and disappointments felt, but this is true of all pursuits. Most will tell you that their only regret is that they didn't start before they did, or that they didn't pursue certain items or areas of collecting, believing they were too expensive or off-limits for some reason or another.

While you may have similar reservations, don't let them keep you from jumping into the collecting waters. You may come to find that your fears were unfounded. You might even discover something even more wonderful to pursue. But you won't know until you actually start collecting, and there's no time like the present to begin.

What They Are and Why We Want Them

PART I

GET THE SCOOP ON...
The new breed of collectors ▪ What makes
something antique ▪ The difference between
antiques and collectibles ▪ Antiques periods
and styles

The Allure of Antiques

Millions and millions of different objects make up the world of antiques, but they all share three common traits: They were made some time ago, they have distinctive stylistic traits that clearly associate them with a phase of cultural history, and they sell in an established market.

In other words, they're old, they have a place in history, and people want them. These basic characteristics have defined the concept of "antique" from the beginning.

People decide to collect antiques for many reasons. Chief among these are the desire to own things of beauty, things of historical significance, things that connect them back to a particular heritage, or things that are functional and that have withstood the test of time. Your reasons are probably similar to these. If so, you're feeding a part of your psyche that you may not have been aware of until now. People have always collected things, be it rocks for making tools and weapons during prehistoric times or Oriental rugs in the modern era. The urge to hunt and gather, in fact, is deeply programmed in our genetic coding. Some people feel the urge to collect more strongly than others, but there's no denying that there are more collectors than there are people who don't feel this particular passion. Some estimates suggest that more than 20 million Americans collect something, with thousands more joining their ranks every year.

The desire to acquire things that are old and of value appears in some of the earliest available records of civilization. During biblical times, for example, the Egyptians filed a claim with Alexander the Great requesting that the Jews return the gold and antiquities that had been taken from them. The Romans were also noted collectors and liked to acquire the plunder from the countries they conquered. They weren't unfamiliar with auctions, either. In A.D. 193, the entire Roman empire was offered up to the highest bidder following the murder of the emperor, Pertinax, by the Praetorian Guard. Archaeologists working on digs often encounter the prior plundering of tombs and graves by individuals looking not just for gold but also for other objects buried within that could be sold to collectors eager to own rare antiquities.

Unofficially...
According to Sigmund Freud, collecting is nothing more than a "redirection of surplus libido onto an inanimate object."

A changing arena

Collecting today is a grander passion than ever before, with more people actively pursuing and acquiring the objects of their desire. The world of collecting, and specifically of collecting antiques, has changed substantially in the past decade as well. Its musty, stuffy image as a pursuit for the wealthy has been replaced by one that is vastly more democratic. Searching for antiques has indeed become a pastime for the masses.

A new breed of collector

Part of the reason behind the evolution of collect-ing lies in the demographics of the American popu-lation today—specifically, the influence of the baby boom generation. As a whole, baby boomers have more disposable income and time to invest in leisure activities, be it racing cars or collecting Coca-Cola memorabilia. For whatever reason, these indi-viduals have also developed into a highly nostalgic generation.

The recognition of these particular trends among baby boomers drove antiques auction houses, long seen as bastions of elitism and wealth in the antiquing world, to change their ways. When their revenues began to flatten in the 1980s, antiques auction houses recognized the need to attract new audiences. Not only were fewer people able to afford the rare and high-priced objects for which auction houses were renowned for bringing to market (although, to be honest, they have always offered pieces in all price ranges), the objects them-selves were becoming increasingly hard to come by.

Rather than continue to cater to the clientele who could afford these items and devote a great deal of time and effort—not to mention expense—to tracking the items down, the major houses decided it was time to bring in younger clients. As a group, these younger individuals, who had money to spend, had largely stayed away from auction houses. They viewed such establishments as stuffy, snobby places that probably wouldn't have anything they liked even if they could afford to buy it. And, frankly, they often felt intimidated by the institu-tions themselves, which seemed like private clubs that you had to know the secret password to enter.

The auction houses realized that to reach these new collectors, they would have to offer items that would attract them. A fresh appeal had to be found, and it largely came by way of celebrity auctions. These highly promoted events, which began with the Duchess of Windsor sale in 1987, caught the fancy of millions of people. These new buyers may have recognized the names Christie's and Sotheby's, but before such auctions, they may never have thought of them as places where anything but rare antiques could be found.

Through such auctions as the Duchess of Windsor and the Andy Warhol and Jacqueline Kennedy Onassis events that followed, average citizens realized that they too could purchase a piece of history, and that they didn't have to spend hundreds of thousands of dollars to do it. Certainly, many pieces that went under the hammer at these auctions did command high prices—JFK's humidor, for example, netted $574,000 at the Onassis auction, and a mere tape measure sold for $48,875. But it also was possible to pick up smaller items—say, a silver coaster with Jackie's initials on it that was undoubtedly part of a set at one time—for significantly less money.

The rise of collectibles

These auctions focused more on newer pieces than on bona fide antiques for the simple reason that they were objects that the celebrities possessed. Although antiques were presented in all three auctions—Warhol, for example, owned an impressive collection of Early American furniture from the eighteenth and nineteenth centuries, which was auctioned along with his more contemporary collections—the newer pieces captured the interest of younger collectors.

Money had little to do with the popularity of these items, as many of them went for tremendously high prices. Rather, the younger collectors felt a stronger connection to items that were more of their generation that those of their parents or grandparents.

For lack of a better term, these pieces came to be designated as *collectibles*. In the antiques arena, this term describes goods that fall into the gray area between old and new. They will eventually be antiques, but they're too young, or they are items that are not traditionally viewed as antiques, such as lunch boxes, old comic books, and old movie and advertising memorabilia. Some collectors prize collectibles as highly as others value antiques that are hundreds of years old.

What causes an item to be considered a collectible rather than an antique is the source of endless debate in the collecting world. While there is no firm definition of "collectible" (or at least, not one that the majority of people can agree on), the following factors are often used to define them:

- They are of modern manufacture—primarily from 1945 on—and employ modern manufacturing techniques.

- There is an established collecting category for them, which means that enough people are actively acquiring them to make them desirable. These items can be found in price guides devoted to collectibles, which cover items that run the gamut from Depression glass and pottery to Barbie dolls and lunch boxes from the 1950s.

Unofficially...
At the Andy Warhol "garage sale of the century" auction in 1988, a $20 Fred Flintstone wristwatch sold for $2,000.

■ They have an established secondary market. Like antiques, they can be purchased from other collectors, from dealers, and at auctions, rather than at retail stores that have received the items directly from manufacturers and distributors.

In some respects, the term "collectible" is a mismatch when used in conjunction with the term "antique," as it often is. Antique is both a noun and an adjective and relates to qualities of age and value, while collectible only very recently became both, and the traditional use of the term has nothing to do with age and value at all. In fact, it's really a misnomer to call certain objects, such as furniture from the Art Deco era, "collectibles" merely because they're too young to qualify as antiques in the textbook sense, which I'll get to later in this chapter. You'll find that many collectors and dealers prefer to call them antiques as they feel that the collectibles designation doesn't fit them at all, while others will refer to them as "semi-antiques," "antiques-in-waiting," or just "old."

From an age perspective, *vintage* is probably the better word to use to describe older items that are not yet antique, but the term has never been widely used, perhaps because of its strong identification with wine production. While you'll hear collectors refer to items such as vintage automobiles or vintage clothing as things from earlier times, vintage as a noun is almost never used in referring to something that is collected.

There is another category of items, also called collectibles, that has virtually nothing to do with the items I've just discussed. They are mass-market pieces, such as plates, figurines, mugs, and plush toys, generally manufactured in huge quantities

Watch Out!
If you're collecting items that are truly antiques, don't refer to them as collectibles. To most antique collectors, the term describes something far different from what you—and they—are collecting.

(literally in the tens or even hundreds of thousands) as commemorative items or in a series featuring the work of one artist or another.

There is no denying that these items have their appeal; witness the feeding frenzy surrounding Beanie Babies, for example. However, they are intended for another audience entirely and do not fall into the definition of the word "collectible" as it is used in the antiques business for the following reasons:

- They are designed and produced for the sole purpose of being collected and are promoted as such. A good example are the collectible Barbie dolls that are designed, manufactured, and promoted as investment pieces, primarily for adult collectors. These are not dolls that kids would play with; they're made to be put on a shelf and admired. Their value is based on what they might be worth if a secondary market develops for them, rather than traditional factors such as age and rarity.

- Their usefulness is often limited. Again, there is a big difference between a Barbie doll that a child can play with and her compatriots that are designed to be put on a shelf and admired. Many collectibles are produced for decorative purposes only and serve very little function beyond this. Items in the other collectibles category were almost always produced to be used, not just admired.

- They rarely appreciate greatly in value and generally come to be worth about what the buyer paid for them. The intrinsic value in these pieces is often quite low. Because of this, they don't hold their value anywhere near as well as antiques do, and they don't even compare well to the other category of collectibles. Their value can even drop, especially if a viable secondary market does not develop for them. Some of the older and rarer pieces, however, have become fair investment vehicles for their buyers.

Many collectors of antiques look down their noses at the first category of collectibles, and they literally sneer at items in the second category, but they really shouldn't. Such items can and have served an important role in the whole conundrum of collecting. Many collectors have started out acquiring these pieces only to have their interests kindled in older and better pieces in the same genre once they've learned more about what they are doing or are better able to afford them.

They are also a reasonable introduction to the world of collecting for children who exhibit an early interest in it. The child with a fondness for Beanie Babies today might be the antique teddy bear collector of tomorrow. I developed a passion for glass objects at a very young age when I started collecting cheap little figurines of horses and dogs, my two favorite animals. Today, as a collector of old and antique boxes in various media, two of my favorite pieces are Lalique powder boxes manufactured in the early 1900s, which I began to covet as my knowledge of glass—and especially art glass—developed and deepened over the years.

Some of the really unique collectibles that are being produced today may very well become worthy of being called antiques when the time comes. For example, such objects as the intricately carved animal figurines produced by Great Britain-based

Harmony Kingdom—especially the earlier and limited-edition pieces—would be some that I'd put in this category because of their fine manufacture and workmanship. To dismiss these objects and some others of contemporary craftsmanship as unworthy of such an eventual distinction would not only be shortsighted but just plain wrong.

For the most part, however, such items currently should be collected only if they appeal to you, and not for any value that they might acquire down the road.

Collectibles vs. antiques

Using the term "collectible" to denote pieces that could someday be antiques but currently aren't because they're too new forces the obvious question: At what age do items earn the "antique" designation? As you can imagine, this determination inspires great debate in the collecting arena. The consensus, if there is one, is this: It all depends on who you ask.

For many years, there have been two common lines of demarcation used in the antiques industry for this distinction:

- Anything made before 1830. This particular year was originally established as a cutoff date by the U.S. government, which, following the stock market crash of 1929, passed a tariff act imposing duty taxes on foreign-made items entering the United States. To help protect the interests of American manufacturers while the economy recovered, the government decided to tax foreign objects made after 1830; anything crafted prior to that year was deemed an antique and was not subject to duty taxes.

The mere passage of time eventually will elevate many of today's collectibles categories into the antiques sector.
—Harry Rinker, *Rinker on Collectibles*
99

The government chose 1830 as a cutoff point primarily because it was a century prior to 1930, which was when the tariff act was adopted. From a historical perspective, it made some sense as well—it's only a decade after 1820, the year generally understood to mark the beginning of the Industrial Revolution and the advent of machine-made products. Since objects made prior to mechanization were handmade, they couldn't be produced in significant quantities, making them rarer, harder to find, and more expensive. For these reasons, they appealed to a significantly smaller audience and didn't pose much of a threat to the American manufacturing industry.

Some people refer to items made prior to 1830 as antiquities because they can be extremely rare, difficult to find, and expensive. However, the term "antiquity" is more appropriately used to describe items of truly ancient times, such as artifacts from ancient Greece, Rome, or Egypt.

66
How old must an item be to be considered a 'collectible'? Less than 100 years old (because at that age it legally becomes an 'antique'), but more than one minute old.
—Ralph and Terry Kovel, *Kovels on Antiques and Collectibles*, July 1999
99

- Anything that is at least 100 years old. This definition, which is used by the majority of collectors and dealers, came about in 1960 when the government revised the tariff regulations it adopted in 1930. The government still uses this definition today, which has a lot to do with it being so prevalent. The other reason why it's accepted by so many people is purely psychological; it's very easy to think of anything durable enough to survive a century as an antique.

- More recently, a third dividing line has also entered the arena. You may also hear the year 1945 used to separate antiques and collectibles, especially by collectors who collect in this category (the one that relates to antiques, not the other one I discussed previously). This is a very liberal date, but it's one that often works well for these collectors because it allows them to call many pieces antique that most people wouldn't put in this category. By this definition, such things as Depression glass would be considered antique, since most of it was made prior to 1945.

For the purposes of this book, items that were made 100 years ago or earlier definitely qualify for the antiques label. However, it's difficult to talk about collecting antiques without considering some of the really lovely objects that are still waiting in the wings, so I'm not going to exclude these items from the discussion. If you're a fan of Art Deco furniture or early Roseville pottery or even movie memorabilia from the 1920s, the information in this book applies to you, too. I personally have a harder time thinking of items that are manufactured later than 1930 or so as antiques because they're too close to where my own memories start, so that's where my own, very arbitrary, line of demarcation is.

As you can see, when you go beyond the generally accepted date at which objects become antiques, it becomes much more a matter of opinion. And perhaps that's as it should be. Far too many collectors get hung up on issues of age rather than focusing on what's really important about an object—its quality and its desirability. As you'll read in Chapter 3, "Understanding Value," age is by no means the most important factor that's considered when assessing how much something is worth. While it's an important consideration, it's not at the

Moneysaver
Not being tied into age when considering buying a piece can save you from spending lots of money on an item that carries a high price primarily because it's old.

top of the list. Remember, "antique" is both a noun and an adjective. It can mean an old, sought-after object of high value, or it can mean an old piece of junk. Calling something an antique isn't necessarily a valuable distinction if other factors, such as quality craftsmanship, classic lines, or historical importance, aren't also in the picture.

Other factors can also influence opinions on when an item becomes old enough to be an antique, including:

- **Location.** If you're living on the East Coast, there's a good chance that you'll use an earlier date at which you consider pieces to be antique than if you lived in the West. While this may seem odd, consider that cities on the East Coast were some of the first to be settled in this country, and the objects you're likely to find in any of them tend to be older as well.

  As you travel west, both the cities and the objects they contain get progressively younger (for the most part, anyway). The great city of San Francisco is a shining exception to this rule due to its historic role as a port of entry; it was much easier to ship pieces of value, especially large items like furniture, by sea rather than by land. But most families relocating to the West went by stagecoach and generally left the majority of these items behind and replaced them with pieces that were made locally. In later years, when relocations were done by train or truck, a greater number of heirloom pieces were brought West, but many large items were often left back because it was cheaper and easier to replace them than to ship them.

▪ **The age of the collector.** As people get older, their perceptions of many things change, including how they regard the world around themselves. Remember "Don't trust anyone over 40," the protestors' adage from the 1960s? If you're anywhere near this age, you know how much your attitude has changed as 40 begins to seem not as old as it once did. Older collectors are generally more likely to dismiss newer pieces from the antique designation— such as 1950s and '60s memorabilia, for example—than are younger collectors with shorter memories to whom such pieces do seem old. While I'll have a hard time classifying objects from the 1950s as antiques for as long as I live, I can see why people in their 20s think that something like a manual typewriter from the 1940s is an antique. The time when these machines were used so far predates their memories and life experiences that they truly seem like relics to them.

▪ **Your emotions and feelings about the object before you.** Here's another interesting fact when it comes to collectors' opinions: They tend to be more ready to classify the things they like as antiques than those they don't. For example, if a collector's taste tends to run to Victorian-era furniture, chances are pretty good that the collector wouldn't think of Art Deco furniture or Art Nouveau lamps as antiques. However, the collectors of such pieces certainly would.

This last point illustrates a key philosophy in collecting: You have to be true to yourself. How you feel about various items and how they relate to your

66
Antiques are revered, sought after, and collected for reasons beyond that of their age, and for this reason the other qualities which they possess must become part of their definition.
—Timothy Trent Blade, *Antique Collecting: A Sensible Guide to Its Art and Mystery*
99

own life experiences should shape your opinions and collecting patterns more than anything else.

Antiques categories—old and new

Before collectibles entered into the picture—in fact, dating back to when the first antiques auction houses were established—a well-defined group of items were traditionally collected as antiques. Even with the collapse of boundaries between old and new that we have today, most people still think of the following items when they hear the word "antique":

- **Furniture:** The largest antiques category, it includes pieces of English, German, French, and American manufacture, and is usually identified by style (for example, Mission or Queen Anne) rather than artist or manufacturer. Of all the categories, furniture is the most archetypical as it contains distinct and obvious stylistic phases that can be more clearly identified than in other kinds of antiques.

- **Silver:** This category includes sterling, silverplate and, especially, English Sheffield plate.

- **Fine Art:** Watercolors, oils, drawings, sculptures, and religious icons all fall within this category.

- **Ceramics:** Another large collecting category, it includes Chinese porcelain, French porcelain, English pottery, German pottery, and American pottery. Most often identified by manufacturer; for example, Rookwood (American), Kähler (Denmark), or Minton (English).

- **Glass:** Pressed glass, cut glass, and cranberry glass all fall within this category. Identified by either type (cranberry, pressed, aventurine), country or place of origin (Roman, Bristol, Bohemian), or artist/manufacturer (Daum, Tiffany, Baccarat, Lalique).

When the supply of traditional antiques began to dry up in the 1980s, the purveyors of such items had to look to new sources for their inventory. By necessity, the traditional antiques categories were expanded to include the following "new" antiques. While little consensus has been reached on what the main categories of antiques are today, adding these to the categories already mentioned will give you a fairly comprehensive list:

- **Textiles:** This category includes oriental rugs and rugs of other manufacture, quilts, household linens, needlework (such as samplers), Navajo blankets, and clothing.

- **Lighting and lamps:** Described by manufacturer (Tiffany, Handel, Durand) or form (lantern, miner's, candle).

- **Metals:** This category includes pieces made of iron, pewter, brass, or copper, ranging from mugs and plates to doorstops and fire irons.

- **Toys:** Dolls, teddy bears, mechanical toys, banks, trains, and other playthings come under this category.

- **Jewelry:** This category includes bracelets, rings, and other items of adornment. Some collectors include watches in this category; others prefer to group them with clocks and instruments.

- **Books and manuscripts:** This category includes first editions and other rare works. A related category, ephemera, consists of other paper items, such as signatures, important letters, and other documents.

- **Clocks and instruments:** This category includes pieces of English, French, German, and American manufacture of all sizes.

In addition to these, several popular catchall categories exist in today's antiques arena. They include

- **Advertising items,** ranging from posters and calendars to service trays, tins, and other items produced to promote various products.

- **Civil War and other military items,** such as swords, knives, guns, letters, uniforms, pictures, and paintings.

- **Artifacts of the Old West,** including paintings, photographs, spurs, saddles, pottery, blankets, and rugs.

- **Maritime antiques,** such as ship models, compasses, logs, and other items found on commercial and noncommercial boats and ships.

- **Household items,** including baskets, food molds, weather vanes, whirligigs, and more.

- **Sporting goods,** such as decoys, fishing tackle, and various gaming equipment (balls, bats, and similar objects).

The majority of the pieces discussed throughout this book will fall into these categories.

Antiques styles and periods

One of the most confusing aspects about antiques collecting for beginning collectors, and even for some who are more experienced, is understanding the terminology used to define and describe antiques. Why this is so confusing is that the same term often refers to a period and a style. A piece of Victorian furniture, for example, exhibits certain design characteristics that mark it as being in this style. That same piece of furniture could also have been produced during the Victorian era or period, which would then make it a "period" piece as well. If that piece had been made, instead, anytime after the era (styles generally extend beyond the period when they were first introduced), then it would be referred to as a "Victorian-style" piece.

To make matters even more complicated, pieces in the Victorian style were not the only ones made during the Victorian period. For example, in the United States, furniture in the Shaker style was also being produced. Then there are broader design movements, such as Classicism, Neoclassicism, and Arts and Crafts, that influenced styles as well.

Unless you're collecting furniture, you don't need to know everything there is to know about every period, style, and movement. Even if you do end up in this collecting arena, you'll probably get to know a great deal about the pieces you choose to collect and not that much about the others. However, it's often helpful to have a general under-standing of what the main periods, styles, and influ-ences are, regardless of what you're collecting, so you can understand what's being said when you hear them and have an idea of what they look like.

What follows are the periods and styles that you're likely to run across during your search for antiques. To make things easier, I've organized them chronologically—this will also help you see how they overlap, when they do. Brief descriptions are also given to provide a general idea of their design elements and when they appeared; however, your best bet for understanding them in depth is through studying books on antique furniture. You'll find several suggestions listed in Appendix C,

"Further Reading." When dates are given, they denote when the style took shape in the United States, not in Europe, as American periods often lagged behind European by at least 20 years.

Jacobean

Unofficially...
Newspaper publisher William Randolph Hearst was so enamored of Jacobean furniture that he brought back roomfuls of it to decorate the California mansion that he shared with actress Marion Davies, according to George Grotz, *Grotz's Antique Furniture Styles.*

King James I (1603–1625) was the ruling monarch when the earliest American colonies were founded. Furniture from this period is called Jacobean in his honor (the English name James is derived from the Hebrew name Jacob). In England, Jacobean furniture was made on a grand scale to furnish large castles. In both England and America, it was almost entirely made of oak because this wood was best suited to the weight of these massive pieces. To help support their weight, Jacobean furniture pieces often had stretchers, or slats, connecting their legs to give them added stability. They're often ornately carved with leaves and floral designs.

Jacobean-style furniture underwent a revival in the United States during the Roaring Twenties. Reproductions of Jacobean furniture, which were often given the generic name "Baronial," were also made during this period.

William and Mary (1700–1725)

An eighteenth-century English style named after the Dutch king and queen who ruled England near the end of the century. In England, these pieces were distinguished by their elaborate lathe-turned legs in the Baroque style, deep carvings, strong curves, and contrasting colors created by lacquering (also called "japanning"), a design touch from the Orient. A simpler version of this style was developed by American cabinetmakers, with a tapering scroll foot (also called a Spanish foot). The wing chair was introduced during this period.

Queen Anne (1725–1755)

A more fluid style than the William and Mary period that preceded it, the lines of Queen Anne furniture were simple and graceful, characterized by scrolls and sinuous "s" curves. If ornamented, the carving is very simple, almost exclusively confined to a shell motif.

Chippendale (1755–1780)

Named after the English cabinetmaker Thomas Chippendale, who published a book called the *Gentleman and Cabinet-Makers Director* in 1754. Chippendale combined elements from two styles—French Rococo and Gothic—and threw in some Chinese ornamentation for good measure to come up with a unique style all his own. Pieces exhibiting Chippendale style did not appear until after his book was printed. Distinguishing elements of Chippendale style include claw-and-ball feet at the ends of cabriole legs and the open back splat on chairs.

Another popular style that cropped up during the Chippendale era was the Windsor chair. Originally an English design, it also became very popular in the United States. It is instantly recognized by its construction: Pieces made in this fashion have a plank seat to which stick legs and spindles are attached. This very durable style is still popular today.

Federal (1780–1820)

This furniture style was influenced by the revival of classical design elements that comprised Neoclassicism, the style that swept through Europe after the ancient Roman ruins of Herculaneum and Pompeii were excavated in 1738 and 1748. It is distinguished by straight lines rather than curved, and classical decorative devices such as the Greek key and the urn.

The American interpretation of Neoclassicism relied heavily on design books created by two Englishmen: George Hepplewhite's *Cabinet-Maker and Upholsterer's Guide* and Thomas Sheraton's *Cabinet-Maker and Upholsterer's Drawing Book*. The styles were very similar between the two of them; Hepplewhite's work can be distinguished by pieces with slender, tapered legs with square edges. Sheraton preferred reeded, rounded, slightly vase-shaped legs.

Empire (1820–1840)

The American Empire style was based on the Empire style popular in Europe during Napoleon's time. In Europe, these pieces had massive proportions and were decorated with such Greco-Roman motifs as acanthus leaves and cornucopias. After Napoleon's Egyptian campaign, motifs such as the sphinx and hieroglyphics also became popular. Veneering was also often used on these mahogany and rosewood pieces. In the United States, pieces were also massive and veneering was also widely used. The Greek scroll, the classical column, and the lion's claw foot were common features. Pieces were often elaborately decorated with ormolu. Empire is sometimes called Late Federal.

Victorian (1837–1901)

Many styles from the past were revived and combined to create furniture during the Victorian era. While furniture made during this period can all be called Victorian, there is no single Victorian style. The styles that were commonly seen in furniture during this period include:

- Rococo Revival (1845–1900): Based on the eighteenth-century European Rococo style, Rococo Revival was widely embraced by Americans when it was brought here via design books. It featured fanciful carvings, curved surfaces, and scrollwork in both "s" and "c" forms. These pieces are also characterized by cabriole legs, which more than suited their curvaceous forms. John Henry Belter was the American cabinetmaker most strongly associated with the Rococo Revival style; he liked it so much that he created a special laminating process that could be curved for use on these pieces.

- Renaissance Revival (1860–1885): Pieces in the Renaissance Revival style are characterized by straight, rectangular forms rather that the curved and flowing lines of Rococo. Decoration was heavy and showy, with lots of medallions and trim. Many pieces incorporate bronze, porcelain, or mother of pearl plaques.

- Gothic Revival (1825–1865): This design style incorporated Gothic arches, quatrefoils, and trefoils to lend a medieval feeling to pieces. It was more popular in England than America and was used more in American architecture than furniture.

- Eastlake Style (1872–1890): Charles Lock Eastlake was an English architect, author, and lecturer who advocated the reform of furniture design, calling for a return to high-quality craftsmanship, an honest use of materials, and the integration of form and function. Pieces based on his philosophies replaced the curving lines of so many of the revival styles with simple rectilinear shapes. His book, *Hints on*

Unofficially...
"Period" antiques
are those made
during the origi-
nal time frame of
the design.
Pieces made in
the fashion or
nature of an ear-
lier period but at
a later time are
correctly referred
to as "in the
style of".

Household Taste, brought his ideals to America when it was published in 1872.

▪ Colonial Revival (1875–1910): Following the Civil War, and especially after America cele-brated its centennial in 1876, a renewed patrio-tism swept the country and awakened an inter-est in America's colonial past. Furniture that was inspired by Colonial styles became extremely popular. Pieces from this period look a great deal like the earliest furniture pro-duced in America, and it is sometimes difficult to tell them apart.

Arts and Crafts (1850–1900)

Based on the Arts and Crafts movement that began in England in the 1850s and spurred by the ideology of Eastlake. This movement, which began in England in the 1850s, was based on a dislike of machine-made objects and stressed simple, hand-made objects that emphasized good workmanship and quality materials. When brought to the United States, it became the influence behind such crafts-men as Gustav Stickley.

Art Nouveau (1895–1915)

Never really popular in the United States, this European movement predated Art Deco by a few years, coming at the close of the Victorian era. It's characterized by a tight "s" curve, called a "whiplash" curve, and ornamentation that made use of organic elements, such as leaves, flowers, and fruit. In the United States, Art Nouveau's influ-ence is seen more in glass and ceramic objects than anything else. The lamps created by Louis Com-fort Tiffany are a good example of Art Nouveau style.

Art Deco (1918–1935)

A twentieth-century French style that took America by storm, this highly stylized fashion made strong use of veneers and lacquer for a sleek, streamlined look. A distinctive element of Art Deco design is the bleached or light-colored wood use to create most of these pieces. Ornamentation was largely limited to simple door pulls and knobs, often made of brass.

Antiques nomenclature

Walk into an antiques shop and you may hear the dealer describe a piece as being "married" or "divorced," or as having "gothic" elements or "cabriole" legs. Does this information have any bearing on what you may end up paying on a given piece? In some cases, yes, as you'll read more about this in the chapters to come. In other cases, what you're hearing are descriptions of specific design elements or other factors that give each antique piece it's own unique quality.

Here are some of the terms you'll hear as you go along:

- **Adapted:** An older, sometimes period piece that has been altered for modern use.

- **Altered:** A piece that has been substantially changed in appearance.

- **Assembled:** A set whose pieces are similar in appearance but do not match. In England, they are referred to as Harlequin sets.

- **Baroque:** Like music in this style, pieces with Baroque styling were popular in the 1600s and early 1700s. Also like Baroque music (think Bach), these pieces were heavily embellished, on a grand scale, and very precise and balanced in design.

Timesaver
Study an illustrated antiques guide before you go hunting for furniture. It can save you many hours of head-scratching.

- **Cabriole:** A design, usually used on the legs of furniture, that curves outward at the knee and inward at the ankle. It almost always ends in a pad foot.

- **Chinoiserie:** Western designs based on those from China.

- **Country:** In the antiques arena, used to describe simple pieces made between the late seventeenth and late nineteenth centuries, usually by rural craftsmen.

- **Divorce:** An item that has been split apart to create two or more new pieces.

- **Gothic:** A design style based on architectural elements commonly found in churches.

- **Marriage:** Two separate pieces that have been joined together to form one.

- **Mission:** The defining style of the Arts and Crafts movement, furniture in this style had a functional "mission," hence the name. Pieces in the Mission style are distinguished by their boxiness and solid appearance. Gustav Stickley is the best-known manufacturer of them, but other designers turned out pieces in this style as well. Architect Frank Lloyd Wright designed a number of pieces in this style to grace the homes he built.

- **Mount:** A pull or other decorative element applied to furniture, made of metal, glass, wood, bone, and other materials.

- **Ormolu:** Gilded brass or bronze, often used on the mounts, feet, and decorative details in late Federal and Empire furnishings.

- **Pad foot:** A simple, curving foot, sometimes set on a cushion-shaped disk. Often used on the legs of Queen Anne furniture.

- **Patina:** The mellow, worn quality that a surface acquires through age and use. It's highly valued on antique furniture.

- **Reeding:** A series of parallel, closely carved ridges or beading.

- **Reconstructed:** A piece that fell apart and was put back together.

- **Refinished:** An item that has had its earlier finish removed and replaced.

- **Reproduction:** Something that is produced as a copy of a style rather than a copy of an exact piece.

- **Restored:** A piece that has been returned to what is believed to be its original appearance. Often used derogatorily.

- **Scroll foot:** Also called a Spanish foot.

- **Shaker:** A furniture style created by the Shakers, a religious sect that came to America from England in 1774. It is simple and functional but by no means plain. Its beauty is in its graceful and delicate lines.

- **Slat:** Also called a stretcher.

- **Splat:** The middle section of a chair back, flanked by uprights on either side.

You'll find other terms listed in Appendix A as well.

Just the facts

- The desire to own objects of beauty is as old as time itself.

- Today's antiques arena includes many objects that once were not considered highly collectible, such as textiles and pottery, that were

added as the sources for traditional antiques
dried up.

■ Many factors must be considered when judging
whether an object is worthy of the "antique"
designation. Age, while important, is only one
of them.

■ Furniture is defined both by period and style.
If a piece of furniture exhibits design elements
of a particular period and was manufactured
during this time, it is called a "period" piece.

GET THE SCOOP ON...
The passion and motivations behind collecting ▪
Tapping into educational resources ▪ The
elements of a collecting philosophy ▪ Being a
wise buyer

Becoming a Collector

The casual collector happens into an antiques shop or show every once in awhile and buys something that catches his or her eye; the seasoned collector shops objectively and carefully with an eye to value. The difference between the two lies not in what each of them has to spend but in how much they know about what they're doing when they buy.

Every pursuit has a learning curve, and collecting antiques is no different. Emotions—and little else—often drive beginning collectors. They lust after certain pieces and strive to own them without knowing whether the pieces are really worth having. While there is nothing wrong with staying at this level, it's an approach that only skims the surface of what collecting is really all about.

Lust and passion are desirable traits for a collector. However, being a successful collector requires the development of a set of skills that goes far beyond emotion. It means having focus and purpose

Chapter 2

> **"**
> I learned to collect by reading everything I could about the things I was interested in, and by asking many, many questions.
> —Antiques collector Roger Allen
> **"**

in your collecting. It takes knowing what to look for and where to find it. In short, it means becoming educated about what you're doing.

It starts with passion

The passion for collecting, most people say, begins much like a relationship with a loved one does. Something catches your eye, or you come across an object that piques your interest. Before you know it, you have a yen. That yen turns into desire, and desire turns into passion.

Ask collectors why they collect the things they do and you'll almost always get an explanation based on how these objects make them feel. "The pieces I love...they give me a high," says private dealer and collector Gene Barth. "They become a living part of me, and I become more alive with them. This, to me, is always how a collector should feel."

If you're just starting out as a collector, this statement may seem a bit extreme. Forming an emotional attachment to an inanimate object, in fact, flies in the face of what most psychologists feel is healthy behavior. But even the great psychotherapist Sigmund Freud professed a deep passion for collecting, which was reflected in the more than 3,000 Greek, Roman, and Egyptian artifacts that he amassed during his lifetime. Perhaps a better way of looking at it is to think of collecting as an extension of who you are as a person. If you approach life with enthusiasm and passion, these traits will also be reflected in your actions as a collector.

If you collect for the right reason—because you love what you are doing—you will derive benefits that go beyond money, status, or recognition, making it one of the most fulfilling experiences of your life. Approach it for the wrong reasons and you'll still gain something, but you'll miss out on the full realization of what your efforts could bring you.

The motivations behind the passion

Passion, clearly, is a key reason for collecting. But passion is only part of the story. Underlying the passion, strong motivating forces drive the deep-seated urge to collect. Some people, for example, find that collecting links them back to cherished childhood memories. Others do it because they feel drawn to the aesthetic values of certain objects. Still others collect because of the challenge presented by doing so, or for the education that their collecting pursuits give them.

66

I'd rather go to a porcelain exhibit than a rock concert.
—Elton John, on the *Oprah Winfrey Show*, September 1997

99

Acquiring objects purely on the basis of passion, however, usually results in a hodgepodge of items purchased for no other reason than the fact that something about them caught the fancy of the purchaser. While the objects they buy may mean a great deal to them, they rarely know why.

True collectors, on the other hand, are much more focused in their approach to the objects they choose to bring into their world. While they may feel a strong attraction to any number of items, they'll usually only acquire the ones that further the vision they have developed for their collecting efforts. They may collect in many categories or choose to specialize in one or two, but their efforts are still more focused. This focus is often developed by knowing the emotional forces that drive them as collectors. Understanding what yours might be can also help you become not just a buyer of antiques but a collector of them.

For old times' sake

Memories and nostalgia are two of the strongest motivations for collecting. They both reflect the desire to connect to the past in some way, to cherished memories or to times that are alluring for their perceived simplicity. Nostalgia, in fact, is one of the key drives behind the surge in collectibles. The broad time frame represented by collectibles virtually guarantees that any collector will be able to connect with something from his or her past.

But when it comes to true antiques, few people alive today were around when these objects were manufactured, so the nostalgic connection takes a somewhat different form. For example, images and emotions from childhood often shape collecting directions. If your beloved grandparents had Victorian furniture, you might feel drawn to antiques in this style because they have positive connotations for you.

People can also feel very nostalgic over eras that have nothing to do with them at all personally but that appeal to their sense of idealism. Antiques of the Old West, for example, often appeal to people who have no direct connection to this heritage but who cherish the hardy, driven spirit of the cowboys. A vacation to a New England fishing village can spur interest in collecting scrimshaw or other nautical objects.

Nostalgia is also a strong trigger for collectors of sports-related antiques, especially items that were used by the colleges and universities that these collectors attended. The glory days spent on a football field can be revisited over and over again through old game balls, helmets, mascots in the form of stuffed animals, even football jerseys and shoes.

History and heritage

Collectors often gravitate toward items that reflect a specific cultural heritage. Even though I never saw

Unofficially...
According to Wendell Garrett, editor of *The Magazine Antiques*, furniture is one of our most tangible links with the past; "it is a reflection of what Horace Walpole called 'the history of the manners of the age.'"

an icon in either of my Russian grandparents' homes, I've always been drawn to them because they symbolize a part of my ethnic heritage that extends back for centuries. When I see one, my mind immediately creates images of my Tartar ancestors as they flew across the steppes of Russia. It's an extraordinarily powerful connection, something which an item of modern manufacture has yet to evoke in me.

There's a certain romance about the past that also proves a strong allure to some collectors. All it took was a hit movie about a doomed passenger ship to ignite the passion for collecting anything related to the Titanic. But the popularity of the movie also brought a collecting category to light that predated the mad clamor for Titanic-related items that set the antiques world on its ear during 1998.

Working 9 to 5

Collectors can also be driven by a penchant for vocation-related antiques. Items such as old Underwood typewriters or metal type slugs and the wooden cases in which they were stored are just a few of the antiques that speak to journalists and others who make their living putting words on paper. They're a powerful connection to what the profession was all about before the computer era.

In the past several years, the contents of several long-defunct pharmacies were put up for auction to benefit various schools of pharmacy. Who lined up to buy the old bottles, scales, and other paraphernalia that were the tools of the trade in these old establishments? Other pharmacists. Industry-specific items find homes with people who appreciate the tools of a profession that means something to them, and only secondarily for their aesthetic value and other aspects.

> **"**
> I like globes. I like how they impart knowledge about exploration, history, and politics.
> —Antiques and art dealer George Glazer, *Elle Décor*, August/ September 1998)
> **"**

Beauty is as beauty does

The inherent beauty of certain antiques is a key motivation for many collectors, especially those with a keen awareness of their senses. The color and line of antiques have strong appeal; how they feel to the hand can also be a powerful allure. There's an immense difference between the feel of a new saddle, for example, and one that carries the patina from years of use. While both may appear luxurious to the eye, the older piece (if well taken care of) will have a particular suppleness that only age can impart.

The highly polished surface of a paperweight begs the lover of such objects to hold it. If you've ever seen anyone close their eyes and run their hands over a piece of furniture, they're depending on what their sense of touch can tell them about the piece more than anything else.

Why money isn't everything

After considering the various motivations that can fuel the passion for collecting, two points should be very apparent to you:

- Your success as a collector is a direct reflection of how well you know yourself and how this knowledge translates into the things you find important.

- While many motivating factors drive the collecting passion, making money at it isn't one of them.

Surprised? The number one rule when collecting antiques is to never purchase them solely as investments. You'll find almost 100 percent agreement in the collecting community on this fact. It doesn't matter what you read or who you ask. Collecting for the sole purpose of financial gain is sheer folly. Make it the leading priority in collecting and you're setting yourself up for failure.

Certainly antiques should be acquired based on their value, but collecting them is more about developing the skills that lead you to the best pieces, not just buying something because of what you might be able to sell it for. How successfully you develop these skills will likely bring you monetary rewards at some point in time, but this should never be the goal of your quest. Remember the story of Claire Beckman, the schoolteacher from Secaucus, N.J., who paid $25 for a rickety old table at an estate sale and ended up with a rare antique worth between $250,000 and $300,000? She didn't buy that table thinking that it would set her up for her retirement; she bought it because she knew enough about antiques to recognize value when she saw it.

Antiques, many experts say, are actually poor investment vehicles. Not only do they not pay off in dividends or interest, they can also lack liquidity. If you need to sell them quickly, chances are good than you'll end up doing so at a loss.

Orville Neely, the husband of an antiques collector, says that his wife's ability to spot value in the items she buys does fatten her pocketbook, but that the thought of financial gain really doesn't motivate her. "My wife buys the craziest things, things I don't think are worth anything," he says. "But she sees something in them that makes her want to buy them. When the time comes to sell them, she almost always makes money on them, but she buys them first because she likes them."

If you allow the appropriate motivations to direct you, you will derive more pleasure from the act of collecting than from the money your collection may someday earn. Let your passion direct you

If you want to invest your money, get a financial adviser. Collect for fun. One is not the same as the other. They are separate and distinct.
—Collector and dealer Marty Ahvenus, in the *Toronto Star*, February 7, 1999

99

Moneysaver
Put more money
into learning
about antiques
than buying
them, especially
in the beginning.
What you know
will go a long
way toward sav-
ing you from the
biggest buying
blunders.

and you may even make far more money at it than you ever dreamed you would. Some of the finest collections have been amassed by people with not much money to spend but who let their love for what they were doing govern their collecting activities.

The people who sell antiques love those collectors who open their pockets and buy because they think what they're purchasing will be worth more in the future. Yes, such a thing can happen. But if it doesn't, all that these collectors are left with are a few nice objects that they probably paid too much money for. Instead of taking pleasure in the other aspects of these antiques such collectors are going to resent having bought them because they didn't live up to expectations.

And why education is everything

What will make you a far better collector than money ever will is the amount of time you spend learning about it. The price you pay for an item, in fact, almost always reflects your knowledge of your collecting category.

Happily, gaining wisdom in the field of collecting doesn't have to be difficult. The process can be as formal or informal as you'd like; in fact, you'll find many good resources far removed from the classroom. When it comes to learning about the fine points of antiques and how to spot them, some of the best teachers are those individuals who are already involved in some facet of the antiques business.

Dealers

Here's an interesting question to throw out to your friends who are antiques collectors. Ask them how they feel about antiques dealers. The responses you'll get will probably run the gamut from "Yech, stay away, I've never met an honest one," to "I know this wonderful dealer who helped me locate the exact piece I've been searching for for years."

Of all the players in the antiques business, dealers are often given short shrift. Some of this is undeniably well earned, as shady operators who indulge in deceptive sales practices occasionally make headlines after being charged with embezzlement or some other fraud-related crime. It happens no more frequently among this group than any other, but in the somewhat small universe of the antiques industry, these events usually garner quite a bit of attention.

Some collectors have a negative view of dealers because they believe dealers hold the antiques market captive. True, dealers often have in their possession some of the best merchandise in the antiques arena, and generally speaking, they charge more for their merchandise than any other source. But some collectors believe they could find the same, if not better, items themselves for less if they just had the time to do so.

While there is some truth to these ideas, time is not the only advantage dealers have. Because they are more involved than the average collector, dealers are on the front lines of the industry, often acting as eyes and ears for the collectors who can't be. They're the ones who go to the auctions and sales that collectors can't get to and spot the items of value that collectors may miss. They're the ones who pay particular attention to trends in the industry and how such developments will affect their bottom line. They're the ones who read all the trade periodicals that collectors mean to get around to when

Those who are most familiar with the broader antique market realize that it is nevertheless a small world filled with people who gossip and who know each other and each other's inventories.
—Timothy Trent Blade, *Antique Collecting: A Sensible Guide to Its Art and Mystery*

they can find the time. They're the ones who keep track of who has what and know when particular pieces are being sold and by whom.

Dealers comprise one of the main categories of influence in the antiques industry, and they can be powerful enough to be the architects of great change should they choose to be. While cultural factors tend to shape trends in the antiques business more often than not, dealers also play a significant role in doing so. It would be difficult for a trend to take shape if dealers didn't stock the inventory that buyers were clamoring for.

The majority of collectors get their first introduction to the world of antiques through a casual visit to a dealer in an antiques shop, mall, or show. For many reasons—some valid, others not—casual visitors to any of these venues are sometimes ignored or spurned, and made to feel like they're not welcome at all. It's hard not to leave with a bad taste in your mouth if it happens to you, but it's important to not let one bad experience sour you on this educational path. "Sometimes a really naive question will get a snappy answer," says antiques dealer Charles Sweigart. "If it happens to you, you may need to recognize that your question might just be incredibly naive and the dealer doesn't want to take the time to bring you up to the next level. Then it's probably time to go onto the next dealer."

If you show a genuine interest in learning, many dealers will be more than happy to answer your questions and point out some of the finer things about items that you're interested in. Even if you don't know what questions to ask, a simple "I'm interested in X, but I don't know much about it," can get the ball rolling.

Bright Idea
Visit shops when you'll have the best chance of being able to talk to dealers. Aim for the middle of the week and either late in the morning or the middle of the afternoon. Weekends are the worst times because these are the dealer's busiest times.

Should you find a dealer who is willing to educate you, ask this individual if he or she minds if you take notes while you talk. Some people find the practice disconcerting and they may feel less free to talk. Others will be honored that you think enough of what they're saying to want to write it down.

As your career as a collector evolves, don't be surprised to find that you spend more time, rather than less, cultivating relationships with a variety of dealers. Not only are they a prime source for buying antiques, they can also be a good source of information for collectors of all levels of experience.

Museums and museum staff

Many people tend to think of museums as being showcases for art and sculpture; however, museums can also have collections that incorporate various categories of antiques, such as textiles, pottery, glass, and even furniture. My long love for paperweights was kindled by the extensive exhibit of them housed at the Art Institute of Chicago that I saw more than 20 years ago. The historical society in a small town where I lived in Minnesota had an extensive collection of antiques—furniture, pottery, textiles, books, even old musical instruments—that had been donated by families in the surrounding area.

Become a regular visitor at your nearest museum and study both its permanent collections and any traveling exhibitions they host. Most museums have regularly scheduled tours led by either highly trained volunteers or members of the museum staff. These are excellent ways to learn more about the exhibits and possibly meet more people who can help you develop your collecting skills. Museum curators are some of the most knowledgeable people around when it comes to the items in their specialty. If there is any such thing as a walking and talking encyclopedia, they're it.

If you go on a guided tour, be aware that you may not be able to ask many questions, nor will what you ask be answered in much depth. Guides are trained to keep things moving and they'll rarely stop to answer a question unless they think the information will be of interest to the entire group. What you can do, however, is approach guides after the tours and mention that you have some questions. If they have the time to talk with you, you'll find them very accommodating and even eager to talk about something they love with another person who shares their passion. Keep in mind, however, that many guides are trained volunteers. While they can be well informed and passionate about the specific exhibit or pieces that constitute their tours, they may not be qualified to answer your questions in much detail. Don't hesitate to ask for a referral to a member of the museum's curatorial staff if you need more help than what the guide can offer.

Getting to know museum staff may also open doors to broader resources than those available to the general public. Items that may be of the most interest to you may not be on display. Some of the best pieces I saw at the historical society in Minnesota were only shown to me when I expressed a strong desire to see them. Once the curator realized how strong my interest was, she was willing to spend an entire afternoon going through the society's collection with me.

Other resources of note at museums include

- Lecture series and classes. Museums that host traveling exhibits often plan educational events around these exhibits.

- Authentication assistance. Museum staff members are often willing to help collectors learn more about the pieces they have.

- Reference materials. Many museums have reference libraries that they make available to members and sometimes to the public. You may even find auction catalogues at some of them.

- Advice on repair and restoration. If a museum doesn't know when and how to do it, who would? Museum staff can also advise on cleaning and storing methods, and provide you with a list of properly trained art conservators.

If you find a museum or two that you really like, consider supporting their efforts as a member. Not only will you be giving back a bit for what you've received, you may also get some great member benefits. Even basic-level memberships often include special programs, exhibition books, lecture series, first chance at tickets for major exhibitions, and more.

Auction houses

If you're fortunate enough to live near one of the leading auction houses, or even a branch of one, you have an extremely valuable educational source that you almost can't afford to pass up. Even if you aren't planning to buy anything (and you shouldn't be at this point, if you're a beginner), you should try to go to the previews held before auctions as often as you can. Not only will you get the chance to thoroughly inspect the items going up for auction, you'll also be able to ask questions of the auction house staff who are there for exactly this purpose.

Many of the individuals who work at the leading houses have the same level of expertise as museum

Bright Idea
Tour any exhibit you like twice: once with a guide, and once on your own. During your second visit, pay attention to the pieces that you find most intriguing. You can learn a lot about your collecting taste by discerning what appeals to you most about various objects.

curators; in fact, they often have received the same training and may have worked in museums prior to joining the house. This education, coupled with the fact that they see hundreds of antiques a year, makes them extremely knowledgeable about their specialty. If they're not overly busy, they may take the time to go through the various elements of value on specific pieces with you.

The revamped approach to customer relations recently adopted by a number of auction houses has also resulted in a stronger emphasis on educational programs than they've had in the past. In New York, Doyle Galleries hosts several lecture series each year designed to educate new buyers and teach them how to collect. Sotheby's and Christie's also use educational programs to bring in new customers and build relationships with potential consignors. Christie's has a Young Collectors program to promote connoisseurship; Sotheby's goes even farther afield with its "Conversations" series, during which a panel of experts discuss virtually any topic.

More information on these programs can be found at the auction house's Web sites (located in Appendix E, "Internet Resources") or by contacting the houses directly.

Antiques shows

Antiques shows are popular events among collectors for a number of reasons. Chief among them is the chance to see lots of antiques in one spot and being able to compare similar items offered by various dealers.

Dealers are often willing to educate collectors at these events if they're not busy. However, the best benefits of going to antiques shows, at least from the educational perspective, are the expert panels and lectures that many of the shows also offer to the public. Topics almost always include a broad discussion on some aspect of the antiques industry and a few presentations on specific categories, and they're usually presented by people with a solid reputation in the business. You may even hear presentations by some of the leading personalities in the industry, especially at shows held to benefit charities. Once you've paid the price of admission, the lectures are usually free.

Friends

A good friend who also collects can be one of your best educational resources when it comes to showing you the ropes about collecting. If this person has been a collector for some time, he or she will be able to give you a real insider's view to what it's all about and steer you away from making major blunders. It's often said that experience is the best teacher, and indeed an experienced collector can be a superb instructor.

Your education can be very in-depth if your friend also collects in the same category that you're interested in, but it's not necessary for both of you to share a passion for the same thing for the learning process to pay off. The basics of collecting are virtually the same no matter what you collect. When it comes to valuing antiques (you'll read much more about this in Chapter 3, "Understanding Value"), many of the same rules apply regardless of the specific item under consideration. In fact, collecting in different categories can even be easier on both of you as you're less likely to be competing against each other for items that you both want to add to your collections.

> **"** Even with the rise of the Internet, antiques shows are still where the action is. —Antiques dealer Barbara Sweigart **"**

Unofficially...
One way to share
the same collect-
ing passion and
keep a friendship
intact, says art
glass collector
Sherry Heller, is
to take turns
buying the
pieces that you
both like when
you go shopping
together.

Friends who collect can also be great resources to borrow books from. As you'll soon find out, collectors who are serious about what they're doing usually have many books related to their passion.

Antiques on the air

Television programs such as the *Antiques Roadshow* are fun to watch, especially when an appraiser gives a value that knocks the socks off the owner of the object. They are also a great educational resource. As a regular viewer, you'll learn a great deal about various collecting categories as the appraisers run through the points they look for when determining authenticity and value.

Most of the pieces you'll see are authentic, but fakes are sometimes pulled out and discussed as well. While it can be difficult to witness the discomfort of the owner when this happens, what you can learn from the experience is invaluable. Almost every time a fake is discussed, the owner mentions that the piece was bought at an antiques shop or auction. Oftentimes, the prices were too good to be true, and under the expert hands of the appraisers, they end up being exactly that.

Antiques Roadshow is the best known of this programming genre, and it's clearly a favorite of antiques collectors and other viewers. According to Betsy Groban, director of WGBH Enterprises (WGBH is the producer of the series), it's the most-watched series on public television in over a decade, with a viewership approaching 15 million at the end of 1999. There are other shows of this genre to watch as well, including:

- *At the Auction:* Filmed on location at Sotheby's in Chicago, this show lets you see what the auction scene looks like at one of the top auction houses. This show is in its sixth season on the Home and Garden TV (HGTV) cable network.

- *Appraise It!:* This appraisal show is shot at the Butterfield, Butterfield & Durning Auction House in San Francisco and Los Angeles. The majority of the show—80 percent—is devoted to appraisals; the remaining 20 percent or so includes feature story segments. This show is also carried by HGTV.

- *The Appraisal Fair:* This program, hosted by Chicago-based auctioneer Leslie Hindman, is in its second season on HGTV. The show invites Chicago-area residents to have family heirlooms and treasures appraised free of charge by seasoned professionals.

- *Treasures in Your Home:* A new show (it premiered in August 1999) on the PAX television network, *Treasures in Your Home* showcases news and features on antiques and collectibles. The show is mirrored on its own Web site (TIYH. com), where viewers can participate in the show's live game segment or bid on featured items. This show features more collectibles than antiques.

Check your local programming schedules for dates and times on all of these shows.

It's even possible to listen to an antiques and collectibles radio show via the Internet. Industry expert Harry L. Rinker hosts *Whatcha Got*, a weekly antiques and collectibles call-in show that airs on KFGO radio in Fargo/Moorhead (North Dakota and Minnesota). The station also broadcasts the show live on the Internet at www.fargoweb.com/kfgo on Saturdays at 10 A.M. CST. Listeners use a

Unofficially...
The legendary reach of the Internet can even make a local AM radio show a global event. Antiques and collectibles expert Harry L. Rinker notes on his Web site that several individuals in Australia and Europe have told him they listen regularly to his show on the Internet.

toll-free number to call in and ask their antiques and collectibles questions.

Antiques in the classroom

Many community education programs offer classes related to art and antiques. Even classes that focus on making or refinishing furniture or creating works of art can be of benefit to collectors. Learning how to do such things as putting a new finish on a piece of furniture or throwing a clay pot can give you a "hands-on" perspective on why certain antiques are so valuable.

Some colleges and universities offer courses in decorative arts and design. Art history courses can also be of value. Depending on the institution, you may be able to audit courses on a space-available basis. Some schools have extension programs that make these classes more accessible to the public.

Online resources

Buying and selling in cyberspace constitutes the big buzz about the Internet these days; however, this worldwide network of computers began as an informational and educational resource and remains one to this day. While most of the sites that you'll find have more to do with electronic commerce, doing a keyword search on antiques or signing onto a major online collecting community like www.antiqnet.com or The Collecting Channel (www.collectingchannel. com) will also link you to educational resources on antiques and collecting as well as other collectors around the world. Several of the top trade publications in the industry also have Web sites where you can view selected articles and gather a wide variety of information on shows, auctions, industry news, and other issues of interest to collectors.

For more information, turn to Chapter 7, "Antiques on the Internet."

Developing a collecting library

In the early stages of collecting, read everything you can, not only about items in the category that you're interested in but about collecting itself. However, you don't have to buy every volume that catches your eye or proves to be a good resource.

A collecting library can be a very expensive thing to amass; you could easily spend several thousand dollars in a year on books, auction house catalog subscriptions, industry newspapers, magazines, and newsletters.

Friends can be good sources of these materials, but even the public library will have general books on the subject that are worth reading. What you won't find at most libraries, however, are guides to specific collecting categories (unless they're very popular). You're more likely to find books on American furniture, for example, than on a specific type of furniture. Both are valuable, but the specialty publications will become even more important to you as you hone and refine your approach as a collector.

Most collectors end up with a combination of the following in their libraries:

- General books on their area of interest that give an overview on styles and elements of value to look for

- General magazines on antiques. Some of the largest and best-known are *Art & Antiques*, *Antique Journal*, and *The Magazine Antiques*. Many library systems carry them, and they can also be found at larger booksellers.

66

Get educated about it. Spend money, buy books. Education is key.
—Antiques dealer Barbara Sweigart

99

- Specialty newsletters on specific collecting categories
- Auction catalogs and prices realized lists
- Price guides related to specific collecting categories
- Specialized guides related to specific collecting categories, such as guides to marks on sterling silver and pottery
- Design and pattern guides, again depending on the category being collected

There are also a number of newspapers that cover the antiques industry. I've listed some of the best-known and most widely read below, ranked by circulation:

- *Antique Week:* This is one of the most widely circulated publications in the antiques industry. It provides both news and educational information as well as lots of display and classified ads.

- *Antique Trader:* Like *Antique Week, Antique Trader* carries a wealth of classified ads placed by people who are buying and selling and display ads for auctions and shows. You'll also find a very comprehensive list of auctions and shows across the country.

- *Maine Antique Digest:* Ask a collector what industry newspapers he or she reads and this one is almost always on the list. This tome has the same content as the others, just more of it. Also a favorite feature: reports from auctions and shows that really take you into the heart of the business.

- *Antiques and the Arts Weekly:* Another favorite among many collectors and with much the same content as the others.

You'll find subscription information for them in Appendix C, "Further Reading".

Books and price guides to consider are listed in Appendix C, along with ordering information. Many of the better antiques books are not available through regular booksellers because their appeal is so narrow. You'll end up having to order them directly from the publisher or picking them up at antiques shows. Some of the better books on antiques are out of print, but you can ask a specialty bookseller or large Internet book company to do a search for you if you have specific titles in mind. Also, check the ads in industry newspapers—you'll often see specialty booksellers listed here.

Issues of price

Some people think that the information contained in price guides is somewhat misleading because the values listed are based on retail asking prices, which are often higher than what many of the items would actually bring if sold. However, the fact that so many of these guides are regularly published underscores how popular they are among collectors.

Price guides describe various types of antiques and list current prices, which are gleaned from sources across the country. Some are general guides that cover the antiques arena as a whole; others zero in on specific collecting categories. I think they're valuable for beginning collectors because they do provide a good overview on various collecting categories and a general idea of the prices for many objects within them. Just keep in mind that the prices they list are on the high side. What you'll actually see in the marketplace can vary significantly from them. You'll find several of the more popular general guides listed in Appendix C.

Moneysaver
Used bookstores often have a good selection of books on antiques. Check them first before you pay full retail on any book unless it's a current price guide.

Developing a collecting philosophy

As I discussed earlier in this chapter, antiques collectors come in all shapes and sizes, and they all have their own collecting goals, which are often shaped by such key motivators as nostalgia, aesthetics, and their own history and heritage. How they realize their goals can happen in a variety of ways. Some collectors are happiest accumulating objects in a wide range of categories. Others like to take a more focused approach and specialize in specific areas. Some are slow and cautious, spending a great deal of time studying before they buy anything. Others like to jump in feet first by buying right away and learning through that process.

No one approach is more right or wrong than any other—it's just the one that best fits the personality and style of the individual collector. The approach that will work best for you is also largely determined by who you are and your approach to life.

Regardless of approach, however, some core philosophies, which I discuss below, guide their efforts more often than not. They're good ones to consider as you develop your own approach to collecting.

Follow your heart

There generally isn't much agreement in the antiques industry, but virtually every expert does agree on one point: You should only buy what you love. "It's what I tell everyone," says Matt Lord, a Seattle, Wash., collector of Roseville pottery. "It's what led me to adding to the pieces that I inherited, and it's what has me keeping them even now when I could get far more for the collection than what I've put into it."

This isn't to say that an object's value should have nothing to do with your buying decision. Quite the opposite is true: Value is and should be a major consideration behind every purchase, which is why it governs so much of the effort that good collectors put into their work. But there's a big difference between making buying decisions based purely on value and buying valuable objects that you love.

With this said, there are times when it might be appropriate to buy pieces that you aren't really in love with. If your collection is based on, say, a historical theme, you may end up buying a few things that support the expression of that theme which you personally aren't all that excited about. For example, you may not be fond of maps or charts, but they're a pleasant adjunct to the model ships, compasses, and other nautical memorabilia that you've been collecting over the years. In this case, it's your love of the collection and your desire to make it as complete as possible that will win out over your feelings about a few pieces.

One of my first collecting friends had a passion for green sherbet cups. She and I spent hours scouring the local antiques shops and malls in pursuit of them. They were never to my taste, but every time I see one today I still recall Cindy's love for them. While I'll never collect these pieces myself, her enthusiasm for a specific object influenced my collecting approach early on and still does to this day.

Stay in balance

There is a big difference, however, between being guided by your passion and emotions and allowing them to overcome your actions as a collector. The love of the objects that you collect should never

> ❝
> Just remember collecting's big rule: Be driven by lust. Love what you collect, whether it's robots, posters, or renaissance bronzes.
> —Deborah Weisgall, *Fortune*, December 23, 1996
> ❞

overwhelm the considerations that you should make when evaluating an object for purchase.

Some of the biggest gaffes in the collecting arena are caused by buyers who let their emotions get away from them. This is especially true when objects have a special significance (for example, if they were once owned by a celebrity). Some of the pieces that went under the gavel in the Jacqueline Kennedy Onassis auction were in very poor condition; a client of a friend of mine who collects Japanese art (who wishes to go unnamed) bought a silk screen at this collection even though it was in tatters. He doesn't care; it belonged to the fabulous Jackie O, and the value in it for him is being able to say that she owned it. Beyond this fact, however, the piece has very little value to anyone except another collector enamored with Onassis.

Being madly in love with something doesn't necessarily mean that it's a wise purchase or something that absolutely needs to be added to your collection. Balance your enthusiasm with some hard reality. Always come back to earth before you buy.

Know what you want

Learning as much as you can about the categories that you're interested in is essential to successfully collecting them. Studying books and price guides, however, will take you only so far in developing your eye. Actually going out and seeing different antiques in as many venues as possible is even more important. Nothing will ever quite replace the value of being able to see and touch the real thing. It is through viewing, examining, and touching items that you gain an appreciation of their attributes. This is what antiques experts call "developing an eye."

You'll find more about what you should be looking for and the attributes that establish the value of antiques in Chapter 3.

Buy the best you can afford

Being a good buyer is not about getting the lowest price. It is about selecting the best objects within the price range that you can afford. Every skill discussed so far is related to accomplishing this goal.

Buying the best that you can afford calls for doing your homework each and every time you consider the purchase of an antique. If you approach each transaction in the same manner, you'll have confidence in your decisions, and you'll make every decision count. If you buy before you have completed your study of a category, your chances of making buying mistakes are greater. New collectors often buy because they convince themselves that they have spotted a bargain. Typically, though, they find that these so-called "bargain" purchases either fall short on quality—that is, they're not good examples of the category being collected—or they miss the target entirely for other reasons.

During the course of doing your research on your collecting category, you may have discovered that the objects you're most interested in collecting are either slightly or completely beyond your reach. If this is the case, don't think about buying pieces of lesser quality just to get into the market, and don't stretch yourself by betting on the come—that is, justifying your purchases because you think you'll be able to sell them quickly and make some money on them. It is often possible to turn right around and sell a piece for what you paid for it or even more, but in general this is poor logic and should be avoided at all costs. Think about revising your ideals instead. You may be able to focus your efforts on a less expensive (or overlooked) segment of the category and be extremely happy there.

Becoming a wise buyer

A large portion of this book is about locating and buying antiques, and for good reason: Buying is the most exciting part of collecting. It is the point at which all of your hard work and study comes together. When you know that you've done everything you can to make a good decision and pay a fair price, it's much easier to put your money down and walk away with the object of your desire.

As you go through the chapters that follow, you'll find specific advice for buying antiques in various arenas—shows, shops, auctions, online, and the like. While your overall collecting philosophies and goals should remain the same regardless of where you're buying, your methods for getting the pieces you're after will vary somewhat depending on the situation. This is one of the reasons why collecting antiques is such a popular pastime—there's lots to be said for the thrill of the chase, and it's never the same from time to time.

By following the educational steps in this chapter and studying the various aspects that determine an item's value in Chapter 3, you'll be in good stead for success as a buyer. While the educational process may seem tedious, it's impossible to overstate its importance. Only by knowing as much as you can about your collecting category will you be able to avoid buying mistakes, and be able to spot such things as fakes and reproductions if they appear in your selected field. Regardless of who you buy from and the types of assurances you're guaranteed, your expertise will be the strongest safeguard against collecting missteps than anything else.

Use every shopping experience as a chance to learn more. Approach each piece critically and apply what you know to your evaluation of it. Questioning is very much a part of the process of learning about antiques, and it's especially important as you become a buyer of them. Don't ever be afraid to ask questions of sellers, no matter where you are and who you're talking to. Don't pretend to know more than you do. No one knows everything there is to know about antiques. What may seem like a silly question to you may be a very good one, and the answer could end up being a valuable education.

On the other hand, don't let your desire to be well educated hold you back from actively getting involved in the antiques arena and acquiring some pieces. You will never know everything there is to know about antiques, either—it just can't happen. Plus, buying can be one of the best learning experiences you can have. If you're feeling fairly comfortable with what you know, go out and test your skills.

Money matters

What collectors spend while pursuing the items they love is a facet of buying that is rarely discussed. Part of the reason for this clearly is linked to the desire to be discreet. However, the majority of collectors also don't give much thought to the expenses involved. They have a general idea of what they spend, which almost always increases as their passion for collecting grows, but that's about it.

There is nothing wrong with buying like this, especially if you're well off and able to afford to collect in this manner. But, the majority of antiques

> **66**
> Collectors should ask a lot of questions, try to get answers from the dealer in writing, and be cautious about spending a sizable quantity of money for something that may exist in great abundance.
> —Daniel Grant, *Consumers' Research Magazine,* November 1997
> **99**

collectors are far from this level of financial security. If you're in this category as well, it's a good idea to develop an antiques budget.

What you want to determine, ideally, is what you spend annually on all your leisure activities (collecting falls into this category unless you're doing it for a living). Once you do, you'll have a better idea of how much you have to spend on collecting. Keep in mind, too, that your expenses as a collector don't begin and end with the price you pay for your antiques. When establishing your financial boundaries for collecting, don't overlook such things as the books you buy, travel costs to various shows or auctions, even admission costs to museums or art shows.

The budget you create should include expenses in the following categories:

- Research. Include the cost of buying books, magazines, and newspapers; travel to and from libraries; museum fees; and parking fees.
- Travel to shows and auctions. Be sure to include lodging, meals, and transportation. Factoring this amount will not only determine how much traveling you can do, but also how far you can go.
- The amount you want to spend acquiring your antiques.
- The costs for maintaining your antiques. Consider such factors as repair, restoration, display, and security. Expenses in this area can be difficult to estimate if you haven't bought much yet. Chapters 15, "Caring for Antiques," and 16, "Protecting Your Collection (and Your Investment)," offer a good rundown on what you may expect. Review them and keep

whatever points are relevant to your efforts in mind as you start buying.

▪ Shipping (if you're having pieces sent to you).

Estimate your costs on an annual basis, since your actual expenses will fluctuate from month to month. There will be times when you'll spend a few hundred dollars on some new books and nothing on antiques, and a few months where you might spend nothing at all. All of your subscriptions may come due in the same month. You might decide to spend everything you have on antiques during the first half of the year and buy nothing after that.

Categorize your collecting expenses as much as possible. Doing so will help you do a better job of staying on track. If you're over in one category—say you've spent more on books than you expected to— you may want to cut back on subscriptions. If your travel budget is nearing its max, you may want to substitute a show closer to home for one on the other side of the country.

There may be times when you'll see a piece that you absolutely must have, but you're a little short on funds. It's all too easy to whip out a credit card and pay for it that way, or to put it on layaway if you're dealing with someone who is willing to do it. Both approaches are fine if they fit into your overall antiques budget.

For example, you finally find the Rookwood vase that you've been searching for. The dealer wants $1,900. Your annual budget for buying antiques is $4,800, and you've already spent $4,000 up to this point. Your purchase wouldn't fit into your budget for this year. Buying it will eat into your budget for the following year, and you'll also incur finance charges if you put it on a credit card. Buy the piece

Moneysaver
Plug your budget into a computerized planner that will allow you to build custom categories to fit your specific expense areas. Such a program can show you in seconds how well you're doing on your budget.

only if you are willing to adjust your budget for the coming year in order to pay for it. Don't increase your budget to cover the expense unless you can really afford to do so. Pay off the outstanding credit balance as soon as possible to minimize finance charges.

If a purchase like this comes on top of other expenses, you'll be over budget unless you honestly factor it into your overall collecting budget. Do it too often and you run the risk of getting into financial trouble. You never want to be in the position of having to sell your antiques to cover your bills because in that situation you'll almost never be able to realize their full value.

Many collectors learned this painful lesson in the late 1980s and early 1990s from a somewhat different perspective when the nation's economy made a large shift away from commodities-based industries to high technology. "I was asked to sell some very fine pieces of art that had been collected by people in the oil and gas business," says private dealer Gene Barth. "There were some great buys to be had as they had to be sold quickly, and pieces sold in these circumstances almost always sell for less than what they're worth."

Just the facts

- The best collectors explore and understand the motivation behind their passion and use this knowledge to refine their collecting efforts.
- Do not collect based on profit motivation. Speculators almost always get burned.
- Educational resources abound in the collecting arena. Anyone who buys and sells antiques and

is successful at it is a potential teacher, as are books and the Internet.

- Develop a collecting philosophy to guide you when you start buying.

GET THE SCOOP ON...
How to value antiques • What all valuable
antiques have in common • Rarity vs. uniqueness • Enhancing the value of a collection

Understanding Value

Chapter 3

W hat's it worth? In the world of antiques, this is the $64,000 question. The popularity of *Antiques Roadshow* clearly demonstrates the public's fascination with knowing the value of what they own. If you watch the show for any length of time, however, you'll see that many different factors go into how a piece is valued, which makes value a difficult thing to assess, much less define.

When considering value, always remember that the antiques industry is a business, and your purchasing power is the object of that business. Thousands of people go to work each day scouring the landscape for objects that they believe you, or someone else, will purchase. And, because of the vagueness that often surrounds the history and manufacture of particular objects, nowhere is the legal concept of *caveat emptor*—let the buyer beware— more applicable. For these reasons, it's important to have a solid understanding of how antiques are valued, as the factors that determine a piece's value will govern what you pay for it.

Unofficially...
The competitive
marketplace of
antiques auc-
tions, according
to antiques
dealer Charles
Sweigart, is a
prime venue for
establishing
value.

All of the effort you put into learning to discern value is what will make you a successful collector. The better your eye, the better your judgment will be. You'll also have a better chance of spotting a real find when strolling through a flea market or when picking through items at a garage sale. True, it doesn't happen very often, but it does happen. Jacques Michel, an antiques picker living in Denver, once purchased an authentic William Merritt Chase painting for $450 right out from under the noses of a roomful of dealers at the city's biggest auction house. He sold it at Sotheby's six weeks later for $468,000. How did he do it? Michel took the time and put forth the effort to develop his eye for value, and he knew which elements to look for. What those elements are is what this chapter is all about.

How value is established

The intrinsic elements of a specific object that comprise its aesthetic quality, such as subject matter, execution, and condition, have a great deal of influence on its appeal to a collector. However, these factors are just the starting point for determining the actual value of an object. A beautiful glass vase, for example, has far more value if it can be positively identified as an authentic piece designed by a widely collected artist. If it was owned by a famous historical figure, the value can go even higher. If the piece isn't in the best of condition, its value can go down, but if it's very rare, condition plays a less important role.

If this sounds somewhat subjective, understand that individual taste and opinion do play a role in valuing antiques. One collector might place a higher value on pieces with historical significance and not care as much about their condition.

Provenance doesn't rank high on the list for some collectors, although they know that this factor can enhance the value of an antique.

While there is room for some opinion on where each factor ranks on the scale of importance, there's little argument as to the factors themselves that are used to determine value. The ones that will mean the most to you as a collector include:

- Authenticity
- Condition
- Scarcity
- Uniqueness
- Provenance
- Historical significance
- Beauty
- Subject matter
- Execution
- Size
- Usefulness

Understanding why these elements are important and how to recognize them in various types of antiques is essential to becoming a savvy and successful collector. Each is explored in detail later in this chapter.

How value isn't established

Many beginning collectors, and even some who should know better, would add two other factors to the list above that, in reality, have nothing to do with value. These factors are price and age.

Unlike the elements of value, price is not static or predictable. It can move up and down based on many factors. Fashion trends, inflation, world news,

Unofficially...
Price is often confused with value. They are by no means the same, and for one simple reason: The individual elements that comprise value are always the same, while price only measures the worth of an object in a certain situation, at a given time, and to a specific individual.

interest rates, money supply, commodity prices, and other similar matters can affect the price of antiques, just as they do the price of bread. But, while these external matters affect price, they do not affect the individual attributes of value.

Antiques can also have many prices. The price you pay to a dealer may be very different than what the dealer paid to acquire the object. Buy something at auction and you'll pay a different price from what you would have if you bought it at a show. Is the inherent value of the object any different? Unless something has happened along the way to enhance or diminish certain attributes of the piece, probably not.

History has repeatedly demonstrated that antiques vary in price over time. If interest in a collecting category has waned, a particular item may not bring as great a price as it did when the category was more popular. Yet, twenty years from now, it could sell for more than what it would today, especially if the category rebounds in popularity.

Age, in itself, also does not equate to value. The age of an object is a consideration, sometimes an important consideration, but it does not have as great an affect on value as the other factors do. Antiques shops are full of objects that are old but so common that they can be bought cheaply. In this context, scarcity is far more important than age.

Authenticity

Whether or not a piece is authentic is, for many collectors, the most important aspect of an object's worth and a major component in considering its value. It's where most collectors start because it often holds the key to other important information. Determining that an object was created by a specific

Bright Idea
Interested in testing your antiques valuation skills? Sign on to the Web site for the *Antiques Roadshow* at www. antiquesroadshow. com. You'll find a wide selection of items to appraise that will challenge your knowledge and help you learn more about the factors that influence value at the same time.

artist or manufacturer, for example, can answer questions about when it was made. Identifying the wood used in a piece of furniture can help you determine its origin and period. Knowing who made a piece and its age also assists in determining scarcity. This information might then be used to determine *provenance*—the history of where the object has been and who has owned it.

Determining authenticity should never be left entirely up to third parties. It's sometimes advisable to get a second or even third opinion before making a major investment, but for the most part you should rely on your own judgement, and your own research, as to whether the object you're looking at is the real thing. As noted in Chapter 2, "Becoming a Collector," this discernment is developed by learning as much as you can about your collecting area and by seeing as many objects in it as you can. By doing so, you'll develop your collector's "eye."

Developing an "eye"

Having a good collecting eye will translate into buying opportunities that will enhance your collection and help you avoid costly mistakes. Keep in mind, however, that at some point, or even more than once, you'll buy something believing that it's the real thing and later find out that it's not. This happens to everyone and is an integral part of the learning curve. When it happens, use it as a learning tool, both for yourself and other collectors.

As a general rule, you should not pay the same amount that an authentic piece would command if you can't prove this factor to your satisfaction. You'll find that reputable dealers will either give you a reasonable guarantee of authenticity or place lesser values on items that they're not sure about. So will collectors and other sellers with integrity. Others

At first you may make many mistakes, but you should always try to learn from them.
—Gene Barth, art dealer and collector

Unofficially...
Comedienne and actress Whoopi Goldberg purchased five Maxfield Parrish prints for $45,000, only to later find that they were fakes. She had to sue to recover her money, according to *Forbes Magazine*, March 24, 1997

won't, either under the theory of "caveat emptor," or because they don't know enough about them, or they don't have enough time to make an informed determination. At auctions, how pieces are described can be valuable clues to their authenticity. You'll learn more about this in Chapter 9, "Buying at Auction."

Is it real or fake?

Authenticity is an extremely sticky wicket. Forgeries, fakes, and improper attributions are serious problems in the antiques industry. This means that you have to be knowledgeable and have reliable sources of information to use for comparisons. You may also have to turn to another collector for advice, or even pay an expert for an opinion.

Even the experts, however, can disagree on authenticity, and they often do. Such things as labels and signatures are the source of endless debate. One expert may judge a piece authentic based on them while another may use the exact same factors to conclude that the object is a fake.

There are many skillfully crafted reproductions and fakes that can fool all but the best experts. However, every antiques expert agrees that one of the keys to building a valuable collection is assuring that the items you purchase are valid examples of your collecting category. Do your research before you purchase anything. Learn how to spot the hallmarks of authenticity as well as the things that brand items as fakes. The more you know, the greater your confidence will be.

Condition

By definition, antiques are old. Because of this, the condition that they are in is a critical factor in determining value. The closer to original condition that an object is, the more it is worth. Any condition that is less than perfect decreases value. However, this does not mean that damaged items are worthless, or that a restored or refinished antique will have greater value than one that isn't. If an object is damaged, repaired, or restored, value will be affected, but the degree of the impact on value will depend on the specific problem and other examples of the same item that exist in the marketplace. In many cases, and especially with furniture, restoring a finish in the interest of improving a piece's condition can severely diminish its value.

The best way to learn how to judge condition is to see as many objects as you can in your particular collecting category. Auction previews are a particularly good venue for this research because they encourage close inspection of the items being put up for bid. As an added benefit, the bigger auction houses will have specialists on hand to answer any questions that you and other potential buyers may have. If the opportunity presents itself, try asking one of these people to tell you what condition an item is in and how this factor is established. If more than one example is being offered for sale, ask the specialist to compare the two and show you why the condition of one is better than the other. Ask about repairs and their effect on value.

Museums are another valuable resource for learning about condition. However, you'll have to do it at arms' length, as touching is discouraged. As I mentioned in Chapter 2, many museums offer guided tours, often led by highly trained docents or even curators who may be pleased to answer questions. If what you want to know is beyond the scope of the tour, try scheduling a private appointment to meet with a curator so you can ask your questions in

Watch Out!
Be particularly skeptical of obvious clues when determining authenticity as they can be extremely unreliable. It's often the subtle details that prove it to be the real thing in the eyes of an experienced collector, not such things as labels or certificates of authenticity.

a more focused environment. You may even get the chance to make a closer examination of certain pieces than the public is generally allowed to do.

Dealers are also a good source of information on condition because it's an important factor in determining how they price their inventory. They also see more antiques than almost anyone else in the business, which, as noted earlier, is an education in itself.

Scarcity

"

The factors that drive value remain constant. Beauty, scarcity, condition—these things hold even for robots.
—Deborah Weisgall, in "Beyond Stocks: Art for Love and Profit," *Fortune*, December 23, 1996

"

It doesn't take an economist to understand that supply has a significant impact on both price and value. There are, after all, only so many paintings by Renoir and only so many pieces of silver by Paul Revere. Many of these now have homes as featured items in permanent museum exhibitions or the homes of wealthy collectors. Thus, the chance to own one of these extraordinary works is becoming rare. Aside from the fact that a painting by Renoir satisfies every element that makes art valuable, the scarcity of the object alone has a definite effect on worth. The same principle applies to all categories of antiques.

This is an area, once again, where knowledge of your collecting category can be extremely important. When the supply of desirable objects in a category is limited, the danger of fakes, forgeries, and reproductions increases. If an antique that your research tells you is extremely rare suddenly pops up, warning flags should emerge along with it. It may be the real thing, but there is a very good chance that it's not. If something seems too good to be true, it probably is.

Uniqueness

Uniqueness is often confused with scarcity, but the two factors are actually very different. If an antique is scarce or rare, it means there aren't many of them in existence to begin with, or the supply of them has been diminished due to tremendous demand. If it's unique, it stands apart from similar pieces due to a style or artistic quality that isn't present in the others.

As an example, lamps with shades that feature the work of Louis Comfort Tiffany are very popular antiques because their beauty appeals to a wide variety of collectors. Many were made, but they're somewhat rare today because they've been actively collected. Tiffany worked in a very identifiable style and many of his pieces look very similar. However, every so often a collector will turn up with a lampshade that can be authenticated as being crafted by Tiffany, yet it exhibits a style that hasn't been seen before. Because the style of the shade is unique when compared to other work by Tiffany, it adds value to the lamp.

Bright Idea
Since most antiques are sold "as is" and guarantees are narrowly construed, be as certain as you can about authenticity before you buy.

Provenance

Tracing the history of an object is known as establishing the item's provenance. Antiques with established provenances are always more valuable than similar items of unknown lineage, and the more history an object can be identified with, the greater its value. Many antiques have interesting histories without particular historical significance, but even the ones with humdrum lives, if documented, are worth more than pieces with little or no provable history.

Establishing provenance is often extremely difficult, which is why it ranks lower on the list of factors affecting value for many collectors. In many cases, it's virtually impossible. However, it is also the one factor that can add significant value to a piece.

For some collectors, researching where a piece came from and who owned it is one of the more intriguing elements of collecting, and they relish the challenge of seeing what they can find out about an object. Even if their efforts are less than satisfactory, they delight in the search and in learning more about something they love.

Never pass up an opportunity to establish the provenance on any item that you collect. If you buy direct from family members or at estate sales where members of the seller's family are present, gather as much information as possible about the object's past. Ask if anyone knows when the piece was originally acquired, by whom, how much was paid, and whether any stories about it were ever told by family members. Is there someone in the family who can give you more information? If so, get the name and telephone number.

Other good sources of provenance information include

■ **Family photo albums.** The sampler that no one knows much about might appear above Aunt Minnie's head in an old photo.

■ **Historical paintings and photographs.** These can yield clues about objects related to important events.

■ **Letters and diaries.** Look to see if mention is made of a specific item.

■ **History or biography books.** Both the text and illustrations in these volumes can reveal important details or links to where other information can be found.

Asking dealers about provenance won't often yield a great deal of information. Don't mistake this for stonewalling. Reputable dealers would rather tell you that there's little they can provide on provenance than repeat information they can't verify.

Bright Idea
Always record as much as you know about the antiques owned by various family members, including yourself. Keep one set of notes with the objects themselves, another set in a secure location where it won't be damaged or lost.

Remember, even if an item is represented as being owned by a certain individual, famous or not, it's only a representation and not necessarily fact. If a dealer has information that he or she feels confident of, you'll hear about it.

With this said, you should try to trace an item's history whenever possible. It can increase value, and it can make for great dinner conversation. Even if you come up empty handed, your stories about what you went through to get there will be colorful enough.

Historical significance

One of the most fascinating facets of value is established when an object or collection is associated with a significant historical event or person. A sword that can be traced to a specific Civil War officer is more valuable than any other example of that weapon. The library of Napoleon would be more valuable than the individual titles owned by historical figures of lesser importance.

Antiques are like time machines. When you consider their many facets, you're mentally whisked back to a previous time. Who can look at a piece of Paul Revere silver and not think about his famous ride? Or hold a Greek urn and not imagine the origin of its creation and the travails it has survived through the centuries? The emotions that antiques generate are one of the greatest pleasures about collecting. Now, imagine how much more intense your emotions will be when the object you just purchased is clearly identified as having a direct association with an established historical event. Historical importance is closely linked to provenance, and is often determined in the same manner as provenance is.

Watch Out!
Be extremely cautious of sellers who use elaborate stories to justify high prices on antiques. They're hoping you'll buy based on hype. Provenance is difficult to prove, and you're better off establishing it yourself than relying on someone else's word.

Beauty

Pretty things sell better than ugly ones do. This seems obvious enough, but the obvious can sometimes be overlooked. When the discussion about antiques turns to such heady topics as provenance, rarity, and uniqueness, it's easy to lose sight of the effect that beauty has on value.

If all other factors are equal, people generally choose the object that they find the most attractive. However, it is also true that beauty is very much in the eye of the beholder. I may see a great deal of beauty in a 1,000-year-old bead, and I would place a high value on it. It may look like a scuffed-up piece of glass to someone else and not worth much at all. For these reasons, beauty is one of the more subjective elements of value. Even still, items that are generally accepted as being beautiful will often be valued higher than those that are not.

Subject Matter

66
Cows don't sell.
—Antiques
picker Jacques
Michel
99

Subject matter is closely aligned with beauty and has its greatest impact on fine art, such as paintings, sculptures, figurines, and other antiques that depict or represent the world around us.

This is another highly subjective factor of value, but it's common knowledge that paintings of young people, and especially girls, generally sell better than those of old men. Scenes that show happy, contented, well-dressed people are often preferred over those that depict the angry, violent, or slovenly. A sun-kissed landscape usually has broader appeal than an angry storm scene. When an artist's work is commonly associated with a specific subject, pieces that depict it will be more valuable than those that don't.

Subject matter can also define a collection. This is often true of items associated with a specific historical event or series of events. As an example, let's say you were interested in Civil War history and decided to collect images depicting famous battles. The subject matter—that is, the events—is a prime focus of the collection. Collectors who share your interests will have a heightened appreciation of your efforts and will place a higher value on the assembled objects due to their focus on a valued subject matter.

As discussed near the end of this chapter, subject matter can also increase the value of an antique for specific audiences.

Execution

What distinguishes a great artist from mere pretenders to the throne? Talent, obviously, but it goes beyond this. The real masters have a certain way of creating things that can only be described as inspired. Faberge had style. Claude Monet knew a thing or two about the use of color. Rembrandt understood light. Michaelangelo could breathe life into marble. The works that they produced have endured the test of time, both physically and artistically.

The way in which an antique is executed largely determines the quality of the piece, which in turn affects its value. As you begin your collection, give careful consideration to quality. Inspect items carefully. Learn about how they were made and why they have endured. Compare items of lesser quality to really fine ones and observe the differences. Train your eye. It will not take long before differences in quality will practically jump out at you. This is the

"

If you've looked at hundreds of the same type of objects, you are going to know quality.
—Dianne Pilgrim, director of the National Design Center at New York's Cooper-Hewitt Museum, *Elle Décor* magazine, November 1998

"

goal you are striving to achieve—to develop a sincere, knowledgeable perspective of your collecting category.

Size

Size, surprisingly, can have a significant impact on value. Bigger isn't always better when it comes to antiques. There are items that, by their nature, are very small. With these pieces, the tinier and finer they are, the higher the value.

The sheer size of some antiques can actually detract from their value. A gigantic antique bar may be absolutely gorgeous to look at, but if it doesn't fit into the average home it's not going to be worth as much as a comparable but smaller piece.

An antique's proportions and dimensions can also affect its value. If a piece is right in every other way but is a little taller or wider than what is really desirable, it won't be as valuable as another piece with the more desirable dimensions. How a piece is proportioned, especially when it comes to furniture, can also be an immediate tip-off as to whether it's a reproduction or not. An authentic, high-style Chippendale is almost invariably larger than later reproductions.

Learning to spot proper proportions is again the product of a great deal of study. Books that specialize in specific collecting categories—especially furniture—will often detail what the ideal proportions are for various pieces. Just looking at a number of objects and comparing them against each other will train your eye to see such factors as well. When in doubt, shy away from purchasing any item whose size doesn't seem right to you, or is unusual when compared to similar pieces.

Bright Idea
Always bring a tape measure and a list of the dimensions of the rooms in your home with you when you're out shopping for antiques.

Usefulness

Usefulness does not affect the value of every category of antique. However, like size, it can be an element used to assess value. Special-use items, such as bars, countertops, display pieces, and the like may be less valuable because their use is limited. Because of this, you can often pick up these objects for a lower price than you might expect.

Auctions are great places for seeing antiques that are less than useful; they're often being offered because the market for them is limited. Sometimes the pieces are just plain strange or odd. It's not uncommon at auction previews to hear collectors speculating as to an item's original purpose, or see them standing before an unusual piece, deep in thought, trying to figure out what it is.

While people can find many creative ways for using odd or unusual antiques in decorating, the appeal of these pieces is limited. If you're ever in the position where you have to decide between an obviously useful antique at a higher price and an odd one that is less expensive, give the matter very serious thought. You might be able to use the odd piece, but you might be almost the only person who can. The safer purchase, if you can afford it, will be the item with broader appeal.

Another aspect of usefulness that is often overlooked is how an unusual or even seemingly useless object can be associated with your primary collecting category to make your overall collection more interesting. Here, usefulness is related not to the object's functionality, but to the presentation of your collection's vision.

As an example, a collector of Victorian jewelry may acquire a set of antique jeweler's tools to display

> 66
> Proportion, dimensions, and size are often immediate indications about both the rightness of a true American period antique and its salability.
> —Appraiser Emyl Jenkins, *Emyl Jenkins' Guide to Early American Furniture*
> 99

along with the collection, or an old display case to showcase everything. A set of nautical prints or maps might go nicely as a compliment to a collection of ship's compasses. These items can often be purchased very reasonably. When they are integrated into a collection, they assume a greater value than they would on their own.

Other factors affecting value

The elements of value discussed to this point apply to virtually all antiques, and should always be taken into consideration when deciding whether an object should be acquired. In certain situations, however, it is also appropriate to consider several other factors, such as regionalism and special interest, when determining value. These are both elements that can make pieces more desirable, and therefore more valuable, to certain collectors.

Regionalism

Pieces that can be linked to a specific city or region often have more value to people who are also linked to these areas in one way or another. A collector of saddles in Texas, for example, will pay a premium for an antique piece created by a saddlemaker from that state. Antiques related to dairy farming have a strong appeal to many collectors in my home state of Minnesota.

Special interest groups

Some antiques have certain elements that make them more attractive to particular groups, and therefore more valuable. An antique watch with a Masonic emblem, for example, will have less value to a watch collector than it would to someone who collects items related to Freemasonry. Antique bottles once used in an apothecary will appeal to collectors

> **"**
> The mystery of value fills the bookshelves of dealers and collectors.
> —W.J. Elvin III, from "Appraising Your Treasures," *The World and I*, February 1995
> **"**

of old glass, but they may have stronger value to a collector who is also a pharmacist. An antique painting depicting pointing dogs may appeal to collectors interested in the work of a certain artist, but it will have greater value to people who breed and train these dogs. An old football may have some value to a collector of sports-related antiques because of its condition or rarity, but it will be worth far more to that collector if he is also an alumnus of the university where the ball was used.

Dealers and other people who are aware of this element of value will often market their pieces in ways that will reach these groups. A very special antique related to a specific profession may be advertised in a magazine or newsletter published for the profession. During the annual Westminster Kennel Club show in New York, dealers will often display antique paintings, drawings, sculptures, and figurines that portray various breeds of dogs, knowing that they have a greater chance of selling such objects to the dog enthusiasts attending the show than at other times of the year.

How to enhance value

As you now know, the intrinsic elements of antiques are largely what establish their value. Some elements, such as subject matter, beauty, or execution, are things that collectors cannot control. An antique is either authentic or not, finely executed or not, beautiful or not. However, collectors can influence other elements of value.

If you're collecting for the right reason—because you love it—the following suggestions will further enhance your efforts. The first two relate to maximizing the value of the objects in your

collection. The rest will help you improve the value
of your collection as a whole.

Establish provenance

As I mentioned above, try to establish provenance
on pieces if at all possible. Doing so not only is a key
element to improving the value of an antique, it will
also help you become a better collector overall. As
discussed in Chapter 2, becoming educated about
collecting is essential to success. However, many collectors get a little lax about it as time goes on.
Making the commitment to doing the research on
the pieces you acquire will keep the educational
process going and help you develop the discipline
necessary for becoming a truly great collector.

Be a concerned caretaker

As mentioned above, condition is a factor that seriously affects value. Always do everything you can to
keep the antiques in your possession in the best condition possible. When necessary and appropriate,
have pieces repaired or restored.

Turn to Chapter 15, "Caring for Antiques," for
more information.

Timesaver
Professional
restorers and
conservators
have the equip-
ment, materials,
and expertise to
properly repair
and restore
antiques. Use
them instead of
trying to do it
yourself.

Demand the best

If you really want to enhance your collection's value,
make sure that every item in the collection is of the
finest quality that you can possibly afford. Quantity
is not nearly as important as quality when building a
collection. Pass on those objects whose condition
makes them poor examples. Search out the really
exceptional items.

Define and refine

As discussed in Chapter 2, beginning collectors
often take a shotgun approach to collecting and buy
things they like without knowing much about them.

There's nothing really wrong with this; however, collections achieved in this manner and left at this level rarely achieve their full value. To fully realize their worth, they must continue to grow, not in size but in definition and refinement.

Defining and refining a collection takes time as well as effort, but they are the hallmarks of both a mature collector and a mature collection. Start by looking at the elements of your collection, not the pieces themselves. Think about the things that fascinate you about them. Look for attributes that thrill your heart. It could be something as simple as the graceful lines of a favorite silver candelabra. Medium can dictate refinement. Maybe you started by collecting pieces by the same artist in various media. You may now choose to refine your collection and focus on pastels only. If antique jewelry is your passion, maybe your focus turns to pieces that exhibit a certain style, such as Art Deco or Art Nouveau, or on specific types of jewelry such as watches or rings.

Your continuing study of your field of interest may have uncovered a specific subset of items in your collecting category that would set your collection apart and make it unique. If so, you may want to consider selling or trading some of your other pieces so you can focus on this aspect of your collection. You'll find more on how to do this in Chapter 12, "Becoming a Seller," and Chapter 13, "Selling Options." As you develop your focus, think about how you can further enhance the objects you own. Display objects so that they can tell their own story. Add items such as prints, tools, memorabilia, and books that support your collection's presentation. A collection that has been lovingly amassed with an eye to the elements that make it truly special will have great value to museums and other collectors.

Be patient

A valuable collection doesn't happen overnight. Like all good things, it is the product of time and effort. Very often, collections don't reach their full potential because collectors get impatient and jump at the first opportunity to cash in on their value rather than waiting to see if the value could be increased over time.

Do everything you can to further your abilities as a collector—study, watch the marketplace, review the results of major auctions, keep up with items of significance that change hands in other venues. If you do these things, you'll not only increase your collection's value, you'll also derive a great deal of satisfaction in doing it.

Just the facts

- All valuable antiques possess the common traits of good workmanship, quality materials, and fine artistic expression.

- The three most important factors to consider when examining value are authenticity, condition, and scarcity.

- Price and value are not the same thing. Price is a measure of value at a given point in time, while the value of an object determines its price.

- The attributes that make antiques valuable do not change.

Finding Antiques

PART II

GET THE SCOOP ON...
The different types of shops ▪ What you'll find
in each ▪ The pros and cons of shops vs. malls ▪
Where you'll find the hidden treasures

Antiques Shops and Malls

B rowsing the inventory in an antiques shop or mall is the first introduction to the antiques arena for many collectors. To anyone who loves old things, the allure of these places is irrestible. Behind each storefront are potential treasures awaiting discovery, and you never quite know what you'll encounter until you go in.

Retail antiques establishments are the most accessible segment of the antiques industry, which is the main reason why they are so popular. Unlike auctions, estate sales, and seasonal markets, antiques shops and malls keep fairly regular retail hours. It's easy to go and satisfy the urge to buy. There are also more of them than any other antiques venue—so many, in fact, that it's virtually impossible to come up with a hard count on just how many there are.

Types of shops and malls

It seems like there are almost as many different types of antiques shops and malls as there are types of

Unofficially...
Getting dealers to open shops and malls in declining retail spots has been a significant component in the revitalization of a number of older urban areas across the United States.

antiques to buy. Each has its strengths and weaknesses, as well as its appeal to various types of collectors. Some are as down home and casual as they can be, with an inventory to match; others are decidedly meant to appeal to collectors who are more at home at black tie events than backyard barbecues.

When you're first starting out as a collector, you'll want to identify shops run by dealers with whom you'll feel comfortable doing business. Keep in mind that the majority of these individuals are reputable and honest, and you'll have nothing to fear about buying from any of them. However, even the best dealers don't know everything about all the items in their shops. You can't rely on a good reputation as a guarantee that what you're buying is authentic. It will still be up to you to determine the quality and authenticity of any object you're interested in.

What you want to find are dealers who are knowledgeable and reliable and that can help you further your collecting career. Here are a few ways to go about it:

- Check the front door. Dealers who are members of local or national antiques dealers' associations often display decals from these organizations on their shops' doors or windows. Other decals that point to a dealer's integrity include those from the Better Business Association or a local chamber of commerce.

- Browse the Yellow Pages. Dealers often run display ads, and these ads may contain information on the dealer's credentials, specific areas of expertise, and other information, such as whether he or she is an appraiser.

- Check listings in national directories or books. Dealers—even the best of them—do tend to come and go. However, if someone's been around long enough to be listed as a resource in an antiques guide or book, they're generally people to do business with. Longevity, however, is not always the best measure. Some of the better dealers you'll encounter along the way are people who are just starting out and are selling their own collections. They're selling what they know, and they're usually extremely knowledgeable about it.

- Ask other collectors. Word of mouth is often the most effective advertising tool there is. If a good friend or someone else you respect has had a bad experience with a particular dealer, they're not going to recommend that you do business with this person.

As you progress through your collecting career, you'll probably visit many different types of antiques shops and malls. Doing so is such a big part of what collecting is all about that many collectors even plan their vacations around going to such establishments. It can be lots of fun (and a great education) to compare the antiques that can be found in different cities and regions. And, again, you never know what you'll find unless you look!

General antiques shops

The majority of collectors feel most comfortable in general antiques shops, and these shops are far and away the most prevalent across the United States. Because they specialize in no one particular type, period, or style of antiques, they appeal to newer collectors who have not yet refined their collecting

Watch Out! Membership in the Better Business Bureau can indicate a dealer who adheres to high ethical standards, but remember that the BBB only records complaints, and the majority of disgruntled customers don't go through the formal process to register one.

style. They also appeal to seasoned pros who appreciate the challenge presented by sifting through the ever-changing assortment of merchandise in which these shops make their trade.

Many collectors get their first introduction to the world of antiques through a casual visit to dealers in shops like these, and that's often the level at which the dealer-collector relationship stays. Because these establishments have such broad appeal, they are generally the most visited. The number of people who come through the doors can make it difficult—if not impossible—for their proprietors to get to know many of their customers well, even if they are successful in developing a fairly loyal following.

General antiques shops are usually not the best places to learn about antiques, especially in any in-depth way. Their broad assortment of inventory is often a reflection of the collecting philosophy and approach of the owners, who probably know something about most of what they have but may lack specific knowledge in categories that do not interest them.

This aside, you'll generally find such shops operated by people with a real enthusiasm and love for the business, who like to share their knowledge with others.

General antiques shops usually contain a broad mix of merchandise, including antiques and newer items in the following areas:

- Furniture. Shops located in small towns can be a good source of primitives and other items with a strong country or rustic flair.
- Household items, including old kitchen gadgets, china, silverware, glassware, stoneware, clocks, and textiles (rugs, tablecloths, napkins).

If the shop is in the country, you also may find a good selection of crockery and items from farm auctions, such as tools and small pieces of agricultural equipment.

- Vintage clothing, including shoes, gloves, hats, furs, and purses.

- Decorative items, such as old photographs, mirrors, prints, and other artwork.

- Paper items, including books, magazines, postcards, and sheet music.

- Toys, dolls, and games.

- Sporting goods, such as old skis, hunting and fishing equipment (including decoys and tackle), and saddlery.

- Fine and costume jewelry.

Because quantity tends to be more important than quality to these owners, you probably won't find many high-end pieces in general antiques stores. If the choice is between buying lots of items that will fill up space or several objects of higher quality that cost more, these dealers are more likely to buy the former rather than the latter, unless they're sure they have ready customers for the more expensive pieces.

The same attributes that attract many collectors to general antiques stores drive away others. These shops can be overwhelming, especially if they are stocked to the gills. You'll usually have to sort through lots of things that may not be in the greatest condition. However, these are also the places where you're most likely to find the best prices— and the best treasures—and the thrill of the chase far outweighs any downside these venues may have.

Timesaver
If you're thinking about hunting for antiques in a city or town that you're unfamiliar with, call the local chamber of commerce first to see if there's a list or map available detailing where the various shops are located.

Antiques malls and cooperatives

These facilities, which are basically buildings that house a number of individual antiques enterprises, are becoming more prevalent, especially in larger metropolitan areas where the cost of running an individual shop can be high. Each person interested in displaying the articles he or she has acquired pays a monthly fee, which covers the space being rented and the renter's share of such things as heat, electricity, cleaning, advertising costs, and other business expenses. In co-ops, in addition to monthly fees, renters share responsibility for assisting customers, ringing up sales, keeping books, and managing other retail tasks on a set schedule. These tasks usually require them to be at the mall about once a week, sometimes more often if the mall is not large. Beyond this, the dealers can come and go as they wish.

These are popular spots for part-time dealers and collectors who think that they may want to become dealers in the future. The risks are significantly lower than if they had their own shops; so, too, are the expenses. Former shop owners sometimes will take spaces in these facilities if they still have inventory to liquidate or they want to keep their hand in the business.

Unofficially...
The first antiques dealers were trash or junk dealers who worked rural market fairs.

You'll generally find the same conglomeration of objects at antiques malls and co-ops as you would at general antiques shops, although the facilities themselves will feature a mixture of spaces rented to generalists as well as specialists. Some malls and co-ops also rent space to non-antiques vendors, such as crafters or sellers of reproduction pieces.

The primary advantage to shopping at these facilities is convenience. Having a number of dealers amassed under one roof allows you to compare prices and quality on items that are duplicated among vendors, a fairly common occurrence in antiques malls. The shopping experience can also be decidedly less taxing than going around to individual shops. They're great places to visit when the weather is bad and the urge to go antiquing hits. They're also convenient if you are buying lots of things at once, as you generally pay for all your purchases at the same time at a central cashier.

On the down side, you'll often get less help in malls than you would in shops that are owned and operated by a sole proprietor. Chances are against your meeting the owner of any particular space, which can make things a bit complicated should you want to get more information on a certain piece or ask other questions of a specific vendor. In a well-run mall, the staff on duty will offer to take messages for vendors who are not there, or they'll let you know when those vendors will be available.

Parlor shops

My first introduction to antiques shops was almost 20 years ago in Charleston, S.C., when a good friend of mine (an avid collector of Civil War objects) decided that we had to make the rounds of the establishments there. My strongest memories of that weekend are of the weather (unbearably hot and humid) and the small, out-of-the-way places we visited (oftentimes, not even marked). In many of them, I felt like I had stepped into a tiny Victorian parlor or reception area where, for some reason, the entire contents of the home had been jammed. There was lots of fancy furniture, ornate rugs, and crystal chandeliers that looked like upside-down wedding cakes, as I recall, none of which fit my preconceived notions of antiques. They appeared far

Bright Idea
Don't let your initial impression of a shop put you off from exploring what's within. Sometimes the best pieces can be found in the places you think are the least likely to have them.

too nice to be old. I didn't dare look at prices. From the looks of things, there was nothing in any of these shops that I could have afforded anyway.

The South is not the only part of the country in which you'll find small antiques shops like this; in fact, they're fairly common, especially in areas where there is a moneyed clientele more interested in acquiring beautiful objects than in finding bargains. Their main distinction from general antiques shops, apart from their size, is in the type and quality of pieces they have available—usually on the highly ornate side—and with prices to match. Their inventory also tends to be more focused than what you'll find in a general antiques shop as it's often a close reflection of the collecting tastes of the owners.

These are not the shops to go into if you're looking for a good deal on an overlooked piece. These dealers focus on high-end, high-quality pieces, and they often specialize in a few collecting areas that they know extremely well. Their clientele usually knows this and are willing to pay a bit of a premium to acquire pieces from them.

If your taste tends to run to the highly decorated and ornate, you'll enjoy shopping in parlor shops. The types of things you're likely to find include

- Crystal and cut glass. These dealers tend to like lots of sparkle and shine.

- Oriental rugs and other articles of Orientalia, such as Chinese porcelain.

- Ornate furniture, especially in Victorian styles.

- Silver and silver-plate service sets, punch bowls, candelabra, and other items, often of English manufacture, as these pieces tend to be more ornate. Victorian silver, in particular, is abundant in shops like these.

- Clocks, such as grandfather clocks and carriage clocks (especially if they're of French manufacture).

Having to pick your way through parlor shops is fairly common because they really can be crammed full of things. It often seems like the people who own them don't know how to stop when acquiring their inventory, or simply don't want to stop. But this is also what can make going into these shops so much fun. In my experience, the proprietors of these establishments are often very passionate about what they do, and they don't mind talking about it at all, especially if you let them know that you're in the looking and learning phase.

Pack-rat shops

Shops in this category are similar to parlor shops in that they are often crammed full of stuff. However, the similarities usually end here. Where parlor shops can be frustrating because their inventory is kept in such close quarters, the shops themselves are usually in good repair and clean. Go to a store run by a pack rat, however, and the first thing you'll probably notice is that the place has dirty windows. But this is only the beginning. Enter these stores only if you have a strong tolerance for dust and cobwebs—you'll find plenty of both here.

These individuals often make their trade by offering items that are of little or no interest to other dealers. Many of the items they will have on hand are only antique by way of age. The items may be of dubious quality, or their value has been affected by lack of care or actual damage. Lots of it is, quite frankly, junk.

Bright Idea
Antiquing can be dirty business no matter what kind of shop you visit. Keep some baby wipes or premoistened towlettes in your car for touch-ups between shops.

My favorite pack-rat dealer never dusts his store. He says it just makes his allergies worse. Cobwebs hang over the fixtures and windows in a very Dickensian manner; if you remember the description of Miss Havisham's room in Dickens' *Great Expectations*, you'll get the idea.

I try to wear the oldest clothes I have when I go to his shop, or something I don't mind throwing into the washer if it gets dirty. But I've found some treasures there, such as an unusual beaded purse that dates back to the late 1890s and an odd little oil lamp that delighted a good friend who collects such things. The chance that I might find even more treasures is what keeps me coming back.

If your time for shopping for antiques is somewhat limited, I wouldn't recommend going into these shops very often, as your chances of finding anything worth buying are far less than in other antiques establishments. Additionally, the merchandise generally is not all that great to begin with. If, however, you do have time and patience, by all means don't overlook these pack-rat shops. Sometimes they are the best places to find the quirky little items you need to flesh out a collection.

Antiques consignment shops

Antiques consignment shops are exactly that—they are places where antiques are consigned for sale. Rather than owning the inventory, the owner sells it for others and retains a percentage of the sale price to cover his or her involvement in the transaction. If you've ever shopped for clothes at a resale or second-hand shop, you're familiar with the process.

It's not uncommon to find consignment pieces in other types of antiques shops; general shops, for example, will take in pieces on consignment if the owner feels there's enough room in the consignee's asking price to add a fair markup to it. In consignment shops, however, much of what you'll see actually belongs to someone other than the proprietor.

The inventory in these shops may be limited to antiques and other older items, but newer pieces and collectibles are often a part of the mix, even in shops that are ostensibly for antiques only. For the most part, items are in good or excellent condition, and prices are reasonable but not cheap. In other words, don't expect to see any bargains. The people who run these shops know how to price things, and they'll price competitively and fairly.

The objects offered for sale in consignment shops tend to be of a far more homogenous mix than you'll find in other antiques establishments, especially if the shop is being run by a nonprofit organization for fundraising purposes. The operators of these shops are particularly savvy when it comes to knowing what sells well, and they can be very selective about what they decide to place into inventory. For them, quality is more important than quantity. You may not find lots of pieces of silverware from various patterns, for example, but you will find complete sets of such items. Other popular items in consignment shops include

- China, sterling silver, and crystal, including serving pieces, platters, and punchbowls.

- Fine costume jewelry and sometimes estate jewelry. If your passion is vintage jewelry from such companies as Miriam Haskell, Eisenberg, or Weiss, these are often the places you'll find it.

- Personal items such as purses, cigarette cases, powder boxes, compacts, and lipstick cases, but

Moneysaver
Consignment items are often marked down over time. If the price on a piece you want hasn't been reduced, ask if the price is firm. If it isn't, make an offer that's 10 to 20 percent lower than the current price. The owner might prefer to sacrifice a few dollars now over having the item sell at a lower price later.

Bright Idea
Great bargains are often available in the back rooms of consignment shops, which are where items are stored that haven't sold but need to be moved off the floor. It never hurts to ask if you can take a look at what's there.

only if they are of good quality and made by companies that are favored by collectors. As an example, I picked up a silver lipstick case, decorated with a little turtle on its cap, at one of these shops. The piece had value not because it was a lipstick case, but because it had been made by the noted designer Georg Jensen.

- Porcelain and pottery, but again, only if they are of good quality and if they are from manufacturers in demand by collectors.

- Furniture of all shapes and sizes. In shops that also accept newer items and collectibles, don't be surprised if you see reproduction pieces of modern manufacture more than true antiques.

- Some household linens and other textiles, but rarely of antique quality.

- Rugs, including Orientals, dhurries, Navajo, and other tribal rugs.

If you have an antiques consignment shop or two in your area, it can pay to get to know the people who run them, especially if you're looking for specific items. Unless you get to these shops on a fairly regular basis, you may miss the better pieces that come through them, as they tend to go the fastest. If the proprietor knows you're looking for something special, he or she can alert you should it come in.

Tea and crumpet shops

These somewhat rarefied establishments are often found in old homes or quaint little buildings in moneyed neighborhoods either in or near large cities. They're usually owned by at least several people—more often than not, very good friends— who have become skilled at spotting value in old things because they've been surrounded by such objects for most of their lives. They may also be avid collectors who decided to turn their passion into a business.

These can be wonderful shops to visit because the merchandise tends to be exceptionally good and tastefully presented. If the owners have the right connections, they'll get first shot at pieces that might otherwise end up at estate sales or auctions, so you may see some wonderful estate jewelry, fine china, crystal, art glass, Oriental rugs, and other quality pieces, especially if the owners have deep pockets.

In these establishments, quality rules over quantity, and the pieces are priced to match. For the most part, these dealers only buy objects in categories that they're familiar with and ones they know they can get a good price for, although a sleeper can be found every once in awhile. Because of this, there generally aren't many bargains at these shops.

The value-added angle to these shops is their ambiance. Walk into most of them and you'll not only smell coffee or tea, you'll be asked if you'd like some. You may even get offered some sort of pastry or cookie (hence the term "tea and crumpet"). Another reason for the name: These individuals often have a weak spot for English antiques, including

■ Porcelain and china, especially by Wedgwood, Spode, Minton, and Doulton.

■ Sterling silver and silver plate.

■ Queen Anne and Chippendale-style furniture.

■ Cranberry glass. I don't know why, but almost every piece of cranberry glass I've ever seen has been in one of these shops.

If you're looking for such items, try to find a tea and crumpet shop. Chances are, you'll have a great time looking at the inventory even if you don't buy a thing.

If there's a downside to these establishments, it's that they can be a little too "precious." Some collectors don't like the close attention that's often paid to customers in these shops. If the owners aren't gunning hard to make a living by what they're doing, you'll also find that they aren't terribly motivated to sell what they have. These are not establishments where you'll have much success in asking if discounts are available. These proprietors often can afford to keep their inventory until buyers willing to pay the full asking prices come along.

Another drawback: These shops can have abbreviated hours of operation, and in some cases, no set schedule at all. If you happen to show up when they're open, great, but you may very well find the place closed if the owners decided to play golf instead.

Timesaver
It's always a good idea to call ahead about hours at any shop. Dealers often travel to buy stock and participate at antiques shows.

In-home shops

Home-based antiques shops have always been in existence to some extent, although it is difficult to estimate their number. With the growing penchant for home-based businesses, it's a fair bet that these shops are probably on the increase as well.

These establishments are often run by people with a deep love of antiques and a real knack for finding them, who have decided to test their mettle as dealers for one reason or another. Often they sell antiques as a source of extra income while they keep their regular jobs. Sometimes it's because they've collected so much that they have to dispose of some of their holdings (which only opens the door for the acquisition of new things). I know of one home-based dealer who got into the business because his friends continuously wanted to buy the pieces of furniture that he was finding at the country auctions and estate sales that he regularly attended. He finally decided that selling some of what he had would allow him to keep buying more pieces.

One of the advantages of buying from home-based dealers can be good prices. Because these dealers have a lower overhead than they would in any other retail situation, they often can afford to pass their savings along to their customers. However, don't expect the prices to be significantly lower, and in some cases they can even be higher than what you'd pay elsewhere. Even though they're running a business from their homes, they're still doing it to be profitable. They won't be giving things away, and you won't find any undiscovered treasures.

Another significant advantage to home-based shops is that they offer the chance to develop a close relationship with a particular dealer, especially if you find someone who shares your passion for a particular collecting category. These are often the best places, in fact, to find people who can be really helpful, especially if you're a beginning collector.

A downside to home-based shops, although a minor one, is that they generally don't have a lot in the way of merchandise, so what you'll usually find is a carefully selected collection of very good pieces. Also, much like tea and crumpet shops, they don't always keep regular retail hours. Some are open by appointment only; however, you'll find that the dealers who are making a living at it (or trying to) will operate much like any other retail establishment. Unless they're primarily selling to private collectors, they'll have to do so if they're going to compete successfully with larger establishments. Another minor downside is the intimacy of these shops. If you're a collector who prefers some anonymity, you'll probably feel uncomfortable in them.

These shops can be tough to track down, especially if they're in cities or towns with lax requirements when it comes to home-based businesses. You'll often come across them purely by chance when you call the number listed in a Yellow Pages ad or in a collecting newspaper or magazine. They'll sometimes have signs out front in the yard. You might also find them through word of mouth or ads in local newspapers, especially weekly shoppers.

Specialty shops

These are establishments that specialize in just one category of antiques—for example, rugs and textiles, glass, Russian folk art, a specific period of furniture, toys, cameras, or phonograph players. They're usually run by dealers who have become specialists in certain areas due to their years of experience and personal interest in such items. Because of this, they're great places for seasoned collectors in search of specific objects to round out or complete a collection. But don't just dismiss them if you're not interested in this category.

Because of the singular direction of such shops, their inventory can be somewhat limited. However, they are often the places where you'll see the rarest objects and the greatest variety of items in a specific category. Even if you're not in a position to buy such things yet, it can be a real treat to see what's in store for you as your collection develops depth.

66

A day doesn't go by that I'm not trying to track down something. My competitors are friendly, but we're all after the same thing.
—Collector and private dealer Marjorie Reed Gordon, in *Elle Décor* magazine, April, 1998

99

The quality of merchandise in specialty antiques shops is usually quite high. These are not shops in which you'll find bargains or hidden treasures.

Shop etiquette

Regardless of the type of antiques shop you go to, approaching the owner about the items within involves following some general rules. Most of these guidelines are fairly straightforward, but you'd be surprised at how often they are violated by people who really should know better:

- Courtesy is first and foremost. Unlike many retail operations, antiques shops are usually owned and operated by people who have a deep love for what they're doing and a strong emotional attachment to it. Showing respect for this will earn you their respect as well.

- Announce your presence with a simple hello, especially if you don't immediately see someone in the shop. The owner may be in back or behind a display case or large piece of furniture and may not have seen or heard you enter.

- If the weather is inclement, try to shake off snow and rain before you enter or right at the front door. If there is a spot for parking umbrellas, use it.

- If the shop is small and you have a bulky coat or packages with you, ask the proprietor if he or she can keep such items for you while you're looking around. (A better idea is to leave them at home or in the car if possible. The area available in most shops for stashing such things is usually pretty limited.)

- Don't carry large or dangling purses. A wrong move with a purse on your shoulder can mean the end to a delicate or fragile antique. This is one of the rare instances when a fanny pack makes some sense. If you must wear a shoulder bag, make sure it's small and on a short strap. One that fits neatly under the arm and hangs no lower than the elbow is the best bet.

- Shop alone or with just one friend. Leave the kids at home if at all possible; even older children who can respect delicate items can be a strong distraction to the task at hand.

- Don't handle delicate or heavy pieces without asking for assistance. The same goes for any items that are in cases, even if the case is unlocked.

- Leave large jewelry at home, especially pieces with prong settings or bracelets that dangle. Rings and bracelets can snag textiles and scratch many materials.

- Leave food and beverages outside.

- Never smoke in an antiques shop, even if the proprietor is doing so.

- Ask questions, but use discretion about what you say. For example, asking about price on a vase and then bragging about the fabulous collection you have at home that you paid next to nothing for will mark you as rude and boorish. On the other hand, commenting on a vase that appeals to you and asking the dealer if he or she has others of the period and type that you collect is appropriate.

- Never disparage a dealer's merchandise or pricing. It is the surest way to be made very unwelcome, and rightfully so. If you don't like what you see, thank the dealer for his or her time and leave.

■ Respect that most dealers will only discuss their sources for their inventory in very general terms. Much of what dealers bring to the table is based on their ability to locate desired items. Trying to find out exactly where a dealer acquired specific objects is like asking a professional in any field to share trade secrets.

■ Leave the store on a good note. Thank the dealer for his or her time and attention. If you liked what you saw, felt comfortable in the shop and hit it off well with the dealer, mention the things you're collecting as well as any specific objects you'd like to find. Be sure to leave a way for the dealer to contact you.

Mall and cooperative etiquette

Many of the same guidelines apply when you visit antiques malls and co-ops; due to the more informal nature of many of these establishments, however, some things are more acceptable in them than in shops. For example, children usually are more welcome in these locales than they are in antiques shops. There also are some rules to follow that are specific to such establishments:

■ Remember that malls are comprised of individual dealers. If you pick up an item from one dealer's spot to compare it to something in another space, be sure you return each item to its original location. If you forget where you picked up something, return it to the main desk or cashier's area. The staff there should

Unofficially...
Many dealers keep "want" lists, which detail the specific items that their customers are looking for. They look for these items when they attend shows and auctions.

be able to tell where the object came from by the coding on the price tag.

- Don't ask dealers for their opinions on items that aren't from their own inventory. It isn't fair to the other dealer, even if he or she isn't there. It's fine to ask general questions. Anything beyond this should be directed to the specific dealer.

- If you need more information on a piece from a dealer who isn't there, ask if you can leave a message to have the dealer contact you.

- If the mall you're visiting has food and beverages for sale (many do), don't take them with you when you shop.

Antiques malls are often too large for adequate policing, which makes theft a problem at some of them. Many have videocameras as part of their security systems, but it's difficult to cover all the nooks and crannies. If you see some objectionable behavior on the part of other shoppers (for example, shoplifting), don't hesitate to report it to mall staff.

Just the facts

- There's an antiques shop or mall to suit every personality and every type of collector.

- You can avoid less-than-reputable shops and dealers by doing some research before you start shopping.

- Don't let a specific type of store or mall deter you from going inside. All are worth experiencing, and you never know what you may find until you go in.

- Treat all dealers as you'd like to be treated, even if they're not especially courteous to you.

Chapter 5

GET THE SCOOP ON...
Leading national and regional shows ▪ The role
of the show promoter/organizer ▪ Special
benefits for showgoers ▪ How to shop
in comfort

Antiques Shows

O n any given weekend throughout the year,
antiques shows are underway all across the
United States. With the American economy
in a long period of sustained growth and inflation at
an all-time low, these events are more prevalent
today than ever before. And they have a long history.
Some of the oldest, like the semi-annual York
Antiques Show and Sale held in York, Pa., are well
over 100 years old. Shows that have been operating
for 25 years or longer have suddenly expanded, and
new events are popping up all over.

Antiques shows, and for that matter antiques
markets, take many different forms, ranging from
megashows that unfold over a period of weeks or
months to volunteer charity functions held over a
weekend. Regardless of their form, however, they all
operate in much the same way. At a designated time
and place, dealers come from various locations and
spread their wares in one spot for the public's
perusal. After the show runs its course, they pack up

and move to the next location or, in the case of multi-week shows or markets, return in a few days to start the process all over again. It's much like an old-time farmer's market—just substitute chairs and glassware for corn and beets. Some markets, in fact, are even held in the same facilities that once housed farmer's markets.

Is there a difference between an antiques show and an antiques market? The two terms are largely interchangeable today, and in this book I use the term "show" to describe both, including those events that actually identify themselves as markets. Antiques markets and flea markets, on the other hand, do differ significantly. Your chances of finding antiques you want to buy are much better at the former.

Benefits for collectors

For collectors, antiques shows provide the opportunity for seeing more items in a day than they probably would during the course of an entire year of visiting shops and going to auctions, flea markets, estate sales, and other venues. These events are also fairly stress-free, with few hard-sell sales tactics. Their very nature encourages browsing, and many attendees go for that reason only. Dealers know this, and they are generally quite willing to leave browsers alone or just answer questions and let it go at that.

Perhaps the most important benefit of these shows, however, is that buyers can purchase items at many of them with great assurance. The top event organizers screen both dealers and merchandise—a process also known as "vetting"—and guarantee the authenticity of their goods based on this process. Shows that follow this process will often note it in their advertising and other promotional materials.

You can also find out who does this by contacting show promoters and organizers.

They may also offer free lectures on various aspects of antiques and collecting as part of their shows, which is a win-win deal for both collectors and dealers. Not only do such events bring more customers in the door, they can also contribute to dealers' reputations as experts in their fields.

Other benefits for buyers include

- Appraisals. Some shows encourage collectors to bring a few pieces along for appraisal. Fees are generally minimal and often include the price of admission to the show.

- The chance to pick up information about other shows and markets in the area. Just about every event has an information table where flyers and brochures are displayed. Information on upcoming auctions is also often available.

- The ability to compare the condition and price of similar items offered by various collectors.

- Silver and porcelain matching services to assist collectors searching for pieces to complete their sets of these items.

- Access to buyer's guides and other antiques publications. As discussed in Chapter 2, "Becoming a Collector," many of the books that are necessary to build a collecting library have to be special-ordered from the publisher or from specialty book dealers. However, you may be able to find them for sale at antiques shows.

- Glass grinding and chip repair. Many shows have at least one booth that offers these services.

66
Ninety percent of our seminars are standing room only.
—*Stella Show Management* exhibitor newsletter, May, 1999
99

■ The chance to see inventory from other parts of the country and to meet new dealers.

This last point also explains, in part, the appeal of these events for dealers. The opportunity to show their merchandise to thousands of people in a very short period of time, even if many of them are browsers, is an irresistible lure. Among all those browsers there are bound to be a few serious collectors who will put their money down. Dealers also like shows because they're great opportunities to expand their existing customer base. Putting out a clipboard with a few sheets of paper on which browsers can list their names and addresses is standard in most dealer booths, and virtually all of them make business cards available for show-goers to take along with them.

Shows also allow dealers to network with other dealers, buy and sell inventory, and spot trends—which, by the way, is another big reason why collectors like them. If you really want to get a feel for what is hot in the antiques arena, try to attend at least one of these events quarterly. Pay close attention to the merchandise you see as well as the prices. If you go often enough and stay with it for a year or two, you'll probably be able to spot various collecting cycles.

66
I always think that antique shows are really designed for wealthy people. Certainly not for a pack rat, bargain hunter like me.
—Milan Vesely, *Money from Antiques*
99

Drawbacks of antiques shows

A major downside to antiques shows (you had to know that there would be at least one) is that they're not necessarily the places at which you'll find great bargains. It costs dealers a fair amount of money to travel to and display at them, which means that they're going to be selling at roughly the same prices as they would if they were in their shops, and perhaps even higher. Your best chance for picking up a bargain is during the final hours of an antiques show or the final day or two of a seasonal market. If they can reach a fair price, dealers almost always are interested in lightening their loads at the end of either event.

Another drawback to antiques shows is that many of them are no longer purely devoted to antiques. Any event billed as "antiques and collectibles" (and there are many of them these days) will feature a mixture of both, with the scales tilting heavily in the collectibles direction as the interest in this area of collecting continues to grow. Unless you're very familiar with a particular show or the company that organizes it, you may be disappointed if you casually wander into a show expecting to greeted by booth after booth of quality antiques.

Finally, the size of many of these shows can be overwhelming and extremely taxing for collectors bent on getting their money's worth and seeing everything they can. While they come in all sizes, the "bigger is better" theory definitely applies to some of the better-known events. After visiting 100 or more booths, you may not remember exactly where you saw the things that interested you most, or even remember their finer details.

The show scene

As with the antiques industry in general, antiques shows have undergone somewhat of a metamorphosis in recent years. As previously mentioned, many shows now on the circuit also include collectibles. Others have narrowed their focus in order to attract more targeted audiences. Still others have changed their scheduled dates, moved from their longtime locations, or even discontinued their operations because the organizers either couldn't continue the

> **❝**
> The largest antique shows... are a test of the patience, endurance, and discerning eye of the most seasoned collectors.
> —Timothy Trent Blade, *Antique Collecting: A Sensible Guide to Its Art and Mystery*
> **❞**

shows in their traditional locations or were faced with rising building rental costs that made shows extremely expensive to hold.

This is a good news/bad news scenario for collectors. The good news is that there are more shows to choose from than ever before. The bad news is that some of the better older shows are either disappearing, changing dates and locations, or not attracting the dealers they once did because of rocketing booth rental rates.

The role of the show organizer/ promoter

To the untrained eye, the differences between the various antiques shows besides the obvious—size, location, and specialty—may be lost. However, these events can vary quite a bit from each other in ways that collectors are only marginally aware of. The biggest difference between them is the quality of the dealers who exhibit at them, which is a factor often controlled by the management of the show.

The antiques industry has a number of respected show management and promotion companies, and dealers compete against each other for the opportunity to exhibit at the events run by these outfits. These managers bear full responsibility for planning, organizing, and running the shows. Some also ensure the quality of the dealers who participate by putting them through a rigorous screening process, which can even include site visits by show staff. Only the dealers who meet the criteria established by the show organizers are allowed to participate.

What this means is that the best shows don't just happen. They are carefully planned, organized, and marketed in order to assure the best return for both organizers and dealers. When everything goes well,

Unofficially... According to their Web site, when Brimfield Associates decided to organize Atlantique City, billed as the largest indoor antiques and collectibles fair in the world, representatives of the show personally visited, screened, and invited more than 65 percent of the participating dealers.

their efforts are rewarded by the scores of customers who will line up hours before the show begins. If they can expect quality exhibitors, good parking, clean facilities, and fair deals, they literally camp out in anticipation—at one show, customers started queuing up 22 hours before the doors opened. It took almost two hours for the waiting crowd to work its way inside.

Shows of note

As is the case with antiques auction houses, a cadre of antiques shows set the standard for the entire industry. If you live where any of them are held, you're probably well aware of their venerated status. If you don't, you may wish to plan an antiquing vacation around one of them.

The shows listed here and in the sections that follow are merely representative of the many fine antiques events that are available to choose from. Many of them are consistently singled out by antiques enthusiasts for various reasons—size, location, quality of dealers, the organizer's reputation, special appeal, and the ability to draw a large and diverse crowd. Some, like the Scott Antique Markets, have a strong regional appeal. Others, like Brimfield, Round Top, and the New York Winter Antiques Show, pull dealers and collectors from all over the country.

As you'll see, many of them have been around for at least 10 years; some of them have been in operation for more than 50 years. The test of time is a sure one with antiques shows. Given the competition in this arena, shows that have survived for a good length of time are doing many things right.

You can find more information on the shows that follow, plus very complete calendars of these events across the country in antiques publications like the ones I mentioned in Chapter 2. Not only do these publications cover all facets of the antiques industry from coast to coast, they provide an insider's view that really can't be beat of some of the more interesting events around the country. The Web sites for some of these publications also provide online show calendars and links to many of the shows that advertise on the Internet.

Brimfield

The thrice-yearly Brimfield Antiques and Collectibles Show began in 1959 as the brainchild of Gordon Reid, who borrowed the show's format from one he had seen in Connecticut. Today it is the biggest of its kind in the United States. Held for six days each May, July, and September in Brimfield, Mass., this event brings together some 30,000–40,000 dealers (you read that correctly) representing every conceivable collecting category, who show their wares across 22 adjacent display fields that are independently run by the 19 operators who comprise Brimfield Associates. The site that houses this event extends a mile and a half lengthwise; some of the fields are a full quarter-mile deep.

For East Coast antiques enthusiasts, this is a can't miss show; but the allure of Brimfield is strong enough to draw collectors from across the country and even overseas. Each six-day event is attended by an estimated 100,000 visitors who browse the 2,000–3,000 dealers in each field. Only the hardiest souls have the stamina to cover the entire show in one visit, although newcomers are tempted to do exactly that.

As big as this show is, it's still growing. According to Robert Brown, the publisher of the *Brimfield*

> 66
>
> Holidays and bad weather can be a boon for bargain hunters—a low turnout means dealers are more likely to cut prices.
> —Helen Thompson, *In Style* Magazine, June, 1999
>
> 99

Antique Guide, every operator at Brimfield has a waiting list of dealers wanting to exhibit there.

Atlantique City

This huge show is an indoor spin-off of Brimfield. Held twice-yearly in Atlantic City, N.J., it's billed as the largest indoor show in the country. From its beginning in 1986, this show has focused on offering the most popular collecting categories, such as Americana, folk art, ephemera, primitives, and similar items. More than 1,000 dealers have booths at this show, which also features a computer-based locating system that links collectors looking for specific items to the dealers most likely to have them.

Round Top Antiques Fair

Round Top, Tex., is the tiniest incorporated town in Texas, with a population of 81. You wouldn't think such a small place could host a major league antiques event, but never say never to a Texan. The Round Top Antiques Fair is held twice yearly (the first week in April and October) in two old dance halls and a couple of tent pavilions just outside of town.

Round Top is a favorite for collectors of Western-themed and Americana antiques. It's also noted for a good selection of country and formal furniture from both the United States and Europe. If you're wondering where Round Top is, it's located between Houston and Austin and can be reached by driving from airports in either city.

Madison-Bouckville

Billed as New York state's largest outdoor antiques show, this three-day show held each August in upstate New York annually attracts more than 1,000 dealers from 26 states and Canada. A big plus for

Timesaver
When you find a show or two that you really like, check to see who is the promoter/organizer. Contact this company and ask to be put on the mailing list so you can plan ahead for next year's shows.

attendees at this show: free transportation to and from the parking area and porters who will transport heavy items directly to buyers' cars, also for free. The show location also hosts a weekly antiques and collectibles festival on Sundays from May to October.

The Renningers Extravaganzas

These shows are held three times a year in Adamstown and Kutztown, Pa. They're some of the largest in the country, featuring merchandise from more than 1,200 dealers from virtually every part of the United States. Adamstown also is the home of the Antique and Collectors Market, which takes place every Sunday; the Antique and Flea Market is held in Kutztown every Saturday.

The Scott Antiques Markets

This mid-America show (it's held in Columbus, Ohio) takes place in four buildings that house some 1,200 dealers from across the country. It's becoming a big draw for residents of the Midwest, but it attracts buyers from other parts of the United States as well. Both antiques and collectibles are offered at this show.

The Ann Arbor (Mich.) Antiques Market

Held at the Ann Arbor Fairgrounds, these seasonal markets (held every third Sunday in April through October, plus a few extra dates in April, September, and November) feature casual, outside tented booths and very formal inside displays by dealers from across the country.

Specialty shows

Specialty shows target collectors who have chosen specific collecting categories, such as dolls, toys, glass, or paper. These events often start off small and gain momentum over the years as a collecting category builds. There are many of these shows to choose from and they're held all across the country; the ones I've selected here represent the diversity of these shows as well as some of the better-known events in several collecting categories:

- **The Allentown (Pa.) Antique Toy Show and Sale:** A toy collector's paradise, with merchandise ranging from dolls to games to mechanical banks. This large show—it usually features more than 350 dealers—is one of the oldest toy shows in the country.

- **The Chicago Toy Show:** Held three times a year (in April, June, and October), this event attracts customers and dealers from all over the world and especially from Europe and Japan, where toy collecting is all the rage. A blockbuster show featuring more than 1,000 dealers, it's held at the Kane County Fairgrounds in St. Charles, Ill.

- **The New York Ceramics Fair:** This new event, scheduled for January 2000, underscores the current passion for ceramics, pottery, and glass.

- **The Baltimore Summer Antiques Fair:** This event showcases rare books from 80 antiquarian book dealers along with merchandise from 450 dealers in other categories.

Information about these shows can be found in the same sources that general shows are listed in, and in specialty publications devoted to each collecting category.

Watch Out!
Be on the lookout for fakes and reproductions at shows. Several collecting areas in which phony and new items currently abound are toys, Roseville pottery, and ephemera.

Charity events

Antiques shows have long been a popular way to raise money for charities. The fact that the money raised goes to worthy causes gives these shows a special cachet among certain collectors, which is one reason why they are so popular.

Because they're charity events, these shows often feature preview parties and receptions (at an additional fee) for benefactors of the sponsoring organization. Benefactors and other show attendees are also treated to such added benefits as lectures by leading antiques experts and exhibitions of various antiques arranged specially for the show.

Charity antiques shows are held in most major cities across the country. A few of the more noted include

- **The Antiques and Garden Show of Nashville:** Held every February to benefit local causes in the Nashville, Tenn., area, this annual charity event is one of the largest of its kind in the United States.

- **Lake Forest Academy Antiques Show:** This June show, held in Lake Forest, Ill., is nearing its 40th year of operations. Not a large show (it averages around 40 exhibitors), it presents a nice assortment of antiques from prestigious dealers in an elegant setting, the former home of meat-packing pioneer Phillip Danforth Armour.

- **The New York Winter Antiques Show:** One of the premier charity shows in the United States, this event supports East Side House Settlement, located in the poorest section of the Bronx. This older show celebrated its 45th anniversary in 1999.

- **The Philadelphia Antiques Show:** A spring show held to benefit the University of Pennsylvania Medical Center, this popular event serves as the anchor for other antiques shows in the area. Early American antiques, folk arts, textiles, needlework, and other items of Americana are showcased.

Charity shows have a certain reputation for being a little on the stuffy side, and some of them can certainly be that way. Don't let this factor turn you away from attending them. They're designed to raise money for organizations that depend on them to be successful, which means that a great deal of effort will go into putting together shows with good dealers, attractive merchandise, and interesting special exhibits and other events, such as preview and opening night parties, to draw collectors.

Going to the shows

Attending most local antiques shows is no more difficult than choosing the ones you want to go to and showing up at the appointed place at the right time, money in hand. However, megashows like Brimfield and shows held in small towns like Round Top take some advance planning. If you're traveling to any antiques show, it's always a good idea to check on available accommodations well in advance of your trip. Shows like these are legendary for monopolizing every housing opportunity within a reasonable distance. Show organizers provide lists of area accommodations to attendees and recommend that reservations be made as early as possible.

If you're planning to attend an outdoor show, you may end up contending with bad weather. Although there are canvas tents and plastic tarps to huddle under when it rains, they afford little

Bright Idea
Put a number of old quilts or towels in the trunk of your car to use for cushioning any fragile objects you may buy.

protection from the mud puddles that such storms generally create. If the show is outdoors in a humid part of the country, mosquitoes will be a pesky problem even when it's dry. After a rainstorm they often come out in force.

Show gear

Always wear casual clothes that you can risk getting dirty and wet. A large tote for schlepping everything around in, basic rainwear, and good bug repellent are three other musts for anyone attending these events. In a pinch, a large plastic bag with holes cut out for your head and hands also will do the trick if it rains, especially if you can cover your head with a hat. Sun protection is also a must. A wide-brimmed hat is a good start, but bring sunglasses and sunscreen with you as well.

Other items to consider bringing that can make life a little easier include

- A two-wheeled shopping cart. These devices can be lifesavers at large outdoor shows. All you have to do is whip out a bungie cord or two and strap your purchases down. Nothing could be simpler. Remember, though, that carts don't work very well when it rains because their wheels are too small for navigating mud. Never leave one unattended if you have items strapped to it; it's very easy for thieves to make off with, especially if the crowd is thick.

- Walkie-talkies or two-way radios. These handheld devices are great for keeping in touch with your spouse or shopping companion. Plus, one of you can go ahead and scope out other parts of the show if negotiating with a dealer takes longer than you'd like. A drawback to these devices: Many of them operate on the same frequency, which can make conversations interesting if not extremely challenging. Always remember that anything you say can be heard by someone else, so be careful disseminating any sensitive information.

- A second pair of shoes and socks. If one pair gets soaked, it's always nice to be able to change into dry ones. Plus, you are less likely to get blisters if your footwear stays dry. Changing shoes during a long day can also revitalize feet and legs.

- A small first-aid kit. It should include bandages (for those blisters), an antibacterial gel or cream in case you get a cut (it happens all the time at shows, especially outdoor ones), and aspirin or some other form of pain reliever (headaches are common, too).

- Antibacterial hand cleaner or baby wipes. Antiques shows, especially outside ones, are dirty places. Being able to clean your hands once in awhile is not only recommended for hygienic purposes, but also can work as a quick pick-me-up when you begin to fade.

- A field identification book or price guide, as well as any other tools to help you inspect any pieces that catch your eye. Most dealers will have such things as black lights available for their customers, although you may need to ask for them. A jeweler's loupe—a special magnifier used to inspect gems and settings—is a handy thing to have on hand and something that many dealers won't have unless they're selling jewelry.

Watch Out!
The crowded atmosphere of antiques shows attracts thieves and pickpockets. Take every precaution to guard against losing your valuables. If you carry a tote bag, make sure it's one with a zipper. Never carry a wallet or checkbook in an outside pocket where it can fall prey to sticky fingers.

- A pad of paper and a pencil or pen for jotting down notes or writing down contact information for a dealer who doesn't have a clipboard to sign.

- A tape measure. Always useful for checking size and dimensions.

- A large-diameter magnifying glass, which can be useful for close-up checks of condition and other small details.

Bright Idea
Pets are welcome at some outdoor antiques shows, banned at others. Call ahead to see what's acceptable at any show you're planning to attend.

What not to bring, sadly, are cameras of any type. Up until recently, it was fairly common to see collectors take pictures of certain items for purposes of comparison or to be able to show them to people at home. Now the practice is discouraged or forbidden at many shows. Why? Thank the con artists and scammers of the world. Get a picture of a desired item, put it up for sale on an Internet site or online auction, lasso an unsuspecting buyer who is willing to pay for the object before he or she takes delivery of it, and you have the perfect setup for an online fraud.

Scoping the action

Show veterans recommend making as complete a sweep as possible of the entire show (or the section you're most interested in) before settling down to the wares available at specific dealers. This will give you an idea of what's there as well as allow you to do some comparison shopping (this also is where the notepad and pen come in handy if you're comparing information from more than two dealers).

Money matters

Cash is the universal language at virtually all places where antiques are sold, and the same holds true for antiques shows. Many vendors at these shows are also willing to take checks with proper identification, and they are equipped for accepting major credit cards.

The high prices at antiques shows are a strong incentive for buyers to want to negotiate. Fortunately, this is an accepted practice. Many dealers will give you 10 percent off if you ask, "Is this your best price?" As previously mentioned, even if the price is firm at first, it may not be by the end of the show. However, if you see something that you really love—even if there's no discount offered—your best bet is to buy it right away rather than taking the chance that it will be around when you come back, or that the dealer will have it after the show is over.

Just the facts

- Antiques shows are one of the most popular spots for collectors to see and buy a wide variety of antiques. However, the opportunity comes at a price, since items are usually more expensive than they are in shops.

- The size of antiques shows varies widely. Bigger isn't always best, though. A small show can yield just as many treasures as a big extravaganza if good dealers are in attendance.

- For the best variety of items to choose from, head for any of the larger national shows.

- Comfort is the rule for dressing at antiques shows. Protection against the elements is a necessity for any event held outdoors.

- Dealers at these shows will often negotiate on price. For the best values, hit the show on the last day.

GET THE SCOOP ON...
Auction traditions ▪ National vs. regional
houses ▪ Choosing houses to fit your collecting
objectives ▪ Auctions by mail

The Auction Scene

Chapter 6

No other antiques venue surpasses the antiques auction when it comes to drama, intrigue, and excitement, and for getting the best buys on good antiques. Yet, for many collectors, auctions are intimidating and off putting. If you're in this category, this chapter will help dispel the many myths surrounding auctions and tell you why these buying venues can actually be some the best and safest for you.

Beginning collectors, especially, are often wary of auctions for the simple reason that they usually haven't attended many of them. It's difficult to feel comfortable with something you don't know much about, and the mystique often associated with auctions can seem more like a brick wall than a portal to doing business. There are also fewer opportunities to buy at auction than at other antiquing venues. They're simply not as plentiful as shops and shows.

However, most collectors find that as their expertise in collecting grows, their interest in buying antiques at auction grows along with it, especially when they realize that they're probably going to get their best deals at them.

This chapter is all about the kinds of auctions (with the exception of estate auctions) that characterized the antiques world prior to the advent of the Internet. Estate auctions, along with estate sales, are discussed in Chapter 8, "Other Sources." For more about online auctions and the role they play in today's antiques industry, turn to Chapters 7, "Antiques on the Internet," and 10, "Buying Online."

The auction allure

When you consider the fact that auctions function as the commodities exchange for the industry, the thought of being a part of the action is extremely alluring. It's a free market, open to all, and one person's money is as good as the next. Why not be in the thick of things, bidding right alongside others with interests similar to yours?

What makes buying at auction very alluring to collectors is the opportunity to, in effect, buy at wholesale at them. You're eliminating the retail component of the supply chain—the gallery or dealer or other collector from whom you would be buying this piece if you hadn't seen it first.

Antiques auctions can get into your blood. In fact, they usually do. At any given auction, the object of your dreams may be put up for sale. If you are astute and have done your homework, you might be the high bidder and walk away with a real bargain. You might not. Regardless, you won't hear many people complaining about the experience.

The auction house tradition

What you'll find at auctions today runs far afield from the fare that once set the standard for the

"
Auctions appeal directly to the competitor in most of us; the daily business of the auction house is...highly adversarial as individuals are locked in combat for ownership of objects that are valuable by virtue of their high quality and their scarcity.
—John L. Marion, *The Best of Everything*
"

business. For many years—centuries, in fact—auction houses like Sotheby's and Christie's had the reputation for being the playground of the famous and wealthy, and for offering items that appealed only to this audience. Whether it was actually the case or not, many collectors perceived these houses as being stuffy and snotty, and they stayed away from them.

Auctions, which have always functioned as trading centers for buyers and sellers, began as very informal arrangements. Whenever someone had something to sell and more than one person was interested in buying it, that person could, and often would, call an auction on the spur of the moment. But when collecting antiques and other pieces of great value became a prized passion for the wealthy during the eighteenth century, the tone of auctions changed.

To service the needs of the buyers and sellers of fine and decorative arts, auction houses were established to act as intermediaries between the two sides of the auction transaction. Sotheby's, for example, dates back to 1744 when London bookseller Samuel Baker, who was seeking a better way to bring together buyers and sellers of private libraries, decided to hold an auction. Christie's, which was started in 1766, also began in London, when fine art dealer James Christie decided to establish a forum for gathering many buyers and sellers of fine art at the same time.

These institutions were first established in the leading population and commerce centers of the time, such as Paris, London, Amsterdam, Brussels, Geneva, and Zurich. As the world's population grew, auction houses were also opened in other major cities, such as Hong Kong and Sydney, and in the

Unofficially...
You can often out-bid dealers at an auction because they require room for a 50 percent mark up on the items they are able to bid on.

United States, Boston, Chicago, New York, and San Francisco, in order to serve a more international market. Many houses were established independently. Some were branches of such well-established houses as Christie's and Sotheby's.

Changes in attitude

Because they started as institutions that catered to the wealthy, auction houses maintained this image for many years. But in the 1980s, as the inventory of available antiques became scarcer and the existing pool of buyers dwindled, auction house management made some changes in order to survive.

But the necessary changes didn't come easily. Many auction houses had difficulty shedding their traditional images, even though it was in their best interests to do so. Some closed, and some merged with other houses. By the early 1990s, however, the new era of the auction house finally emerged, designed to reach out to whole new audiences of collectors. Not only did the houses offer objects that once would never have crossed their portals, new categories of collectors were encouraged to come in to see what might catch their eyes.

The auction house today

The names Sotheby's and Christie's have long been synonymous with good taste and breeding. To this day, a certain cachet is still associated with these houses based on their venerated position in the industry.

Their financial reserves and other resources—such as highly trained experts in various aspects of fine art and antiques—place them heads above virtually all other houses. But none of this should deter you from considering them as sources for acquiring pieces for your collection. Yes, they were more stuffy

Unofficially...
According to Christopher Hartop, director of specialist services at Christie's, half of his employer's efforts go toward servicing the needs of individual collectors, not dealers.
—"Auctions Without Anxiety," the *Wall Street Journal*, July 2, 1999

than not at one time, but they are anything but that today. Any collector can call to ask for advice and assistance from these institutions, and they are encouraged to do so. The best collector is a well-educated collector, and it is very much a part of the approach of the modern auction house to do whatever is possible to aid this particular education.

Outdated myths and legends

Even though auction houses have largely reshaped themselves, many collectors still hold vestiges of their earlier images. These are a few common misconceptions:

- "I'm not rich enough." The big ticket items do attract the most attention when it comes to media hype, but the truth is that many items available at auctions are well within the reach of the average collector. According to a 1995 article in the Christian Science Monitor, 80 percent of the merchandise sold by Sotheby's went for less than $5,000, and 25 percent for less than $1,000. Wisely, such houses as Christie's and Sotheby's now put a lot of promotional effort behind their less-expensive auctions in order to capture what they call the mid-market—collectors willing to spend in the $500–$2,000 range.

- "I have to know what I'm doing (or at least give the impression that I do) before I'll be taken seriously." There's some truth to this statement, but you'll find that auction houses—especially the top ones—are exactly where you can get a lot of the education you need, not only about auctions but about antiques in general. In fact, previewing lots prior to auction is acknowledged as one of the best ways to learn about antiques, and you can do it at virtually all auction houses.

■ "I'll never be able to follow the auctioneer's patter." The stream of rapid talking that char-acterizes auctions is known as the "auctioneer's chant." It consists of a series of numbers (rep-resenting the bids) connected by simple filler words that are used to remind bidders of the last number bid and give them time to think about whether they want to bid higher. At some auctions, such as those for cars or tobacco, lots are presented quickly—tobacco auctioneers, in fact, may sell upwards of 600 lots per hour—and it is difficult to keep up with the fast-paced chant unless you're familiar with it. At the auctions that collectors are most likely to attend, items are presented much more slowly, more along the pace of 60 items or so per hour.

■ "Auctions go too fast. By the time I'll be ready to bid, the lot I'm interested in will be gone." True, auctions can be fast paced, but they don't all go at the same rapid-fire speed all the time. Part of the auctioneer's responsibility is to judge the tenor and mood of the crowd and present items appropriately. If they feel they should spend more time on important lots, they will. If they think it's appropriate to spend some time educating buyers a little, they'll do that too. Even if the bidding is frenetic, it doesn't mean that you can't participate. There is always time to make your intentions known before the final gavel falls.

■ "If I scratch my nose or wave to my spouse, they'll consider it a bid." This is how bidding is often portrayed in the movies, and it's a great dramatic (or comedic) device. The truth is, it almost never happens. Most auction houses assign numbered paddles to bidders before the auction begins, and most bidders use them.

Auction houses generally prefer the use of bidding paddles regardless of the situation. They don't like to overlook bids and little gestures such as nose scratches or ear pulls can escape their notice if bidding is active. In either case, such occurrences are rare as auctioneers keep a very close tab on the active bidders for each lot. If you're not one of them, they'll ignore your gesture or ask you if you meant to place a bid. Rarely does an erroneous bid put an undesired object into the hands of an unsuspecting waver or bidder. When it does, the item usually is re-auctioned or offered to the next-highest bidder.

▪ "I may end up paying an inflated price because the auction house will have people bid up the item." Such activity, known as shilling, is against the law. This isn't to say that it doesn't happen, but the chances of it happening to you, especially if you're doing business with a reputable auction house, are virtually nonexistent.

So, with these myths dispelled, here's the bottom line: Auctions can be great places to find antiques at good prices and a lot of fun to go to. You won't know which ones are the places for you until you do some research on them and actually attend a few. With so many different types of auctions available to you, don't cheat yourself by not exploring this particular arena.

Moneysaver
Many auction houses charge a buyer's premium, which can add 10 percent or more to the price you pay for any items you purchase. Even this premium, however, is far less than the average markup at retail.

Each type of auction, as you'll see in the descriptions that follow, offers a unique forum for buying and selling antiques, and there's a good chance that you'll find one or more of them a good fit for the collecting category you wish to pursue. In some cases, they may be the only venues in which you'll see certain types of antiques, especially very rare and costly pieces.

You'll find contact information in Appendix D for all the auction houses mentioned in this chapter, as well as for a number of other well-known establishments.

Once you identify the auction houses that most interest you, contact them to see if they offer subscriptions to their auction catalogs. Most do, and they'll usually offer lists of the prices realized at auction as well. Be prepared to pay handsomely for these subscriptions; $30 for one catalog is fairly standard, and an annual subscription can cost as much as $150 or more. Many houses will also sell individual catalogs. Some will offer a free sample so you can get an idea of the items they offer for sale.

Some houses even offer preview videos for certain auctions. This can be a great way to see items if you're not going to attend the auction in person, but they still don't replace the scrutiny through which you should put any object you're considering buying. For more on how to do this on an absentee basis, turn to Chapter 9, "Buying at Auction."

National auction houses

Such establishments as Butterfield & Butterfield, Christie's, Du Mouchelle Art Gallery, Phillips Son & Neale, Robert W. Skinner, Sotheby's, and William Doyle Galleries are widely acknowledged as some of the leaders of the American antiques auction industry. This is based on such factors as size, age, and the services they provide to buyers and sellers.

As part of the overall redefining of the auction industry, many houses have made major changes in their structure and in the way they do business. Butterfield & Butterfield, for example, is now part of the auction empire owned by online giant eBay (it also owns Kruse International, the largest auctioneer of cars in the world). Both Christie's and Sotheby's have crossed what used to be a sacred division between art dealers and antiques houses and acquired renowned art galleries (Christie's bought Leger, a famed London gallery, while Sotheby's purchased the Andre Emmerich Gallery in New York). Online bookseller Amazon.com bought a 2 percent share in Sotheby's in June 1999, and announced plans to launch a joint online auction site—sothebys.amazon.com—which will offer art, antiques, and collectibles. You can look for more of these deals to take place in the future as the auction industry continues to redefine itself, especially as electronic commerce and online auction sites continue to develop.

While it's too early to tell how these partnerships will work out, it's more than likely that they'll end up in favor of collectors, especially those collectors with interests in more than one category. There's more convenience in dealing with one or two houses instead of many, and the services provided to buyers and sellers are often more comprehensive following a merger. On the other hand, the dominance of such major superhouses and Web sites may have negative implications for the industry as a whole if it forces smaller dealers and auctioneers out of business. Customers could lose the more

66

For as long as anyone can remember, auction houses and dealers have been clients and co-conspirators; now that the houses have entered the retail fray, they're becoming competitors.
—Robert Becker, from "Where the Auction Is," *Town and Country,* January 1, 1997

99

personalized, customer-centered services they can expect from local businesses.

Big league specialties

You'll see most major collections, large pieces of antique furniture, important paintings and sculptures, celebrity auctions, and other important antiques and artwork offered at the largest auction houses. They have a well-established reputation for handling such items, and when it comes to presenting them to the public, they often have the largest resources for pulling in the kinds of crowds that will bring the best prices.

These houses do business year-round; there is, however, a high season when the grandest and most expensive items are auctioned, generally autumn through early winter. This allows the auction houses to capture buyers after they return from their summer vacations and before the holiday season begins. Less grand auctions that they also conduct include the following:

- Skinner Auctioneers' Discovery Sales: Skinner, a Boston-based auction house, promotes these sales to beginning buyers. They often contain the contents of various estates, which means a lot of variety both in items offered and prices.

- Sotheby's Arcade sales: This lower-priced branch of Sotheby's conducts auctions that feature furniture, art glass, pottery, and other decorative items.

- Christie's East sales: Another lower-priced branch of a major auction house, the sales conducted by Christie's East are also designed to attract the mid-market instead of the high rollers.

These events are the ones preferred by many beginning collectors because they're usually void of the hype that can surround the higher-ticket events.

Value-added services

What makes establishing a relationship with a large auction house desirable is the wealth of information and services that these institutions have to offer. Many have satellite locations in various parts of the country for the convenience of buyers not located near their main places of business. San Francisco-based Butterfield & Butterfield has offices in Los Angeles and Chicago; Christie's, which like Sotheby's also has a real estate division, has more than 100 representatives in 41 countries. At one point, Sotheby's had more than 200 specialists in 70 different collecting categories.

All three of them also have Web sites where the following information (in varying degrees) can be found:

- Auction schedules.
- Catalogs.
- Lot prices following sales.
- Frequently asked questions about antiques.
- Information on appraisals and consignments.
- Auction terms glossaries.
- Newsletters and e-mail notification of news and events of interest to collectors.
- Information on financial services, such as advances on consignments and loans secured by art collections that are not being sold.
- Online absentee bidding. Butterfield & Butterfield has used this feature extremely well

Moneysaver
Catalog subscriptions can be costly. If you have a friend who collects the same things you do, see if the two of you can share the expense.

in its multicity auctions held simultaneously in key cities across the country.

Many of the larger houses offer even more services for buyers. Christie's, for example, has an international art studies program for students of all ages. Sotheby's also has a similar program. New York-based William Doyle Galleries, which is noted for its specialty couture sales, hosts a lecture series that highlights such topics as specific collecting categories and ways to discern value.

Locating major auction houses

You'll find information in Appendix D on all the major houses discussed here. Most can be accessed through their Internet sites, and this is often the best way in which to get to know what they offer and ask questions of them. These addresses are listed in Appendix D as well.

Regional auction houses

With the collapse of trade boundaries created by advances in telecommunications and a more globalized economy, many regional auction houses function like national houses do—in other words, they have a national presence and they attract buyers from all over the country (and even internationally) in some form or another. Others are either smaller in size and presence and direct their marketing efforts to residents of the region in which they're located, or they specialize in antiques and artifacts from their particular area. Examples of regional houses include

- America West Archives. This Cedar City, Utah, auction house specializes in historical documents, letters, photographs, papers, and other materials related to the Old West.

Unofficially... One of the best sources for auction houses of all types is the Maine Antique Digest newspaper. The online version of the paper at www.maineantiquedigest.com provides a comprehensive listing of auctions all over the country.

- Cincinnati Art Galleries. Located in Cincinnati, Ohio, where Rookwood pottery was manufactured, this gallery specializes in Rookwood pottery auctions.

- Manheim, Penn.-based Conestoga Auction Co., Inc. Located in the Conestoga Valley, this company pays tribute to the area's pioneer heritage, specializing in firearms and Native American relics.

- The Treadway Gallery, located in Zanesville, Ohio, is another that specializes in American pottery from the surrounding region, such as Roseville and Weller.

- Neal Auction Company. Located in New Orleans, a city renowned for its various antiquing spots, this auction house attracts both national and international buyers to its estate auctions, which feature American, English, and Continental furniture; silver; porcelain; paintings; prints; sculpture; jewelry; and Oriental rugs.

- The Coeur d'Alene Art Auction. Wildlife, sporting art, and art of the American West are the specialties for this regional auction house located in Hayden, Idaho.

Other well-known regional houses are listed in Appendix D.

Why you'll want to do business here

If you're collecting antiques related to a specific region or historical event, these auction houses can't be beat for variety and selection. For example, if you're collecting Civil War memorabilia, houses south of the Mason-Dixon line are going to be your best bet for picking up these items. If fishing and

Unofficially...
With the costs of doing business through major auction houses on the rise, many fine things are now sold through smaller houses, often outside of major cities.

maritime antiques are more to your liking, check out auction houses in Maine and Massachusetts.

Regional auction houses often sell collections from prominent local collectors that are thought to have a stronger local appeal than they would if consigned to one of the larger national houses. Very fine antiques can be found at this level; it's definitely worth your time to identify a few of the houses that you think will fit your collecting goals and establish relationships with them.

Since these houses are smaller than the national establishments, they often know their customers quite well, and they use this information to help them personalize their services for these customers.

How to find them

Regional auction houses often advertise in the leading industry publications, found in Appendix C, "Further Reading." You'll also find them listed in various Internet directories. Many have some type of Web site, although the information contained there may be no more than a brief description of the house, an auction schedule, and contact information. Advertisements for specific auctions conducted by these companies are also often listed on the Web.

Specialized auction houses

Specialized auction houses are exactly what the name implies: They focus their efforts on specific collecting categories. In many cases you can identify the specialty of the house by its name; for example, Baltimore Book Co. Inc. specializes in—you guessed it—books and other ephemera. Chuck de Luca Maritime Antiques (located in York, Maine) specializes in nautical antiques as well as fire department antiques. Other specialty houses of note include

- Bill Bertoia Auctions. If you're looking for antique banks and toys, this New Jersey-based auction house is the place to go.

- Early Auction Co. Based in Milford, Ohio, Early Auction specializes in art glass, although general antiques auctions are also held.

- David Rago Auctions. Another auction house in New Jersey, this one specializing in items from the Arts and Crafts movement.

- Swann Galleries. Rare books, autographs, photographs, and other pieces of ephemera are available at this New York auction house.

Given the number of antiques houses in the United States, at least one is probably dedicated to your specific collecting category.

Why you'll want to do business here

The value in dealing with specialized houses is the specialty itself. The people who run these establishments are experts in a particular collecting category and they'll know everything there is to know about it. They know who owns what and when special pieces or collections are coming up for auction. This very focused approach can make them valuable resources for collectors who are taking a similar approach to their collections. If you really aren't interested in seeing anything but what you collect, you can cut right to the chase at these auction houses.

Finding specialized houses

Auction houses specific to a collecting category are often listed in price guides and general collecting guides. Other sources include:

- Ads in industry newspapers and magazines

Watch Out!
Auction houses that specialize are rarely going to have bargains since they attract so many collectors of that specialty.

- Notices in collector's club publications
- Internet antiques indexes

Dealers also have a group of houses that they frequent, and they may be willing to tell you about a few of them, especially if they're not planning to attend any sales themselves in the near future. Remember though, auctions are a primary source for dealers to acquire their inventory. They may not be willing to divulge this information unless you have a very good relationship with them.

Local auction houses

There is at least one auction house in virtually every city in the United States. For the most part, they fall into the following categories:

- General auction houses. Some houses will auction off just about everything—from appliances to livestock to collectibles. They'll have very active auction calendars with something scheduled at least once a week and even twice weekly during certain times of the year.

- Antiques auctioneers or estate liquidators. These establishments will schedule an auction when the situation warrants one—in other words, if they've acquired enough pieces to hold a good auction, or if they've been hired to conduct an estate auction.

- Specialty houses. They may specialize in one collecting category, more than one, or in a very specific segment of a category (for example, twentieth century furniture or a combination of glass and pottery). Again, they'll usually hold auctions when the situation warrants it, which may be no more often than once or twice a year. Between auctions, these houses often function more like antique shops or galleries.

Again, due to the collapse of trade boundaries and more efficient communications networks, local auction houses can draw regional and even national audiences. How far their circle of influence extends will have a great deal to do with their finances. Local houses intent on building a broader customer base will advertise in industry publications and spend some money promoting themselves on the Internet and in antiques guides. If they're not interested in stretching their boundaries or can't afford to do so, ads in local papers and the phone book will be about the extent of their marketing.

Events run by local auction houses can be real hit-or-miss propositions, depending on the type of establishment. However, they're worth considering for the following reasons:

- They're close. If you can't get to auctions in other parts of the country, they may be your only opportunity.

- You'll get the opportunity to see who else is collecting in your category. Local auctions are great places for networking and for meeting dealers and other collectors with interests similar to yours.

- They're great places to get your feet wet. The atmosphere at many local auctions is decidedly laid back. In fact, many collectors start with these auctions just to hone their skills before moving on to other venues.

Unfortunately, you won't know whether such auctions are worth your time unless you preview them. Most local auctions don't have catalogs, and if

Bright Idea
Many smaller auction houses don't follow regular schedules and only hold auctions when their inventory reaches a critical mass. When you find houses that you like, ask if they send out notices to customers on a mailing list.

Watch Out!
Always check the
reputation of an
auction house,
especially a local
house. They tend
to come and go,
and they can
leave disgruntled
buyers and sell-
ers in their wake.

they do the information they contain is usually
sketchy—often just lot numbers and brief descriptions. Because the quality of the pieces being
offered can vary so widely, you may end up waiting
an entire day before you see something worth bidding on, so they're not places to go if you're short
on time. On the other hand, they can be great
venues for whiling away the hours on a rainy afternoon.

Other types of auctions

The auctions discussed next are grouped together
for one of two reasons: They're either less common
than the ones mentioned above, or they appeal to
very select audiences. Even though they may be
somewhat off the beaten track, they too present
good buying opportunities, especially if your needs
are very specialized.

Country

Typically low-key affairs conducted on-site at a house
or farm that is being sold, these auctions are decidedly different from the more formal events held by
auction houses or galleries. Since the entire contents of the estate are usually being sold, there will
be items in virtually all categories to look at. There's
a good chance that most of them won't appeal to
you in the least—unless you are in the market for,
say, a cow milker—but there will be plenty of people
around you who will be extremely interested in such
devices.

Why spend your time at these auctions? If you're
collecting in a country-related category, these are
the places where you'll find what you're looking for.
Other reasons to attend these events include

- No buyer's premiums. Unlike auctions held in many other venues, there typically are no additional charges to the buyer at country auctions.

- No reserves. A reserve specifies the lowest price a seller will take on an item. If the item doesn't meet its reserve, it doesn't get sold. You'll rarely see them at country auctions and others held to liquidate estates.

- Less competition from other collectors. These auctions are often held during the weekend, but some take place during the week, which makes it harder for collectors who work to attend. They're also low budget, which means that advertising is often limited to a display or classified ad in the local paper or some flyers distributed in whatever town the auction is held in. However, you will see a lot of dealers at them as they are prime venues for finding pieces in some collecting categories—not necessarily antiques categories, however.

Even though country auctions are often a little (or a lot) on the seedy side, don't judge them by their appearance; as Mary Emmerling puts it in *Mary Emmerling's New Country Collecting,* "Don't judge an auctioneer by his overalls." Dealers in rural locations can be, and often are, just as sharp as their counterparts in the city. If a good antique comes up at a country auction, you won't be stealing it unless it has escaped the scrutiny of everyone there.

Charity

Auctions have been popular fund-raisers for non-profit organizations for years and they're often a fertile source for collectors. The items in these auctions

Unofficially...
Many small and medium-sized newspapers are establishing Web sites, and these can be great places for spotting country and farm auctions. Try doing a search on a town or city name to see what's available.

are generally donated for tax purposes and by people with a genuine interest in whichever charity is benefiting from the auction. While there may be a nice selection of pieces to view, and some real treasures among them, many of the donated items may be there because the original owner found it difficult to sell them. This is especially true if the item has limited interest—that is, its appeal is local or regional or geared toward a very specific collecting category.

These auctions may be limited to antiques or may contain a little bit of everything. If they're being held to raise funds for a local public television station, they're usually telecast. However, the public is always given the opportunity to personally inspect items being auctioned, and you should always take the opportunity to do so.

Catalog or mail order

These auctions offer special merchandise geared to attract the interests of a well-defined collecting audience. While you may not be aware of them, they're actually quite common because they're a fairly inexpensive way for a specialized house or dealer to reach a broad audience. Once interested bidders receive their auction catalogs, they place their bids by phone or mail during a specific time period. When the deadline for the auction is reached, the house or dealer reviews all the bids and awards each lot to the highest bidder. Buyers can also specify their high bid amounts and let the house do their bidding for them until their maximum is reached. This format, by the way, is also used by eBay and other online auction establishments.

Although these auctions are fairly popular, especially for people who can't get to auctions in person, you may see fewer of them as the antiques arena continues to take shape on the Internet. Some houses and dealers who currently hold these auctions are also making their catalogs available on the Internet. It's cheaper for them than mailing catalogs to all their customers, and they can also reach far more people by doing so.

Just the facts

- Auctions can be the best venues for picking up antiques at a good price.

- Viewing the items available for auction is an ideal way to learn more about antiques in general.

- Ask for information from a variety of auction houses—national, regional, and specialty— when determining which ones you want to do business with. Each will have something different to offer.

- Use the Internet to track down auction venues across the country. Many houses maintain an online presence exactly for this reason.

Still More Places for Finding Antiques

PART III

GET THE SCOOP ON...
Using the Internet to search for antiques ▪
Buying opportunities on the Internet ▪ Finding
online research sites ▪ Online communities for
collectors

Antiques on the Internet

The Internet is changing everything, and the antiques business is no exception. A quick search through any of the Internet search engines turns up not just hundreds, but thousands of Web sites dedicated to antiques and collecting, ranging from auctions and virtual antiques malls to chat rooms and information databases. Virtually every entity in the industry has a presence on the Web, or soon will.

For collectors, the Internet offers unique opportunities for pursuing the objects of their desires. It will never replace some of the traditional aspects of collecting that are so alluring—such as being able to see things in all dimensions and actually touch and feel them, or talking face-to-face with other collectors and dealers—but you can do so many other things. If you can't travel physically to a show or an auction, you can probably get there in cyberspace. Need to look up a price? Go to an online database.

145

Trying to learn more about a certain period or style? With the Internet, you can tap into informational resources around the world.

Welcome to the virtual world

Even if you're an old hand at using a computer, you may not have had much reason to surf the Web until now. If so, the following overview will give you an idea of how it's done and what awaits you there. (If you've spent a good deal of time in cyberspace, you can skip forward to the next section.)

The Internet started out as many individual computers that were joined together to form a communications and research tool for the federal government, research institutions, and libraries. By its nature, the Internet is dense with information, and weaving your way through its content can be time-consuming. A recent cartoon compared an Internet search to reading *War and Peace*. But, just like that great novel, there are treasures to be found if you plow through it.

The World Wide Web, which was developed in the early 1990s, added graphics and sound to the Internet and opened the door for much broader applications. It was during this time that the majority of consumers got their first opportunities to explore the Internet when such online service providers as America Online, CompuServe, and Prodigy added Internet portals (or passageways) to their basic offerings.

Boarding the on-ramp

Accessing the Internet still requires signing on for service with one of these companies or through any of the many Internet Service Providers (ISPs) located throughout the country. There are many ISPs to choose from, and more of them are cropping up on a regular basis. This can make the choice of a provider difficult, but not impossible. Here are some of the questions you should ask any company you're interested in using:

- **Cost**   Most providers now offer a fixed monthly fee with unlimited online time, with prices currently ranging from about $9.95 to $21.95. Some, however, base their charges on actual time spent online. Ask to see if there is a free or low-cost trial offer for the first month so you can try out the service. Also ask if there are any start-up fees in addition to monthly charges. Some ISPs, especially start-up companies, offer special rates if you prepay your contract for a specified period of time. If this option appeals to you, make sure the contract has an escape clause in case you find that the service isn't meeting your needs.

- **Access**   The ISP should offer an 800 number for access in your area. Be sure to ask if there is an extra charge for using it. Try calling the number a few times during the time of day you're most likely to be using it. If you are greeted by the shriek of a modem connection more than once or twice, consider a different company with a lower user-to-modem ratio. Another handy feature, especially if you travel and want to check your e-mail while on the road, are access numbers in cities in other parts of the country.

- **Modem speed support**   Even the fastest modems can't work to optimum speeds if the lines to them aren't providing rapid access. While most computer users are connecting to their ISP over plain old telephone wire, faster connection options, such as Integrated Services Digital Network (ISDN) or Digital Subscriber Line (DSL), are becoming more widely available. Ask to see if the ISP provider is supporting these connections or plans to do so.

- **Technical support**   Problems always happen when you least want or expect them to, which is why good and available technical support is so important. Ideally, support should be available 24 hours a day, seven days a week, and accessible through a local phone number or an 800 number. Avoid systems that offer online or e-mail supports as you have to be able to sign on to use it.

- **Services**   E-mail is a standard offering with most ISPs. Other services of interest to many Internet users are Web page hosting and e-commerce support.

Once you have signed up for the service you've decided to use, and it's installed on your system, getting on the information superhighway is really just a few keystrokes and mouse-clicks away. One of the nicest things about today's computer systems is their intuitiveness (or the sense you'll have that they are intuitive). Rather than having to face a dark screen with a blinking cursor and figure out what to do next, these systems usually tell you what to do. If you take a wrong turn, starting over is as easy as clicking on the "home" or "back" button on your Web browser (the software that allows you to navigate the Web), which will take you back to where you began.

Searching for information

Search services, such as Yahoo! (www.yahoo.com), AltaVista (www.altavista.com), Excite (www.excite.

Moneysaver
Keep track of how much time you spent online. If you're averaging fewer than 20 hours per month and you're primarily using your online service provider to send and receive e-mail and access the Web, you're a good candidate for an ISP that offers service based on actual connect time.

com), Infoseek (www.infoseek.com), Lycos (www.lycos.com), and others are your tools for finding information on the Internet. They operate in a similar manner to electronic Yellow Pages (which, incidentally, also can be retrieved online) by employing programs, called search engines, to search for information. Each has different protocols for entering search terms. Some will tell you to type in a phrase, such as "antiques in Indiana." Others will prompt you to enter keywords separated by "and," "or," or "not," or even plus and minus signs, such as "antiques + Indiana," or "antiques – Indiana." Each will yield a different search; "antiques and Indiana" or "antiques + Indiana," for example, will give you Web sites that have both antiques and Indiana in the descriptions. "Antiques not Indiana" or "antiques – Indiana" will give you listings of antiques that exclude any information pertaining to Indiana.

Click on a site that interests you, and you'll zip to that location in a matter of seconds. What you find there may or may not be of interest or relevant to your search. If it is, look around. If not, click on the "back" button and go to the next item on your list.

While information on the Web can be reached through any search service, no one service will take you to every possible site because they're all configured differently. New information is also constantly being added to the Internet. If you can't find what you're looking for with one search service, try your search using another one, or use a meta search service, such as Metacrawler (www.metacrawler.com), Dogpile (www.dogpile.com), AskJeeves (www.askjeeves.com), or Copernic 99 (www.copernic.com). From the user's end, these search applications work the same as any search service; however,

Timesaver
Use the bookmarking function on your search engine to mark the sites that look interesting so you can find them again. You can always delete them later if they don't prove to be useful.

Timesaver
If you think you know where you want to go but you don't know the address and you don't want to deal with a search engine, try typing in the name with a "www." at the beginning and a ".com" at the end. If it's a nonprofit organization, substitute ".org" for ".com."

instead of maintaining their own databases, they take your query and submit it to several other search services. The other services process your question and return lists of sites to the meta search service.

Because of the huge number of Web sites dedicated to antiques, it takes practice to fine-tune your keywords and key phrases in order to get to the sites that will be of the most use to you. Experience will teach you to try several different combinations until you find the ones that work best. Searches can be very specific, such as "Tiffany vases," or more general, such as "antique American furniture." The responses will vary widely. With practice, you'll learn how to achieve the best results. Broader searches are sometimes best because they may take you to wonderful and unexpected Web sites. But they take time, so be patient.

Browsing a site

Web sites usually are designed with color pictures, text, and graphics. Most are pleasing to the eye and organized to encourage exploration. Some play music while you browse, and a few even have short videos.

The majority of today's Web sites are user friendly once you understand how they're organized and how they work. Think of them as books. They start with some sort of an introduction page, or home page. Some home pages are as simple as a graphic with an icon. Click on the icon and you'll go past the home page to other pages with more information. Other home pages are more graphically dense and illustrate what the site has to offer right away. In either case, they work in much the same way by guiding you to other pages in the site. These pages may have links (called hyperlinks) to still more pages in the same site, or they may have links to other sites with similar information. You can tell a hyperlink from plain text because it will usually be underlined or highlighted in some way. If it's really a hyperlink, when you move your cursor over it, the cursor will turn into a hand.

A single Web site may consist of hundreds of pages or just a few. The more complex sites will allow you to search within them for more information. At eBay (www.ebay.com), the largest online auction site, you can type in "English tea caddy," and a list will be returned with all the possible items listed for sale at the site. You then browse around by clicking your mouse on each item listed. If you see a piece you like, you can print the photograph and information about the item, make further inquiry, or bid on it (more about this later).

Buying online

E-commerce has become the most exciting segment of the online community, and certainly the most hyped. It's hard to believe that buying and selling over the Internet was little more than a concept just a few years ago, but it is decidedly big business today and everyone wants a piece of the pie. The mad scramble to establish e-commerce sites is driven by big numbers; in 1999 alone, e-commerce sales were expected to total $20.2 billion. The key players in online commerce have pushed hard to ensure that online transactions are as safe as any other, and their efforts have been amply rewarded by the sheer numbers of Internet transactions that are being conducted each day.

Most sites that allow shopping have virtual "shopping baskets" where you can place selected items as you continue looking for other things. (If

Unofficially...
Forty percent of Web users will be online buyers by 2002, generating $400 billion in e-commerce transactions, according to researchers at International Data Corp.

you change your mind at any time, you can remove items from your basket as well. Some sites allow you to save your purchases for a later date so you can think about them for awhile.) When you are done browsing, you proceed to "check out," where your online purchase will be completed. You'll be asked for your name, address, telephone number, e-mail address (for order confirmation), and credit card number.

You'll be notified via a pop-up box if the site you're using is secure or not (unless you've chosen to disable this feature on your computer). If you're transmitting to an unsecure site, you can abort the transmission and make other payment arrangements if you are uncomfortable or uncertain about the transaction. Keep in mind, however, that the technology used in most Internet transmissions makes it virtually impossible to intercept a credit card number. Data is transmitted in packets of electronic information that are reassembled at the receiving end. Intercepts are rare; however, the possibility of them happening is a factor to consider before buying on the Internet. Your best bet to ensure against credit card interception on the Internet is through using secure sites. You'll be able to tell what they are by a security icon—usually a lock—that will appear in your Web browser's window when you go to sites that use secure servers.

Staying connected

Using the Internet effectively takes skill and patience. Until you learn how to narrow your definitions when you do a search, your inquiries will turn up hundreds, even thousands, of Web sites, and yes, you'll wander down a number of them before you learn how to recognize the ones you really want.

Going down those side roads gets even more frustrating when your journey gets interrupted by a computer crash, which can happen for a number of reasons and usually when you least want it to. Your best defenses against such crashes include:

- Using up-to-date hardware and software. While it's possible to surf the Web with older machines, newer systems use technology specially designed for Internet applications, which vastly improve your chances of completing a search without the computer freezing up on you. The Web is graphically dense (and getting more so by the minute), and it takes a computer with lots of speed and processing capacity to access it comfortably. This isn't to say that the older PC you have at home won't work well for you now and for some time to come. The time to upgrade a computer system or buy a new one usually comes when there's something you want to do with your existing machine that you can't do now, such as edit video or develop graphically-dense Web sites, or when you spend so much time on the Internet that processing speed does become more important.

- Having clean phone lines. Crackly, staticky phone lines can wreak havoc with online communications. If the clarity on yours is poor, ask your phone company to run a check on your lines to see if there are any problems that they can correct.

- Using surge protectors. Just a slight interruption in power can end an online session; a surge protector can smooth out the peaks and valleys of electrical service and keep you

Moneysaver
If you're thinking about upgrading an older computer for Internet use, compare the upgrade costs to the price of a new machine. You may find that you can get a brand-new computer for a few dollars more than what it will cost to upgrade the old one.

communicating. At a minimum, your computer should be plugged into a power strip that has a surge protector built into it. More powerful devices with additional features also are available.

- Repairing any faulty connections or lines in your home. Telephone outlets with faulty wiring also are a source of communications problems. A phone with a short in the cord can foul up all the telephone connections in your house, including the one that your computer uses. Check the phones first by unplugging each one to see if transmission quality improves. If this doesn't fix the problem, test the outlets by unplugging phones from them as well.

The modem, which is the piece of equipment that allows your computer to talk to other computers, needs clean phone lines to work its fastest and best. Even if the modem on your machine is fast—these days, a modem running at 56 kbps (kilobits per second) is fairly standard—its transmission speed will drop over dirty lines.

Types of sites

The Internet basically is an electronic library and a huge shopping mall where new items are being added by the minute. The information and buying opportunities it contains are almost beyond comprehension. Until you actually conduct a few searches and familiarize yourself with the information relevant to your collecting category, it is hard to accurately describe the depth of the Internet pool.

While many Internet sites have content pertaining to a specific function, such as information, community, shopping, or research tools, the current trend is toward developing sites that can offer as many different functions as possible. For example, an auction site may include a list of dealers, collector clubs, and insurers. An online antiques mall may have links to price guides, reference materials, and auctions. Online periodicals have links to dealers, auction houses, discussion groups, and suppliers. And, of course, there are the advertisers. They're the ones hoping that you'll stay long enough at the site to become loyal to it, and in the Internet world, loyalty results in revenues.

From the consumer's point of view, these Internet sites really aren't a bad idea as they can make accessing information on the Internet much easier. If you can get most or all of what you need at one site, why go elsewhere? The constant barrage of advertising can be annoying, but most Web surfers learn to filter it out over time.

Electronic commerce sites

As previously mentioned, the World Wide Web has been a tremendous boon to the antiques arena, opening it to new markets and new groups of collectors. People who once only dreamed of being able to attend certain shows or auctions can now use the Internet to get them there, thanks to all the different sites for electronic commerce that have been established in the past few years.

Retail sites on the Internet range from electronic storefronts for restaurants where you can place an order for takeout or delivery, to full-figured online establishments that offer a little bit of everything. New companies join the milieu on a daily basis, and there's something new to look at every time you sign on.

Watch Out!
Internet "cookies" are used by many Internet sites to collect information on the people who visit them. If you don't want to add yours to the data being collected, refuse to accept cookies when the system asks if you want them.

Unofficially...
There are thousands of antiques buying opportunities— one directory listed more than 1,500 direct purchase sites—and more are added every day.

It is impossible to quantify the number of sites for purchasing antiques that exist on the Internet. Nor is it possible to determine whether purchasing items through the Internet is any more or less preferable to buying through conventional establishments. Your satisfaction is rarely guaranteed in either instance, especially when dealing with older antiques (those made prior to 1870). Older objects are often excluded from even the best guarantees. However, there are ways to assure customer satisfaction, which will be discussed in more detail in Chapter 10, "Buying Online."

For antiques collectors, e-commerce sites of interest run the gamut from classified ads to the arena that is currently occupying the spotlight: online auctions.

Online auction sites

The granddaddy of these sites is eBay, which pioneered the concept of the online auction for such companies as Amazon.com and eHammer. While eBay and the others bill themselves as auction sites, they really function as clearinghouses. They do facilitate auctions, but they never have the goods being auctioned in their possession. Nor do they collect money from sellers; the final transaction takes place directly between the buyer and the seller (sometimes facilitated through an escrow service). It's the same sort of purchase you may make at any garage sale, antiques mall, or dealer transaction, except that the price you pay is determined by bid as opposed to negotiation.

Other differences between online auctions and the traditional auction model include the following:

- Items are offered separately rather than in lots, although a seller may sell multiples of the same item to one or more buyers (known as a "dutch" auction).

- There are no catalogs describing the merchandise, nor are there specialists available to discuss the condition and provenance of an item. The seller posts all information and is responsible for the accuracy of its content.

- The company offers no guarantees concerning condition and authenticity of the merchandise. Instead, it is up to the buyer and seller to come to agreement on such issues themselves.

- Items are not sold in a day. Most auctions extend over a period of five or more days. Some go on as long as 10 days.

- There are no buyer's fees beyond what the seller asks for (usually postage, and sometimes insurance on higher-priced items).

All online auction sites ask you to register before you are allowed to submit a bid. Usually, you only have to register once. When you complete the registration form, the Web site sets up an account for you. Each time you come back to the site, the Web site software recognizes you; this allows the site to develop a profile and transaction history on you and all the other users of the service. This is how you can check out the people with whom you are dealing (it's also how they check you out). It also speeds up your future transactions since the computer already has your basic ordering data on file.

When you go to an auction site, you'll notice that there are established categories for the items being offered for sale. Be sure to check all categories that interest you; sometimes you'll find items that you would expect to be listed in one category actually listed in another. For example, you may find

Watch Out!
Experts recommend using something other than the main screen name for your Internet account for identification purposes when registering for online services. Divulging such information can make you vulnerable to anyone interested in stealing your online identity.

Bright Idea
Check eBay's auction spotlight for the hottest items currently being bid on at that site.

a piece of estate jewelry listed under either "jewelry" or "arts and antiques," or even "beads." If you are looking for a particular type of item, it is best to use the search feature, which will help you find it regardless of the category in which it is listed.

When you've located an item that you want to purchase, you submit a bid. Some sites have an automatic bidding process that allows you to enter the maximum amount you're willing to pay. As the auction goes on, your bid will automatically be increased until it reaches the amount you've set. If at that point you're outbid, you'll be asked (via e-mail) if you want to increase your maximum bid.

You'll also be asked where you'd like to start your bidding. Items are listed with a seller's reserve (the minimum acceptable price) if there is one. As in regular auctions, a bidding increment is displayed so that bidding proceeds in an orderly fashion.

Once your bid is posted and is accepted as the current high bid, you will be identified as the current high bidder. This is where the automatic bidding function takes over. If a subsequent bid is entered higher than your current bid amount, the software automatically raises your bid by the minimum increment required to again put you in the high bidder slot. If bidding reaches the maximum amount you've set, you'll be asked if you want to revise your maximum. If you don't, you're done for that auction.

Eventually, the time period for the auction expires and the high bidder is declared the final buyer. Seller and buyer are both notified by e-mail so they can arrange payment and delivery. For high-ticket items, escrow services are available to protect the interests of both buyers and sellers.

Auction sites also may include general information on collecting and collectors' bulletin boards. They also have links to online booksellers and purveyors of other services of interest to collectors.

For more detailed information on bidding on items at online auctions, turn to Chapter 10.

Internet antiques malls

Electronic antiques malls are basically traditional antiques malls translated to cyberspace. However, unlike earth-based malls, dealers can rent booths in several different areas and offer the identical merchandise in each. It's the electronic equivalent of a perpetual antiques show, but it's going on simultaneously wherever the dealer has established a spot.

Online antiques malls usually have names like The Antique Attic, The Village Antique Mall, Antique Villa, or The Antique Store; in other words, they have names like real malls. And, just like walking through a real mall, browsing an online mall will reveal many different types of dealers. Many are highly specialized regarding the type of goods they carry. Items are displayed through photographs and written descriptions. Buying usually requires contact with the dealer either through e-mail or over the phone. As in face-to-face transactions, it is up to you as the buyer to know what it is that you're purchasing and to be able to authenticate it. Some dealers provide guarantees as to authenticity and many will allow you to return an item if you're dissatisfied with it. Usually the return must be made within several days of receipt.

It's a good idea to check the reputation of any online mall with which you're interested in doing business. Hallmarks of a well-established and reputable site include the following:

Bright Idea
Use a credit card for online purchases whenever possible. It will make it easier to cancel a transaction should you need to.

- Statements of membership in online merchants' associations or other professional associations on the home page.

- Notices of any awards the site has won, also displayed on the home page.

- Criteria used to screen participating dealers. You may have to go beyond the home page to find this. One common place for such information is in the area that gives dealers information on renting online space. Often, this will tell you if any meaningful quality controls are in place.

A good check and balance to use when transacting with a specific online dealer is to run the dealer's name through the electronic version of the telephone book. Such services as Switchboard (www.switchboard.com) let you search for individuals by name or address and also has a Yellow Pages section. Most search services have similar directories available. Check to see if the address and phone numbers match. If there are representations in the Yellow Pages ad, do they match those at the Web site? If discrepancies exist, ask questions and ask for references. Take the time to follow through. Remember, a guarantee is only as good as the person making it.

Online dealers

Many antiques galleries and dealers with regular shops also have retail sites online. Although some dealer Web addresses only provide contact information, it is increasingly common that you can examine and purchase items while online. Dealing direct with established galleries through their Web sites can be particularly helpful when the gallery is a specialist in a particular collecting category. The Internet also allows you to open the door to dealers and galleries in cities that you may rarely get to, if at all. You can establish a relationship with gallery management through your "virtual visits" that you may otherwise have a difficult time arranging. Dealers often publish newsletters, have special shows, and serve as finders for the serious collector. The Internet can help facilitate this relationship.

Many of the more comprehensive dealer sites also have such value-added features as recent sale results and articles about featured artists or objects.

Making direct purchases from dealers over the Internet differs from face-to-face business transactions in several ways. In some respects, the arms-length nature of the Internet can work to your advantage as it can help you avoid the "sizing up" and hard-sell tactics some dealers use. Unless the time comes for you to talk directly to one another, your impressions of each other are formed solely by your online communications. There is no way for a dealer to be able to judge you on anything other than your knowledge.

You'll find more detailed information on online malls and dealers in Chapter 11, "Buying from Dealers."

Online communities and clubs

Bringing people together from all over the world has been one of the Internet's strongest attributes from the start. In the early days of the 'Net, online bulletin boards and newsgroups allowed participants with similar interests to both post and answer questions and relay information to others. In many cases, information of interest to participants was

Watch Out!
Treat online sellers the same way you would a dealer with whom you have never met or transacted business. Build relationships through small purchases before putting yourself at large monetary risk.

made available in online archives consisting of files created by various members and uploaded to the newsgroup site.

Major online services took this concept a step further when they established "online communities" that combined bulletin boards and newsgroups with other content, such as articles pertaining to the issue at hand and links to other areas of the service that may be of interest. Like newsgroups (which still exist, by the way), these online communities focused on specific interests or concerns—for example, women's issues, health, personal finance, or hobbies.

Online communities were a big selling point for online services in the early 1990s, and they continue to be very popular for their ability to bring people of similar interests together from all over the world.

Locating online communities

Finding online communities can be a bit tricky as there really isn't a way to do a search for them. AOL has one for its members who are antiques collectors, which can be accessed by typing the keyword "antiques." EBay also functions as an online collectors community, offering bulletin boards, live chats, and links to other sites of interest. Collectors Web (CollectorsWeb.com) is another site with a message board where collectors can chat.

It's also possible to find online collecting communities by searching other antiques-related sites, and it's a good idea to keep checking sites that you like as content is constantly being added to the Internet. As an example, one of my recent searches turned up a community center, expert chat, and bulletin boards at David Rago's Web site (www.ragoarts. com)—all of them added since my last visit there.

> 66
>
> I still correspond via e-mail with a woman I met in the mid-1990s through AOL's hobby and home-crafts community. We're close friends, yet we've never met face to face.
> —Bead artist and collector Carol Kaplan
>
> 99

Collectors' clubs online

Thousands of collectors groups are present on the Internet. Some are comprehensive online communities that offer a variety of services, including bulletin boards, classified ad listings, events schedules, and live chats with experts. Others are organized as newsgroups for information exchange. Still others exist as nothing more than listings in online directories.

Finding these clubs can be difficult; a search with the keywords "collectors club" may yield thousands of sites. A better way to do it is through the Club Directory, a service of Collector Online (www.collectoronline.com). The site lists more than 800 collectors clubs, and their Web sites if they're on the Internet. Select one that interests you from the list, click on its name, and you're automatically transferred to the club's home page.

Other sources for listings of collectors' clubs include

- Online telephone directories.
- Auction and dealer Web pages.
- Online antiques malls.

You'll find several sites for antiques newsgroups listed in Appendix E, "Internet Resources".

Information-based sites

The more traditional role of the Internet as an information source has taken a lesser role thanks to the explosion of e-commerce, but this is another area in which the 'Net really shines.

Auction houses online

If you're surprised to see auction houses listed here instead of in the e-commerce section, here's the

reason: While most of the top auction houses currently have a presence on the Internet, they aren't
conducting many online auctions yet. A few have
taken place—Butterfield & Butterfield, for example,
hosted a live auction in 1999 in partnership with
Galerie Koller in Zurich, Etude Tajan in Paris, the
Dorotheum in Vienna, and Swann Galleries of New
York. Called the "Art on Paper" auction, the event
was conducted live simultaneously at each location
and over the Internet. Butterfield & Butterfield,
which acted as the agent for the sale of O.J.
Simpson's estate, also accepted online bids when it
was auctioned off.

At this point, most of the top auction houses are
in the process of establishing sites for online trading, making their first forays into this particular
arena, or joining forces with other online entities in
order to do so:

- Butterfield & Butterfield has a deal with eBay
  to offer "co-branded" fine arts and antiques on
  eBay's Web site.

- Sotheby's and Amazon.com have plans for a
  joint fine arts and antiques auction site called
  Sothebys.Amazon.com. The new Web site will
  feature coins, stamps, sports and Hollywood
  memorabilia, fashion, animation art, toys,
  dolls, and other collectibles, as well as general
  art and antiques, books, and jewelry. Property
  to be auctioned will be consigned through
  Sotheby's by a select network of approximately
  1,000 dealers and art world professionals.

- According to the *Wall Street Journal* and the
  Maine Antique Digest, Christie's is discussing
  plans with Disney for an online site. Although
  Christie's has yet to strike its deal, there is no

doubt that it too will soon be conducting online auctions.

From the collector's perspective, all of these transactions are positive events, and the results that they will yield will add an important dimension to the world of antiques online. For now, however, auction house Web sites are good places to visit for other reasons. You can purchase auction catalogs online, research archived catalogs, review the results of recent sales, view pieces that are being offered for auction, get information on appraisal services, and ask questions of experts via e-mail. If there are classes being offered, information will be listed. Calendars of upcoming auctions are also available online.

More on attending live auction house events online (when they become more widely available) can be found in Chapter 10.

General reference materials

The number of reference materials that can be accessed through the Internet is staggering. Magazines, newspapers, books (both general and specific interest), videos, and price guides all can be tapped into electronically. There are no subject or geographical limitations. Even foreign language problems can be overcome through Web sites that offer information in various languages.

In the early days of the Web, much of the general reference information online could be accessed for free. This has gradually changed as the providers of such information developed ways to charge for this information. While it's still possible to tap directly into sites maintained by major newspapers and magazines such as the *New York Times*, the *Wall Street Journal*, *USA Today*, *People*, and others, you

Moneysaver
Most public libraries offer access to fee-based databases for free.

generally won't be allowed complete access to all the information available online without paying a fee.

Every search service has a news and media section where searchable newspapers, magazines, books, and other media are listed. What is available depends on the service, so it's a good idea to check with more than one.

Trade periodicals

Almost every major trade periodical in the antiques business, along with every major newspaper and magazine, is now available in an online version. This includes the *Maine Antique Digest*, the *Antique Trader*, *Antique Times*, *Antique Jewelry Times*, and a host of other titles. In most cases, the publisher includes a searchable database of previous articles, dating back for months and even years. Many also contain links to other Internet sites of interest to collectors, such as online malls, collector's clubs, and informational sites.

Price guides

Major price guides available online include the one maintained by the *Maine Antique Digest* (www.maineantiquedigest.com). The Kovels also have a free online guide (www.kovels.com) that includes listings for more than 200,000 items. Specialty price guides are coming online as well; the Slawinski Auction Company (www.slawinski.com) recently launched one dedicated solely to Victorian furniture and accessories. Every article listed is illustrated by professional photographs that allow the buyer to compare the condition as well as the price of similar objects.

Libraries, museums, and more

One of the truly marvelous advantages that the Internet provides to its users is the ability to access the vast information from and about libraries, museums, and private collections around the world. It is hard to imagine any group that can make better utilization of this type of resource than antique collectors. After all, antiques are history, and a lot of history is locked up inside libraries and museums.

Many nonprofit organizations are banding together to offer broader access and more efficient use of their resources. Solinet, for example, is a nonprofit library cooperative that provides resource sharing for more than 800 libraries of all sizes located throughout the southeastern United States and the Caribbean. While it's only available by going to a public library, you can access information from books, magazines, newspapers, photographs, and other resources throughout the system. In some cases, information is only available in hard copy; however, synopses are often available. In other cases, full-text information is available online and can be retrieved. Although Solinet is the largest network of its type, similar information sharing arrangements exist throughout the United States.

Museums also are mounting efforts to make their information and services more accessible to the public. The American Association of Museums (aam-us.org), for example, is the sponsor of the Museum Digital Library Collection (museumlicensing. org), which was formed to make the information resources of museums available to a wider public through digitized collections. It's also where you can find links to hundreds of other museums with Internet presences.

Professionals online

The Internet is an ideal tool for tracking down such experts as appraisers and conservationists worldwide.

Many have personal Web sites that you can find by doing a keyword search. Others have an online presence through Web sites maintained by professional organizations and associations.

Appraisers and appraiser associations

Appraisers are well represented on the Internet, either through individual Web sites or through sites maintained by the American Society of Appraisers (www.appraisers.org), the Art Dealers Association of America (www.artdealers.org), and the International Society of Appraisers (www.isa-appraisers.org). Information on insurance, tax issues, and other topics of concern to the appraisal industry also is available at some sites.

Dealer associations

Many local, state, and national dealer organizations maintain Web sites. Since these associations exist primarily to promote the business of their membership, the information you can expect to find while visiting these sites is primarily the name and location of member dealers along with a description of their specialties. While many of these organizations tout services such as dispute resolution, these representations should be taken with a grain of salt.

Perhaps the best use of these sites is to determine how long the organization has existed and how long the dealer you are inquiring about has been a member. This is always helpful information and can be a decent indication of long-term business stability. Art and antique dealers spring up and expire quickly. Finding a gallery that has successfully maintained a business presence for a number of years suggests reliability.

Bright Idea
Check the criteria for membership in various appraisal associations to find an appraiser that will suit your particular needs.

Preservation and conservation societies

Preservation and conservation societies, such as the American Institute for Conservation of Historic and Artistic Works (aic.stanford.edu) and the American Numismatic Society (www.amnumsoc.org), abound on the Internet as well. Many have comprehensive Web sites that contain a good deal of practical information, including directories of restoration and conservation specialists, conservation material suppliers, and helpful hints for cleaning, storing, and caring for antiques. Again, these societies exist primarily to promote their membership and to serve as clearinghouses for issues affecting their specialties.

Keeping information straight

Organizing the information you glean from the Internet is an essential element to the work that you conduct online. Just as collecting antiques requires patience, so too does developing and maintaining electronic resource files. Fortunately, most computers come equipped with some sort of data management or contact management software. The software used for accessing the Internet also has these functions built into it. The hard part is developing the self-discipline to use these programs. The benefit is that as your interest in collecting and your collection grow, so too does your information pool.

It's best to keep your collecting data separate from your personal or business data. If you maintain a directory of names, addresses, phone numbers, e-mail addresses, and Web sites, break your list down so you can find the names quickly. Obvious categories would include auctions, dealers, appraisers, collector clubs, price guides, specialists, and general and specific resources. Do the same for other information

Watch Out!
Subscribe to newsgroups and electronic newsletters with caution. Choose only those that you feel will help you keep abreast of important information.

Bright Idea
Be sure to save
your old e-mail,
even if you need
to put it onto
disks to relieve
congestion on
your hard drive.
These messages
contain a reliable
written record of
your discussions,
inquiries, and
agreements.
Make hard copies
of important
communications
in case your
computer crashes
or a disk devel-
ops problems.

that you retrieve from the Internet. Your system doesn't have to be complex, but it must be functional.

E-mail letters, like business letters, are an invaluable source of information. Most mail management software allows you to create folders for specific contacts. Many will automatically transfer old mail to these specific folders. Take the time to set these systems up as you go. Over time you will find that retrieval is far easier when a consistent method of archiving has been followed.

Managing e-mail is particularly important if you subscribe to a newsgroup or other electronic information service. Active newsgroups can deliver hundreds of pieces of e-mail to your account daily. Before you realize it, you will be inundated with enough newsletters and e-junkmail that you won't have time to read them all.

Depending on the quality and quantity of the information you get from these sources, it may be best to delete as you go. Useful nuggets of information can be extracted and dropped into subject specific files. The rest is like old newspapers that take up space and serve no useful function. Toss it out on a regular basis. If you organize your standard files weekly, you should pay the same amount of attention to your online files.

Just the facts

- The antiques industry is erasing its physical boundaries through the Internet.

- Learning how to configure your searches will return good sources of information.

- Apply the same cautions to online transactions as you would any that you conduct face-to-face.

- Staying on top of electronic communications can solve data management problems in the long run. Review and edit online information on a regular basis.

GET THE SCOOP ON...
Buying from estate sales and auctions ▪
Establishing a relationship with a picker
▪ Why timing is everything ▪ Out-of-the-way
spots to search

Other Sources

Venues such as shows, auctions, and shops are always going to rank at the top of the list when it comes to prime locations for finding antiques. They're the best if you want to see a lot of pieces in a relatively short amount of time, and they're generally the safest bets for the majority of collectors. However, they are by no means the only sources of antiques that are available, and, frankly, they don't appeal to everyone. If you're somewhat of a contrarian or a real treasure hunter, your preferred path may be the one less taken. If so, this chapter is for you.

What follows is a rundown on just about every out-of-the way place or source where you might find an antique. Your chances of finding the object of your desire will be better at some of them; estate sales and auctions, for example, are renowned for the treasures that they bring to light after many years of being hidden away in one person's possession. Other venues are decidedly dicey and are best approached with the knowledge that there might be

173

more value in your search than in the objects you'll find. But if you're really willing to turn over every rock and look around every corner when building your collection, you won't want to neglect them.

Sleuthing the estates

When individuals die, their families often have the responsibility for settling the estate that they leave behind. After the members of the family take what they want, they often decide to dispose of the remaining items by holding an estate auction or sale.

Depending on the taste and the financial where-withal of the deceased, these venues can be great places for antiques hunting; on the other hand, they may not be worth going to at all. Unfortunately, unless it's an estate auction and you can preview the items several days prior to auction, you won't be able to make a determination (unless you're familiar with the person who died and you know the sorts of things that he or she owned). Estate sales operate just like garage or yard sales: You may or may not find something wonderful, but there's no way of finding out unless you go.

The newspaper ads announcing estate auctions and sales, which is how the majority of them are pro-moted, may not be of much help, either. Most describe the items being offered in very general terms. Unless valuable items that will draw certain buyers are being sold, all you'll usually see for descriptions will be words like "antiques," "col-lectibles," "vintage," or "old." However, if an estate sale does contain antiques, this fact is generally highlighted within the ad. They may give the name of the deceased or refer to the individual in more general terms, such as "well-known collector" or

Unofficially...
Estate sales and auctions are also held, although less frequently, to liquidate the assets of individ-uals preparing for retirement, or as part of a divorce settle-ment.

"member of prominent Midwestern family." If items have been added to the sale that didn't belong to the estate, which is sometimes done to round out a weak sale, this also will be noted in the ad.

At both estate sales and auctions you can expect to see objects ranging from good pieces of furniture to household linens that have seen better days. Everything is sold "as is." If you're looking for antique silver or porcelain, these are pretty good venues at which to find it. Other potentially valuable items you might spot include

- Artwork. If the kids don't like it, they'll sell it.

- Costume jewelry. Families usually keep fine jewelry and let the cheaper pieces go unless there's someone in the family who likes it.

- Oriental rugs of various ages, but not necessarily old enough to be antiques.

- Various forms of antique glass, such as art glass or cranberry glass.

- Personal items, such as clothing, purses, and cigarette and powder boxes.

Unofficially...
It may seem predatory, but if you're a close friend of the family it's worth talking directly to family members prior to a sale, especially if there's something in the estate that you're particularly interested in owning. You may end up getting it for less than you'd pay if it went through the sale.

What you generally won't find, sad to say, is antique furniture. Unless the deceased collected it, the furniture you'll see will generally be of twentieth century manufacture. Reproductions also are commonly found. If furniture is what you're seeking, country auctions and sales are your best bets for finding it. The contents of many rural homes and farms are far older than what you'll see in the city. They can be good places for picking up a wide variety of pieces, especially if you're looking for such things as pie safes and other more rustic items.

Most auctions that involve estates are handled by auctioneers or estate liquidators, who specialize in coordinating such efforts. If this is the case, you'll find the name of the company holding the auction included in the ad. These auctions are the ones to search out, as you'll usually find the best prices at them. Sales, on the other hand, can be conducted by any of a number of entities—liquidators, dealers, even family members. Estate sales handled by liquidators, once again, are your best bet. If family members decide to do a sale on their own, the prices can be extremely off the mark (usually too high) unless they really know what they're doing. Sentiments often get in the way of a reasonable price. So do fights.

Dealers will price fairly but a little higher than liquidators usually do, especially if they have their own shops where they can take items that don't sell at the estate sale.

How estate auctions work

Estate auctions are conducted in much the same manner as general antiques auctions are with the following exceptions:

- They generally offer items from one person's or family's estate rather than items that have been collected from many sources, although it's also common to see the assets from several estates combined to make a larger and better sale that will attract a greater variety of buyers.

- They're usually not limited to antiques. You'll see a little bit of everything at these auctions because they really are meant to clear the slate of an estate.

- Because it's often necessary to settle an estate quickly, items offered at auction may have lower reserve prices—that is, the lowest price the estate will accept—than they would if they

Watch Out!
Be wary of estate auctions advertised in the newspapers that are not held by an auction house with which you're familiar. Sometimes they are made up almost exclusively of cheap reproduction furniture and cheap oriental rugs that have been added to the sale by those who run it.

went through an antiques auction. If the estate being auctioned doesn't contain many pieces that would command decent prices, it may be held as a "no reserve" auction, or reserves may be placed only on items of higher value.

Estate auctions are conducted in much the same manner as other auctions, which are discussed in Chapter 9, "Buying at Auction."

The ins and outs of estate sales

Estate sales are usually held in the home of the deceased, although they may take place in other venues, such as an auction gallery, if the sale is held after the home is sold. I've even seen them held in meeting rooms at motels. Some are "come one, come all" events where everyone is allowed access to the items inside at the same time. If it's a very large sale (or a very small home), some sort of crowd control may be imposed. A common method is to allow one group of buyers in as another group leaves.

Sales associates will be on hand to keep an eye on things and to maintain the overall appearance of the sale by rearranging and consolidating items as the sale progresses. They will assist buyers with such things as lifting heavy objects, opening display cases, unfolding and folding large household linens and the like. They can usually answer general questions, but they may not know very much about individual objects. If you can't figure out what a particular item is or what it is used for, they probably can, but this usually is the extent of their knowledge.

Like garage and yard sales, the items in an estate sale will bear price tags. Sometimes there will be additional information noted on the tags, especially if it will enhance the piece in the buyers' eyes. The information may or may not be accurate. If you're

Unofficially... Numbers are sometimes assigned to buyers at larger sales. It's always good to go early to estate sales, but especially so if you're going to be assigned a number. If you don't, you may wait half a day to get in, and you'll miss the best pieces.

new at collecting, a general antiques and collectibles price guide can help you identify pieces that you're not that familiar with. You can also see what kind of deals you're getting by checking prices at the sale against those in the guide.

Since the idea is to liquidate, prices at estate sales tend to be fair—more than what you'd pay at a garage sale, but less than if you bought from a dealer. The people who run estate sales do so on a regular basis and have a very good idea of how things should be priced for the fastest sell. Most of them base their fees for conducting the sale on a percentage of the overall sales amount, so it's to their advantage to price fairly but not cheaply. For these reasons, estate sales are not venues where price negotiations are encouraged.

This does not mean, however, that the prices you see on the first day of a sale are firm. They usually are for that day only, and only until the end of the day. By the conclusion of the first sale day, about half of the anticipated gross receipts of the sale have usually been tallied. Prices will be reduced for the next day, so this can be a good time to make an offer. If it's more than what the reduced price will be in the morning, you may get what you want. If it's not, you can take your chance that it will still be there in the morning and buy it then.

You may also be able to leave a written bid for the conductor of the sale to consider at the end of the first sales day. Many estate sales allow this practice as a convenience to customers who are interested in specific items but may not be able to attend the second day of a sale. If your bid is deemed fair, you'll be contacted before the beginning of the second sales day and asked if you're still interested in buying the item.

Watch Out!
Don't carry a large purse or backpack to an estate sale. If you aren't asked to check it at the door, you'll end up having a hard time squeezing through the crowd.

Items on the second day of a sale are often marked down as much as 25 to 50 percent depending on their original price. Even at this point, however, you can still offer a bid that is lower. As the end of the sale looms closer, your chances of having it accepted will increase.

Usually the only items that are left at the end of an estate sale are the things that no one wants, so your chances of getting the piece you're interested in at an end-of-the-sale price aren't very good (unless, of course, the item is something that no one else wants or that other buyers think is still too expensive). This is when the best deals can be struck, so if you're a gambler you may want to wait to see what happens. The person conducting the sale might ask you what you're willing to pay for the piece just to get it sold.

Estate sales offer no warranties or guarantees on the items that are sold. These are very much caveat emptor situations. You're going to live with whatever it is you buy, so make very sure that the items you take with you are exactly what you want. If you inspect them thoroughly, you won't be greeted with any huge surprises when you get them home.

Finding auctions and sales

Newspapers are generally the best places to find advertisements for estate sales and auctions. Ads can appear in both the general and the classified areas, so be sure to check each. If the estate belonged to a local celebrity or someone known to have collected antiques, it may also be listed in such publications as the *Maine Antique Digest* and some of the other industry papers and magazines listed in Appendix C, "Further Reading."

Bright Idea
Auctions and estate sales often have truckers available to deliver heavy items that you might buy. If you're shopping for large pieces, a call ahead can save you from having to move these items yourself.

Reading auction and sales ads

As previously mentioned, many ads for estate sales and auctions don't contain much specific information on the items that will be offered for sale. However, they almost always will indicate the scope of the auction—that is, how much of the estate is being sold, if more than one estate is being offered, and so on. The following descriptions are most common:

- "Complete" or "in entirety." This means that everything in the estate is being offered for sale.

- "Partial contents." This indicates an estate that is not being fully liquidated for one reason or another. Sometimes the family wants to keep the better pieces, or, in the case of retirees, only the pieces they no longer want to hold onto are being offered for sale. This description is also often seen when sales or auctions are held to liquidate disputed items in divorce cases.

- "Highlights only." The estate has been edited, which means that only the best pieces will be offered. Smaller, less important items may have been consigned or donated.

Other terminology used in estate auction and sales ads includes:

- "Partial listing" or "in part." These statements usually precede the list of items in the estate that are being included in the ad. More important items are printed in larger type. As the list winds down to lesser items, the type will get smaller.

- "Many more items too numerous to mention." You'll see this at the end of the long list. It usually indicates such things as sets of dishes, glassware, tools, clothing, and other items that are available in quantity but not important enough to highlight.

- "Unreserved" or "without reserve." This means that there are no set prices that must be met. The seller will accept the best offer made.

Always remember that auction and sales ads are designed to lure buyers, and therefore only the most popular types of pieces will be highlighted. If you don't see things that interest you, it doesn't necessarily mean they aren't there. If you have the time to look, you might find a good addition to your collection at a great price.

Pickers

This somewhat unsavory term applies to people who act as freelance buying and selling agents, mostly for dealers. They may be dealers themselves; however, they're more often just people who have the time to search out antiques and have an eye for spotting pieces with value that other people have overlooked.

Pickers may or may not have a great love for antiques. If they don't, their efforts are more profit-directed and they'll work hard to find pieces they know they can sell. These people also tend to know exactly what the dealers they work with are looking for and will generally buy only the items that their clients want. If they're doing it because they love antiques, they'll keep their eyes open for pieces that interest them and may buy them even if they don't have an immediate sale in mind.

Some pickers work full-time. Others do it as a supplement to their regular jobs. They usually don't have shops, just a place to keep the items they've

Unofficially...
The practice of adding pieces to an auction or sale that didn't belong to the estate being sold is called "salting."

collected. It's not unusual to see a picker pull up to an antiques shop with a trunkful of small items or pulling a little trailer with larger pieces. It's their traveling shop.

Pickers base their business on working with dealers because this is where their chances of selling are strongest, but some will work directly with collectors. Be aware, however, that these people don't carry huge signs identifying them as pickers. They generally don't even have business cards. You'll have to go by instinct when identifying them. Sometimes a shop owner will point one out to you. You'll also see them at some of the other venues in this chapter.

If you do meet a picker, nothing prevents you from establishing a working relationship with this person. Understand, though, that you won't necessarily get good prices from pickers. They often do find great deals, but they're generally not going to pass along those incredible savings to you. In order to keep prices relatively stable in the market (and preserve their dealer relationships), many of them charge about what you'll end up paying for the item if you bought it through a dealer. If you do establish a relationship with a picker, be prepared to pay cash at all times. Most pickers don't want to reveal their income sources (or pay taxes on their sales).

Scouring the classifieds

Keep an eye on the newspaper for any information about your collecting category and monitor business news, economic developments, and other information for trends that may affect your collection. After you're done reading all the other sections, spend some time going through the classified ads as well. You'll see ads for garage sales and auctions, but don't stop there. Also look through the ads placed in various categories such as furniture, artwork, jewelry, and clothing. Many newspapers even have classified categories specifically for antiques and collectibles.

This isn't something that you have to do every day, as most ads are placed once and run for a week or two. Sundays have always been prime classified ad days. Fridays and Saturdays are big in areas where garage sales are held on the weekends. If you live in a city where these sales are held during other parts of the week—in Minneapolis, for example, it's common to see garage and yard sales on Thursdays and Fridays but not on the weekends—you'll need to scan the paper on whatever days of the week are most appropriate. Weekly shoppers and other free newspapers are also good places to look for garage and yard sale listings.

For the most part, newspapers are better sources for sales and auction listings than they are for items offered by individual sellers, but you may find items that you feel are worth checking out. Always take the wording in classified ads with a grain of salt—remember, they're worded to entice buyers. Many people also don't know everything they should about what they own, and things they think are in good condition may not look the same to you. Always call the seller to ask for all the details about anything that interests you before going to see it. Ask about condition, size, medium, and anything else that would affect your decision about going to see this piece. If everything checks out, then make an appointment to view it. Try to arrange to see the piece in the seller's home or in a neutral location such as a coffee shop or restaurant. And don't be surprised if the neutral location ends up being an

Moneysaver
If you're not much of a newspaper reader, see if your local paper has a special weekend rate. Thursday through Sunday delivery will give you all the classifieds you need to read.

antiques shop. Dealers also place classified ads to help bring new customers through the door.

Putting the word out

If you pick up business cards from dealers, either at shops or shows, turn them over to see what's on the backside of them. We're accustomed to reading only the front of cards, but people in the antiques business often use the back of their cards to advertise what they're interesting in finding and buying. You don't necessarily have to go so far as to have cards printed up announcing your buying intentions, but the theory behind doing so is a good one to keep in mind.

Let people know what it is that you're looking for as much as possible:

- If you're a member of a collecting club, be sure to network with the other members.

- Tell your friends and family members. They may not have the items that you're seeking, but if they know what you're looking for there's a chance that they'll keep their eyes out for it as well.

- Online chat rooms and bulletin boards are also good places to post your wants and needs.

One more tip when it comes to putting the word out. If you have a relative who has an antique that you covet, be sure to let that person know that you'd like to have it when the time comes. This may sound crass, but you'd be surprised at how often collectors find out that they've missed out on really nice family heirlooms because they didn't speak up. Both of my grandmothers had beautiful Russian samovars, and I would have loved to own either of them. Since I never said anything to them, both pieces were given to other family members.

Watch Out!
Never include personal information such as your name, address, and phone number when posting messages on an online bulletin board. Leave only online contact information, such as your screen name.

Garage and yard sales

Sometimes, but not very often, you can find good antiques among the objects at these sales. The adage "One man's junk is another man's treasure" applies to a certain extent, but the treasures you're likely to find are probably not going to be really valuable pieces. Still, it's often worth going around to these sales, especially if you have the time to do so. They're good arenas for making lowball offers and picking up pieces at a steal; most sellers are just trying to get rid of what they don't want, so they often haven't given much thought to how much their belongings are really worth.

Long-time garage sale aficionados suggest the following:

- Always carry cash, and in small bills. Most sellers won't take checks.

- Scout the ads in the paper, and make a game plan. Don't just drive around aimlessly looking for sales.

- Start early, especially if you're going to sales in good neighborhoods where the chances of finding quality pieces are higher.

- If you have lots of sales that you want to visit, see if you can get a friend (or even your spouse) to preview some of the sales while you shop at others. If you're both equipped with cell phones, you can trade information on the spot.

- If you see it and you want it, buy it. If you don't, the next person will.

- If you see an item that you'd like but you're not sure that you want to pay the asking price (even after you've negotiated it), ask the seller

Unofficially...
According to
Peggy Hitchcook,
author of *The
Garage Sale
Handbook*, a
well-orchestrated
garage sale can
bring the seller
anywhere from
$500 to $1,300
in a weekend.

to give you a call after the sale if the item is still available. Be sure to leave your name and phone number.

■ In the early or mid-afternoon, make one last sweep of the sales you visited earlier in the day. This is when sellers are winding down their efforts and they'll be very motivated to let things go for a song. They may even be giving things away.

Garage sale etiquette dictates that you should not ask a seller to hold an item for you. Doing so can prevent a sale, especially if you later decide you don't want the object. Either buy it when you see it or take a chance that it will be there when you come back. If a seller is willing to put something aside, make sure you call him or her if you decide you don't want it so the item can be sold to someone else.

Bankruptcy sales and auctions

These events are held by government bankruptcy trustees to liquidate certain holdings of a bankrupt individual or company. These are real hit-and-miss propositions, and unless you are very avid about your collecting, they may not be worth your time to track. They can, however, yield some real treasures. H. Christopher Clark, an attorney and former trustee in Denver, recalls one estate that contained a significant amount of very fine antique furniture. "The debtor really didn't know what he had," Clark says. "To him, all the old furniture in his home was just that—old."

Bankruptcy sales and auctions are advertised in the paper. If the sale is large enough, and especially if a business is being liquidated, the ad will state as such. If not, they'll often appear along with all the other classifieds. You won't know that you're buying from a bankrupt estate until you call about the merchandise and reach the office of the trustee, who will almost always be an attorney. Keep an eye out for the sales and auctions that are identified as being held by the bankruptcy court, as these are often the venues in which you'll find the most items to look at.

Items with obvious value in a bankruptcy estate will have been appraised. The debtor is given the first shot at doing this; however, if the trustee suspects that pieces have been undervalued, independent appraisals will be ordered. These valuations will usually fall into the fair-market category; in other words, they won't be based on what the piece would bring if it had to be sold immediately, but rather on what it would bring if offered for sale in a competitive marketplace. These are the prices the trustee will try to get for items either at sale or auction. For this reason, you won't necessarily get any bargains, but you may be able to find a nice item to add to your collection.

City and state auctions

These auctions are periodically held to sell unclaimed property from safe-deposit boxes, morgues, and the like. At one auction held a few years ago in Texas, such items as antique harmonicas, an autograph book with the signatures of Franklin and Eleanor Roosevelt, and a pair of French opera glasses dating to 1891 all went under the auctioneer's gavel.

Other items that can be picked up at these auctions include jewelry, coins, stamps, and just about anything else that fits into a safe-deposit box or is carried on someone's body. Watch your local paper

Moneysaver
Although firm prices are placed on items in bankruptcy sales, trustees will accept offers if items don't sell in a certain period of time. If you're interested in something and willing to take a chance, leave a bid with the trustee. You'll be contacted if it's the best one offered.

and newscasts for these events, which often garner good media attention. Also check the official Internet site administered by your state government to see if they're holding auctions of unclaimed merchandise. In Texas, for example, many of the items auctioned by the state are listed at the state comptroller's Web site.

Flea markets

I used to spend many hours at flea markets with a very dear friend, which gave me a fondness for these venues, and I'm certainly not alone in this. Picking through the items at flea markets, in fact, is one of the top-ranked leisure activities in the United States.

Back when I was going to them regularly, they were good sources for small items, such as Depression glass, pottery, and even some furniture. Over the years, they've become less so, primarily because many of the people who were once likely exhibitors at these events now hold garage or yard sales on a regular basis instead. The costs are lower because they don't have to pay for space, as they would at a flea market, and they can usually skirt such issues as obtaining licenses and charging sales tax when they're selling at home.

If the flea market is actually a huge outdoor antiques sale, like the ones held at the Pasadena Rose Bowl in California or the Brimfield, Mass., show described in Chapter 5, "Antiques Shows," your chances of finding worthwhile pieces are considerably better. However, most of today's flea markets are general emporiums that offer a little bit of everything, new as well as old. If you're collecting items that were manufactured in the twentieth century, you'll have better luck. You'll almost never find anything made before 1900 at any of them.

Unofficially...
The first flea market was held in Paris, where it was called a *marche aux puces,* or "the market of fleas." The reason for the name is that there are so many second-hand articles of all kinds for sale that they are believed to gather fleas.

If you're looking for the odd and unusual, however, flea markets are worthy places to visit. And if you've never been to one, you really should go. They can be loads of fun, and even if you don't find antiques at them, you'll probably locate lots of other things to buy.

The rules of the road for shopping at flea markets include the following:

- Arrive very, very early. If it's a good flea market, it will also attract dealers who will peruse every interesting piece even as they are being unloaded from cars and trucks. If you roll in at 9 or 10 A.M., you'll miss the best selection.

- Wear comfortable clothes. Flea markets are the venues for your oldest jeans, most broken-in shoes, and your big floppy hat. Also, dress in layers so you can cover up or strip down depending on changes in the weather.

- Carry a large tote or backpack for small objects. Flea markets may be the only places where such accessories are welcome. Include a small towel to cushion fragile objects.

- Always bring sun protection. Even when the early morning is foggy or overcast, those weather conditions can disappear in a hurry and leave you baking in the sun.

- Bring cash. Some well-established dealers will take checks. Some are even set up for accepting credit cards. Most, however, will want to do cash transactions.

- If you find yourself buying more than just a few items, ask the sellers if they'll hang onto them for you until you're ready to leave. Be sure to get a receipt as proof of sale.

Moneysaver
Flea markets are one place at which you'll want to pay cash if at all possible, as many vendors will give you a discount if you do. Be sure to ask for a receipt.

■ Do a quick once-over of the entire place, if possible, before settling down to do business with any one vendor. It's a good idea to get a feel for what's there first, especially if you see the same item offered by more than one seller.

Flea markets are premier haggling spots, and the sellers at them expect it. Always ask if you've been quoted the best price; when you do, you'll usually get a price that's about 10–15 percent lower than the first one. While you're bargaining, experts say, it's a good idea to lay claim to the object that you're haggling over by putting your hand on it. This is a signal to any other interested parties that you're in the process of negotiating a price. If a seller is bargaining with another customer on a piece that interests you, don't interrupt. You may end up losing out on it, but it's not considered good form to do so.

Still more sources

Antiques pickers are renowned for leaving no stone unturned when it comes to finding antiques. The following sources are ones that they frequently haunt because they occasionally yield the great find. However, it takes a lot of dedication to go to these lengths to hunt for antiques, and most collectors just don't have the time:

■ Thrift shops. Clothing, books, small household items, and children's toys are generally what you'll find at most shops. Ones that are run by service organizations like the Junior League will have better merchandise because items being sold are usually donated by members of the organization. They are encouraged to donate items in good condition, as the profits from the sale of these items are used to fund various charitable efforts. Shops run by

Goodwill Industries and the Association of Retarded Citizens (ARC) are other places to search for antiques. Generally, however, they're better sources for collectibles than they are for more valuable older items.

Bright Idea
Most thrift shops put out new merchandise on specific days of the week. Find out what this is, and you're most likely to find the best pieces.

- Bulletin boards at supermarkets. Many supermarkets allow people to post notices for a variety of goods and services; you never know what you might see there.

- Used furniture stores. Again, you're more likely to find pieces of twentieth century manufacture, but you'll be in luck if you're looking for furniture and other household items from the '20s, '30s, and '40s.

- Junk shops. I have heard stories of very valuable paintings being discovered in these places. I've never found anything of value in them myself, but I don't have much patience for digging through piles of junk. Just about anything you'll find in these shops will be in bad shape and in serious need of some cleaning.

- Church rummage sales. Of all the places listed here, they may be your best bet as items donated to these sales usually come from the members of the church that's holding the sale. Again, they'll have a strong interest in donating good items because of their affiliation to the institution.

With the exception of used furniture stores and junk shops, be prepared to pay the sticker price on anything you see. Chances are that it's already fairly low. Shooting a low-ball bid in the other establishments is always worth a try. You may be bidding on a piece that the owner is tired of looking at and wants to get rid of.

Just the facts

- Making the extra effort to search such venues as estate sales, bankruptcy auctions, yard sales, and the like may lead you to a hidden treasure.

- Know your shopping venue well. In some situations, prices are firm. In others, negotiation is allowed and sometimes even encouraged.

- Be in the right place at the right time. Earlier is better at many of the less-traditional places for antiques shopping.

- Always bring cash. It does speak a universal language.

Buying Antiques

GET THE SCOOP ON...
Buying at live auctions ▪ The lowdown on
warranties ▪ Bidding tips ▪ How to spot a scam

PART IV

Buying at Auction

Chapter 9

Buying antiques at auctions is one of the most rewarding experiences a collector can have. Whether it's in the hushed atmosphere of a Christie's auction gallery or a crowded room at an estate liquidator, nothing can match the adrenaline rush when the gavel falls, the word "sold" rings out, and you know that the item of your desire is yours.

Buying at auction and being successful at it requires a set of skills that should be consciously and carefully developed. It is folly to think that you can walk into an auction on a whim, start bidding, and have any measure of success when you do. As is true with all buying venues, a great deal of preparation and research should first take place.

Learn everything you can about the auction process, including the quirks, and you'll come away a winner when the time comes for you to raise your bidding paddle.

How auctions work

All auctions work in essentially the same way, no matter what types of items are offered or by whom.

The house assembles objects (called "lots"), determines the prices they might realize, and sets a date for the auction. It then markets the items to potential buyers through advertisements, auction catalogs, and, increasingly, on the Internet. If the auction is "live," that is, attended in person by bidders, items are also available for viewing for a certain time prior to their sale. Finally, at the specified place and time, each lot is sold to the highest bidder. Anyone who has registered as a bidder and exhibited the ability to pay can participate. This open competition is what makes auctions exciting.

After the auction, goods are delivered, payments are cleared, and any disputes that may have arisen are resolved. This process is repeated over and over again at live auctions, through mail auctions, and on the Internet.

The buyer's role

As a buyer, your involvement in the lifecycle of an auction starts when the items going through auction are being marketed to potential bidders. But your real work actually begins much earlier. Your knowledge of your collecting category is key to your success at auction. Your studying is validated when you're a successful bidder at auction.

Remember, auctions are the only venue in which the buyers, not the sellers, determine the final price. The decisions that you and the other bidders make will have a significant influence on establishing the value of a particular item, and could even impact the values in the collecting category as a whole.

Apart from bidding on items, buyers have other responsibilities in the auction process as well. Specific auction venues may impose additional requirements on the buyer, but the following are always necessary for any auction venue:

- Reviewing the auction catalog (if available) for items of interest as well as the terms and conditions of sale

- Previewing items of interest to establish value and determine condition

- Registering as a bidder, which means understanding the terms and conditions of the sale and agreeing to be bound by them

- Establishing your financial ability to pay for items that you buy

- Bidding in a manner acceptable to the house

- Arranging for packing, shipping, and storage of any items you buy, if necessary

- Contacting the auction house immediately if there is a problem with the item that you purchased. It is far easier for an auction house to refund money before the consignor of the item is paid.

Any other responsibilities required of you as a buyer will be spelled out in the terms and agreements for the sale. Review this information thoroughly so that you won't have any unpleasant surprises. For example, many auction houses will charge you if you leave merchandise you've bought at the house past a certain length of time. It's a good idea to know these things up front so you can make any necessary arrangements and avoid these situations from happening.

The auction catalog

Auction catalogs are prepared for most significant sales and are an essential component to the

Bright Idea
The responsibility of the auction house usually ends when ownership is transferred to the winning bidder. Remove the items you've bought as quickly as you can. If something happens to them after you've bought them and before you pick them up, you, not the auction house, is liable for it.

research that you should do before attending an auction. While the format of the catalogs themselves will vary from house to house and even from sale to sale, you can expect to find the following information in all of them:

- General information about the sale itself.

- Terms and conditions of sale.

- Descriptions of the items being auctioned. This information will include a few words about what the item is; for example, an American Renaissance parcel-gilt and inlaid walnut center table, and the elements of value that were used to determine the piece's selling estimate, including its history and condition.

- An estimate for what the piece is likely to bring at auction. This amount is usually expressed as two figures signifying what the auction house's experts believe is a reasonable selling range for the item, based on their experience and research.

- A glossary of terms used to describe the items being auctioned, and what the terms mean.

Learning to read auction catalogs takes practice. Fortunately, many good auction houses recognize this and give clear examples and specific descriptions as well as a good glossary of terms that explains the terminology used in the catalog.

It's all in the details

The way an auction catalog describes an item reveals important clues as to how the value of the object was established. However, these sometimes very subtle clues can escape the eye of a novice collector. Learning how to spot them and what they signify is an important part of the educational process that auction buyers go through. The catalog's glossary of terms will describe what the distinctions are, but you still have to learn how to spot them.

The following descriptions are an example of how you'll see pieces described in a catalog. Take particular note of the significant differences between them created by the inclusion or deletion of a few key words:

- *George III mahogany corner chair, c. 1770.* A description worded in this manner means that the object is an authentic piece of the period indicated.

- *Side chair, Baltimore, c. 1775.* This description indicates a side chair with design elements that mark it as a piece manufactured in Baltimore during the stated period.

- *Louis XV style gilt-bronze-mounted and parquetry bureau.* This description, which includes the word "style," indicates that in the opinion of the auction house the item is an intentional reproduction of an earlier style.

The following descriptions illustrate what you might see in a catalog for Frederick Remington paintings. Remember, all opinions rendered are those of the auction house alone:

- *Ascribed to Frederick Remington.* This indicates that the piece is an authentic work by the artist.

- *Attributed to Frederick Remington.* Probably a work by the artist, but there is less certainty as to authorship.

- *In the style of or in the manner of Frederick Remington.* The painting is the work of an artist working in Remington's style.

Bright Idea
If you're thinking about buying an item in a category with which you aren't very familiar, check the glossary of terms to make sure you're correctly interpreting the catalog's representations on the item.

▪ *After Frederick Remington.* This means that the painting is believed to be a copy of a known work of the artist.

The terms "signed and dated" and "signed and inscribed," or just "signed," "dated," or "inscribed" usually mean that the named artist signed, dated, or inscribed the painting with his or her own hand. Such terms as "bears a signature," "bears a date," or "bears an inscription" normally mean that someone else has added the information to the painting.

Prints, rugs, silver, porcelain and other collecting categories have similar distinctions in the manner in which they are described. Be sure to carefully review each glossary of terms to make sure that you understand what you are purchasing.

Terms and conditions

As you read through an auction catalog, you may notice that a portion of the description on certain objects is highlighted in some way, either by printing it in ALL CAPS or **bold type**. These typestyles are used to identify the elements of an object that fall within the auction house's warranty.

When you buy at auction, you enter into a legal contract. Under the terms and conditions of sale, the contract will contain both your responsibilities and those of the auction house. When auction houses guarantee the goods they sell, they carefully ensure that the warranties they give are narrowly defined. Since the terms of the contract are dictated by the auction house, the document favors that party. These contracts are written with many exceptions and disclaimers designed to protect the auction house, not the buyer. On the occasions when actions against auction houses are brought, the

Watch Out!
Never assume that a good faith mistake on your part will be corrected by an auction house. There are no money-back guarantees unless the house itself is in major error.

plaintiff almost never wins. Customer claims are rarely upheld, so understand your rights.

Every auction house has its own set of specific contractual terms. While there isn't room to discuss all of them here, the following points are covered by all of them:

- How items will be paid for
- Any additional fees that the buyer is responsible for
- Limits of warranty
- Exclusions to the warranty
- The auction house's liabilities regarding loss from fire, theft, and other casualties
- Information regarding disputes and how they will be handled
- Limits of liability regarding packing and handling of purchased lots

When you register as a bidder, you are acknowledging that you are familiar with the terms of sale. You also have to agree to these terms and consent to be bound by them. The agreement is sealed with the drop of the auctioneer's hammer. If you are the high bidder, you have entered into a legally binding agreement. The only thing you can do about lopsided terms is to refuse to participate, but that deprives you of the experience. The better option is to understand the terms of sale and know what your rights are in case of a dispute.

The terms and conditions of sale can be found in the auction catalog. If there isn't a catalog, be sure to ask for a copy of the terms and conditions when you register as a bidder.

Timesaver
Make arrangements for packing and shipping prior to auction.

The cost of doing business

When you consider that dealers usually mark up their goods from 100 to 200 percent, the cost of buying at auction seems like a bargain. It can be, but there are additional costs and fees that you'll incur which can significantly increase the amount you'll end up paying. These costs and fees can add as much as 25–35 percent to the asking price of an antique.

The terms and conditions of sale will spell out in great detail what your final cost will be for anything you buy. This amount will include

- The bid price—that is, the price at which a lot is sold to the purchaser. This is also known as a "hammer price."

- The buyer's premium, a percentage of the purchase price that the auction house takes as a fee.

- Any applicable state and local taxes, and any other taxes that may be assessed.

The aggregate of these amounts is the true purchase price that you'll pay at auction.

Other fees that you may be assessed include

- Storage. If your payment doesn't clear in a timely manner, the auction house can charge a fee for storing the items until they can be released to you.

- Packing and shipping. Some auction houses have shipping departments that offer these services; buyers can either elect to have the auction house handle these items or they can arrange for such services independently.

- Interest on fees, commissions, premiums, bid prices, and other sums that are not paid promptly to the house.

Here's how these fees can stack up: Assume you just bought an antique chest at an auction in New York, and your bid price was $4,000. Your buyer's premium will be $600, or 15 percent of the bid price. You'll also be assessed $330 for state taxes. The item will have to be packed for shipment, so add another $150 for crating charges. Shipping may cost another $500. The final cost on your chest (at a minimum) will be $5,580, or 28 percent more than your bid price.

Bright Idea
Carefully calculate the expenses that you will have to pay if you are the successful bidder. Adjust your maximum bid amount to avoid any sticker shock later on.

Payment methods

Auction houses expect successful bidders to make payment in full immediately following the sale. Make your payment arrangements in advance of the auction to avoid the risk of penalties that are assessed on anyone who has difficulty making full payment. These fees can be steep.

All auction houses accept cash, cashier's checks, and personal checks with approved credit. Some also take credit cards, but purchases made in this fashion are often limited to a maximum dollar amount, generally around $25,000.

If the purchase price and other charges exceed $25,000, you will probably have to make other payment arrangements. This usually means arranging for a wire transfer or another method for delivering certified funds. Again, make these arrangements prior to attending an auction if you think you'll be making large purchases. If your check is drawn on a foreign bank, you can expect a special handling fee to be charged as well.

Auction houses will extend credit to preferred customers. The interest rates on these credit lines can be significantly higher than what you'd pay if you took out a loan yourself. If you find yourself in the position of considering this approach, do it on the shortest terms allowed by the house and plan to arrange for a more favorable loan somewhere else when you can.

Buyer's premium

A nasty surprise to anyone unfamiliar with auctions, the buyer's premium is pure profit for the auction company because it is assessed in addition to what sellers pay the house for auctioning their goods. It is simply the price you have to pay for doing business with an auction house, like the dealer's prep charge that car dealers tack on to the price of a new vehicle. Unlike the dealer's prep charge, however, which you can get dropped or reduced if you're a savvy car buyer, the buyer's premium is a given—no haggling is allowed at auction houses.

Be sure to determine how much you will be charged for the buyer's premium before you enter any bid. Many auction houses charge from 10 to 15 percent of the bid price. The international houses, such as Sotheby's, Christie's, and similar sized firms charge 15 percent of the bid price up to and including $50,000, and 10 percent of any amount in excess of $50,000. Smaller regional houses may charge 10 percent of the successful bid price up to certain levels and from 5 percent to 7.5 percent thereafter. Some local auction houses may not charge a buyer's premium at all.

Taxes

Sales taxes can constitute a significant portion of the final purchase price. Be sure to check the terms and conditions of sale to see what your obligation will be.

Loss and damage

Upon the fall of the hammer, the risk of loss due to fire, theft, or other damage passes to the buyer.

Make sure your items are immediately protected by the terms of your insurance policy. As I'll discuss in Chapter 16, "Protecting Your Collection (and Your Investment)," many of the policies written to cover antiques and other fine items provide immediate protection.

Storage charges

Auction houses give buyers a specific time period in which to remove their property from the premises once payment has cleared. Failure to remove items during this time frame can result in the assessment of storage fees. The auction house will add additional charges if it has to make further storage arrangements for items still in its possession after a certain period of time, usually 60 days after purchase.

Shipping and transportation

Buyers also bear responsibility for packing and transporting any items bought at auction. The auction house usually will take care of packing and make arrangements for shipping, and they charge buyers for these services. The biggest expense, however, may be for transporting your purchases to your door. Large items, such as furniture, can be extremely expensive to ship.

Certain property sold at auction may be subject to the provisions of the Endangered Species Act of 1973, the Marine Mammal Protection Act of 1972, the Migratory Bird Act of 1982, and other environmental laws such as the New York State Environmental Conservation Law. If the property you purchased is subject to these laws, you may not be able to transport or export items without a special license. For a fee, the larger auction houses can usually help you obtain the appropriate license; however, they will not guarantee your ability to

Moneysaver
If you are attending a large regional auction, check with a dealer or two from your area to see if they can help you with packing and delivery. They may have space on their own trucks that they'll be willing to let you have for a fee.

obtain a license, and the failure to obtain one will not be a legal basis for rescinding the purchase. In other words, you'll still be responsible for paying everything stipulated by the terms and conditions of sale.

Depending on the item's medium, such as whale bone, ivory, or the skins of endangered species, you may not be allowed to resell the object in the United States. Even if this happens, you'll still have to pay the auction house whatever you owe.

The standard limited warranty of authorship

Over the years, auction houses have developed a practice of describing the goods they sell by type, age, authorship, period, culture, or source of origin. The language that is used to describe an item is very carefully drafted. Depending on how an item is described, there may be no warranty applicable to the object, or the warranty will be so narrow as to be of practically no value.

What, then, is warranted? Not much. For example, authorship might be guaranteed for five years from the date of sale, but the warranty is only good for the original purchaser of record at the auction, and only if the item is in the same condition as it was when it was purchased. The warranty cannot be assigned—in other words, it must be reestablished if the object is resold.

Consignors and their agents (auction houses), incidentally, must have the legal right to sell an item; however, several major auction houses have been accused of putting objects on the auction block knowing that title defects exist. When a true owner discovers an object in the hands of another individual, he or she can sue to recover it. If the

Watch Out!
Always review the actual terms and conditions applicable to the auctions you attend before you participate. These terms will define your rights and obligations.

claim can be established on behalf of the true owner, a series of lawsuits can erupt. You may have seen, for example, headlines in the past several years about lawsuits filed to reclaim artworks seized from European Jews during World War II. The rightful owners of these works, or their heirs, have won several of these cases, and the courts have also awarded damages to the unfortunate buyers in at least the amount of the original purchase price.

Exclusions from the standard limited warranty

As mentioned earlier, to the extent that any warranty is given for an item, in some cases it will only apply to those representations that are printed in highlighted type. When this convention is used, the auction house gives no guarantees as to the accuracy of any comment other than in these statements, although the tough competition for client loyalty between auction houses necessitates that they make every effort to present accurate information. And even if a specific statement about an object is made in highlighted type, other exclusions can come into play that will limit the usual warranty. At least four other exceptions usually apply to and limit the guarantee offered by auction houses:

- If an item is dated as having been created prior to 1870, the date is generally excluded from warranty unless the item is later proven to be an outright forgery. It can be difficult to establish the age of an antique prior to this year. For this reason, the best guarantee usually offered is the fact that the specialists responsible for the object have reached a consensus that it was created on or about the date they have assigned to the object.

- The warranty given by auction houses does not apply when a difference of opinion about authorship exists between the seller's specialists if the differences are noted in the catalog or by the auctioneer. The standard terms and conditions that apply at most auctions grants the auction house the right to make modifications to the descriptions contained in the catalog. If a modification is announced publicly prior to the commencement of bidding, it is up to the purchaser to take it into consideration.

- The third exception applies to the general consensus about the authorship of a given piece. If, at the time of sale, it is the opinion of the scholars and specialists who have examined the object that it is an authentic work of the specified artist, then the subsequent decision by these experts that they were mistaken will not nullify the sale.

- If, however, the specialists were duped, the auction house will sometimes rescind the sale. Sotheby's found itself in this situation in 1996 when it was forced to refund the purchase price of a George Innes landscape. The same expert who had originally authenticated the piece ended up declaring it a phony when he saw the piece again several years later. According to the account published in Forbes Magazine, the appraiser had based his earlier authentication on a photograph. Up close, he saw that the artist's characteristic brushstrokes were missing.

  Douglas Esposit, the purchaser of the painting, demanded a refund, but was told that the auction house did not guarantee the

Unofficially...
It is not a crime in the United States to sell fake art and antiques as long as the fact that they are fakes is not known by the seller.

authenticity of any paintings dated before 1870. A well-planned protest on the eve of the Onassis auction brought attention to his plight, and Sotheby's did refund his money.

- Even when a fake slips through undetected, the buyer must demonstrate that the forgery is less valuable than the original would be worth as of the date that the customer demands the purchase be rescinded. Although diminished value is usually apparent, it requires expert opinion to establish, and the buyer, not the seller, bears the responsibility and the expense for establishing this factor.

- Finally, the date of an object is not warranted if this fact can only be established by a scientific method that was not generally available until after the date the catalog was published or that was unreasonably expensive to use if available prior to that date.

From time to time, each of these exclusions has come into play and prevented a customer from rescinding a purchase. However, by their nature, these provisions cover the odd circumstance that may arise.

The day of the auction

As the day of the auction draws closer, you'll need to take time to attend the preview in order to examine the items that you're considering buying. Even at smaller local auctions where specialists are not employed, the preview gives you a chance to make a close examination that will reveal attributes that are hard to see in photographs or when sitting in the audience. You can ask questions about condition, prior ownership, the results of recent auctions, and

Watch Out!
Don't assume that the glossary of terms in an auction catalog stays the same from sale to sale. Always look things over to check for any changes that may have been made.

Bright Idea
If the auction company does not sell items in a number sequence, find out when the item you are wanting to bid on might come up on the block for sale so you don't miss it.

upcoming sales. You should never miss the chance to preview an auction in which you intend to participate. Carefully consider bidding on items that you have not examined. Most auctions sell on an "as is" basis.

Go to the preview prepared to obtain the information you need to make a buying decision. While there, pick up a copy of the terms and conditions of sale if you haven't seen it already. Ask how the staff prefers for bids to be entered and review the registration process. Familiarize yourself with the terms and conditions of sale, warranties, payment terms, and other business concerns.

Auction houses normally schedule previews during the week prior to the auction. Usually, you can also preview items in the hours immediately preceding the beginning of the auction. But check with the auction company to find out when it allows objects to be examined. Auction houses are not stores, and access to lots is often limited due to insurance and security issues. Most auctions make a special effort to advertise when viewing is allowed, and you should make every effort to be there during these periods.

Registering for an auction

Before you can bid at an auction, you must first register as a bidder. Doing so helps the auction run smoothly and provides information to the staff that will allow them to prepare the necessary documents related to your purchases, such as transfers of title, bills of sale, bills of lading, payment invoices, and tax forms.

When you register as a bidder, you must acknowledge that you are familiar with the terms of sale, agree to these terms, and consent to be bound by them. Registration does not obligate you to actually participate in the sale; it merely facilitates an orderly transaction should you elect to do so.

Generally, you'll be asked to provide fairly basic information, such as your name, address, phone numbers, and other contact information. Be sure to bring a form of picture identification, such as a driver's license. Some registration forms ask for other information that the house can use to build a personal profile on you. You're under no obligation to provide this information. Some houses, especially the larger ones, will ask for a bank reference.

After you register, the staff will give you a card or paddle with a number on it, which you will use to bid. Since the auctioneer is not likely to know your name (and doesn't have time to stop the auction to ask) he or she simply makes note of your number. That way, the auctioneer can be assured that the correct person was awarded the purchase.

Once you have your paddle, go into the auction room and take your seat. Dealers like to sit near the back of the room so they can keep a close eye on the bidding action while concealing their own bids to a certain extent. Sitting near them can be an education in itself, and a back-row seat does afford a better view of the overall action. However, if you're intent on watching how the auctioneer operates, sit closer to the front.

The auctioneer will begin the action by introducing a lot by its name and number and opening it up for bid.

Placing your bid

Bidding at auction can be the most intimidating aspect of buying at auction. Understanding how bidding is done and how it progresses can take some of the fear away.

Bright Idea
Listen carefully to hear the increment being used during bidding. From time to time the auctioneer will increase or decrease the increment to speed things along or break a deadlock.

Auctioneers usually start the bidding by asking for a specific amount. This amount is generally based on about half the lowest estimated price published in the catalog. For example, bidding on a vase with a low estimate of $1,000 may start at $500. Bids then increase by specific increment. The following pattern is fairly common:

BID RANGE	BID INCREMENT
100–500	Auctioneer's discretion, usually between 10 to 50
500-1,000	by 50
1,000–2,000	by 100
2,000–3,000	by 200
3,000–5,000	by 200 or 500
5,000–10,000	by 500
10,000–20,000	by 1,000
20,000–30,000	by 2,000
30,000–50,000	by 2,000 or 5,000
50,000–100,000	by 5,000
100,000–200,000	by 10,000

Anything above 200,000 is usually set by the auctioneer at his or her discretion.

Entering your bid requires nothing more than raising your number so the auctioneer can see it. He or she will either nod, point, or otherwise acknowledge you. Spotters assist auctioneers at large auctions to make sure that bids aren't overlooked. Don't shout out your bid as this is generally thought to be bad form. However, you definitely should say something if your bid wasn't noticed. It happens rarely, but it does happen.

Understanding the reserve

Lots in a reserve auction have a minimum amount—the "reserve"—that must be reached before the item is sold. This is a confidential figure established by the seller with the auction house.

Reserve prices are usually set at half to two-thirds of an item's low estimate. Thus, if an object is estimated to be worth from $800 to $1,200, the reserve would likely be set at between $400 and $534.

Reserves may be higher or lower than this amount, but this formula is a good estimate. It is very unusual for a reserve to be equal to or higher than the lowest estimated value, and it never exceeds the highest estimate.

If a reserve on an item is not met, the auctioneer will withdraw the item from auction.

Wise bids

You'll want to develop a sense of timing when it comes to jumping into the bidding process. Remember, the auctioneer will usually open bidding at about half of the lowest estimate on an item. However, he or she will retreat from this number if no one bids at this level. If you bid too quickly, you may prevent the auctioneer from dropping the asking price. If you wait until the last possible second, you may end up being excluded by a fast hammer. On the whole, it's best to formulate a clear strategy in advance and follow that plan. This means that you should establish a good opening bid in your mind.

If the opening bid you thought was reasonable is higher than the bid being asked by the auctioneer, go ahead and raise your paddle. If the opening ask is only a little higher than you think is appropriate, wait a moment to see if others agree with you. If you're right, the auctioneer will retreat toward a lower figure.

Always set a hard and fast limit on the amount that you're willing to pay on any one item, and never exceed it. A good auctioneer knows how to build excitement and spur on a bidding war in a

Unofficially...
Auctions that are advertised as "unreserved" or "without reserve" mean that any bid on an item will be accepted.

spirited auction. An onset of auction fever can be a very expensive illness. Learn to set boundaries and stay within them.

Auctions tend to ebb and flow. Good auction houses and auctioneers orchestrate how lots are presented for maximum effect. The most valuable lots are often spread out to keep the excitement high for the entire auction. This, however, can also work against the house. If buyers are tired and tapped out at the end of an auction, higher-priced lots that are offered then will often sell for a song. If you can stick it out until the end, you may get some great deals.

Absentee bids

Virtually every auction house allows buyers to place absentee bids. These bids usually take two forms. Either the bidder arranges with the auction staff to bid on his behalf, or the bidder communicates bids by telephone. This is a very common practice and some of the largest purchases in history have been effected by long distance, including van Gogh's *Irises*, which in 1987 sold for $49 million to an absentee bidder. In either event, you must make arrangements in advance of the auction in order to absentee bid.

If you elect to use the auction house staff, you'll have to establish the maximum amount that you are willing to pay for a specified item. A staff member will then enter bids on your behalf. This service is usually free of charge, although the standard terms and conditions apply to the sale.

The other popular method of absentee bidding is to bid via telephone. At the large auction houses, a telephone bank is manned continuously to facilitate absentee bids. The auction house calls preapproved bidders before the lots they have specified

Unofficially...
Forty percent of the lots sold by Sotheby's are by absentee bids, according to John L. Marion, former chief of Sotheby's, in *The Best of Everything*.

are offered and keeps them on the line until they drop out of the bidding or are awarded the item.

If you want to participate in an auction as an absentee bidder, contact the auction company in advance for the necessary forms.

After the sale

If you are a successful bidder at auction, the auction house will expect you to complete the necessary legal and financial arrangements by the close of the auction. You'll be asked to sign various forms designating transfer of ownership, payment terms, and the like. If everything is completed to the auction house's satisfaction and your payment method has cleared, you'll be allowed to take the item or items with you that you've bought. If this isn't the case, or if you've purchased items that must be shipped, the auction house will retain them until you can make further arrangements. Once they're home, all you have to do is enjoy them.

Warning flags

Caveat emptor—let the buyer beware—is the rule and not the exception when buying antiques at all times. Unfortunately, auction houses sometimes engage in tricks and devices that deceive customers. Art dealers and others consign works that they know are not authentic. Auction houses and dealers sometimes "salt" estate sales with inexpensive reproductions and pieces from other less reliable sources without disclosure. False bidding can take place.

Not all the blame for these problems falls to the auction houses—they are sometimes victimized as much as buyers are—nor is there an easy answer to keeping such problems from happening. You can protect yourself as a buyer to a certain extent by putting time and effort into learning how to

Unofficially...
Items that don't sell during an auction are sometimes still available for sale after the auction is over. Buyers can either meet the reserve or make an offer.

become a savvy collector. The more knowledgeable you are, the greater your ability will be to make independent judgments and spot things that don't quite ring true about antiques and the people who sell them. The more experience you gain, the less likely it is that you will be victimized.

Keep an eye out for any of the scams noted above, as well as a few others described below, which are relatively common. Spotting any of them should deter you from doing business whenever and wherever you see them.

Salting an auction

As discussed in Chapter 8, "Other Sources," salting is most likely to take place at estate auctions where items that didn't belong to the estate are inserted to make the sale stronger—and thus more attractive—to potential buyers. It's a problem only when assertions are made that every object in the sale belonged to one person. If the auction house discloses that other objects have been added, and these items are pointed out in the catalog or list of pieces for sale, there's really nothing wrong with it.

Bait and switch

As noted above, auctioneers can make changes to the stated description of a piece prior to the commencement of bidding on it. If you hear this happening frequently during the course of an auction, however, it can be a sign that merchandise is being substituted for the original items listed in the catalog. Often, the substituted pieces are not of the same quality. An unsuspecting buyer can end up paying a high price for a piece of lesser value.

False bidding

It is easy to manipulate bidding by pretending to accept bids when no competitive bids are actually being made. This can be done by auctioneers to build false interest in an object. Such bids may be made by friends of the auctioneer or the seller. While the practice is somewhat common, this doesn't make it ethical.

If you're new to the auction game, this practice may be difficult to spot. Your best defense is in attending lots of auctions so you become familiar with how they operate.

Watch for subtle signs between the spotters and the auctioneer. Pay attention to who is bidding and who is winning. Be suspicious if you notice that a certain bidder often participates but never wins. He may just be bidding up the price. An auctioneer might also run up a series of artificial bids to force a legitimate bidder to place a higher bid. The indication of false bidding occurs when the auctioneer retracts the highest bid and awards the object to the next highest bidder, concluding the sale. In situations where auctioneers make legitimate mistakes on taking bids, the sale is usually reopened at a lower bid amount, not just concluded.

Keep in mind, however, that many auction houses will bid on behalf of the owner up to the reserve price. This is legal and an accepted way to protect the seller's interest when a reserve is in place. A house that bids beyond the reserve, however, is unethical and unlawful.

Fakes and forgeries

A serious problem in the antiques business, some fakes are so good that even the experts have difficulty spotting them. A fictitious history of ownership will often accompany these pieces as well, making the establishment of true provenance virtually impossible. Even the finest auction houses in the

66
Fakes are a growing cottage industry.
—Victor Wiener, executive director of the Appraisers Association of America, in "The Boom in Fakes," *Forbes*, March 24, 1997)
99

world make mistakes when judging the authenticity and quality of art. Being a wary buyer is the only attitude that you can afford to take.

Question everything you're told, and purchase only those pieces that you have independently determined are worth your while. If there's hype surrounding an object, ignore it unless you can determine that it's warranted.

Unless you are absolutely convinced that you have discovered an authentic piece, limit your bidding to amounts that would be appropriate for unauthenticated items. If you are looking to build a valuable collection, purchase with the assumption that the item is not what it purports to be and pay accordingly. Then have it examined by experts (if you were unable to do so earlier). Occasionally, you can get a real bargain. Often as not, however, you get what you paid for and nothing more.

Just the facts

- Set a firm limit on the amount you are willing to pay on an auctioned item. Be sure to budget an additional 25–35 percent of the bid amount to cover additional costs.

- When you bid at auction you are entering into a legal contract. Make sure you understand your rights before you bid.

- Make sure you understand what attributes of an item the auction house is willing to stand behind. Be careful to study the glossary of terms in the back of auction catalogs before you bid.

- Fakes are a common problem in the antiques business. Carefully weigh claims of authenticity against the object's attributes and get a second opinion whenever possible.

Chapter 10

GET THE SCOOP ON...
How to buy at online auctions ▪ Finding the
site that's right for you ▪ Safeguarding your
purchases ▪ Online frauds to avoid

Buying Online

In February 1999, when Butterfield &
Butterfield sold property seized from O.J.
Simpson's home as part of the civil settlement
won against him by the families of Nicole Brown and
Ron Goldman, it became the first traditional auction house to move beyond merely offering clients
the ability to place bids online. It provided bidders
with the opportunity to view streaming video, hear
the auctioneer, and even chat with other buyers. It
gave the antiques industry the opportunity to see
into the future, when live online auctions will be the
norm rather than the exception.

But for now, Butterfield & Butterfield remains
the exception. It takes a very fast computer and a lot
of bandwidth to deliver the video and audio signals
that a live auction produces, technology still beyond
the reach of the average bidder. Most computers in
use today receive information through telephone
lines, which have a hard enough time handling the
signals they currently transmit; pushing video and
audio through them is like squeezing an elephant

through the opening in a sodapop can. Still, the push is on to find an efficient and cost-effective way to deliver such signals to eager consumers.

Unofficially...
According to AuctionWatch, online consumer-only auctions constituted 1.5 million users and generated $1.5 billion in revenues in 1998. By 2001, an estimated 17.5 million users will be generating $15.5 billion in revenues.

In the meantime, online auctions will continue to follow a model based on the mail and catalog auctions that have been a part of the traditional auction arena for many years. It's been the approach that makes the most sense, and, surprisingly, except for the inability to allow bidders to touch and feel the antiques, it's also been able to deliver a good sense of what it's like to bid in person. You can monitor the action in these auctions to see what the current high bid is on any item. If you're participating in an auction and have elected to use the company's automatic bid feature, you're even notified if someone has outbid you. It truly is just about the next best thing to being there, and it's definitely an arena worth participating in...if you know what you're doing. If you don't, you'll get scammed here, just as you would anywhere else; unfortunately, your chances of it happening in cyberspace are even higher.

Online auctions—the good, the bad, and the ugly

The greatest advantage to buying at online auctions should be extremely apparent by now: convenience. And, frankly, they're a lot of fun. Leading companies such as eBay and Amazon.com have invested millions of dollars in creating friendly online communities designed to make you want to visit often and stay awhile when you do. Even if you're not interested in actually participating in an auction, you may find it tempting to sign on for a few minutes to see what's going on. And once you're on, you might just find something that catches your eye.

EBay even makes it possible for buyers to monitor auctions when they're away from their computers with eBay A-Go-Go, a notification system that links to a pager or cell phone to provide immediate auction alerts to registered users.

Another extremely large advantage to bidding online: no buyer's premiums! Not yet, anyway. With these auctions, the seller bears all the costs of the auction until it closes. The costs to the buyer generally include a phone call or two and shipping fees, but sellers sometimes even pay these. Sales tax will be charged by anyone who buys and sells antiques and other items as a business, but the reserve set by the seller often includes this amount as well.

The downside to Internet auctions, unfortunately, is rather steep. With fraud rampant, just about every trick in the book has been played to success in cyberspace, some of them with some very interesting new angles. If there is a loophole to be found in the system, online scammers will find it. When one hole is plugged, they'll find another one.

The fact that fraud is so rampant goes back to the main flaws inherent in the system: You can't actually see and feel what it is you're buying, and you can't get a good look at the person who is selling it to you. So you can never be sure that you'll get what you've paid for, and sellers can never be sure that they'll actually receive payment.

The auction companies themselves can't be of help because they never physically take possession of the items being sold. They act purely as intermediaries or middlemen, facilitating transactions between buyers and sellers. While they do their best to provide a safe and sound environment for such transactions, their responsibility ends there and

Unofficially... Online auctions prompt nearly five times as many complaints as any other aspect of online commerce, according to the National Consumers League.

they emphatically make this point in their disclosures.

As part of the user agreement, you will be required to release an online auction company or anyone affiliated with the company from liability if your online transaction goes sour in any way whatsoever. It is up to you and you alone to do whatever is necessary to assure the validity of your online transactions. Online auction houses will give you advice and support for doing so (more about this later in this chapter), but that's as far as most will go.

Spotting the scams run on buyers is often difficult, but it can be done. You'll find some tips on what to look for and how to avoid the more obvious ruses later in this chapter.

Unofficially...
According to *Fast Company* magazine, there were an estimated 1,500 auction-related Web sites in more than 40 product categories by the end of 1998.

Becoming a cyberbidder

The basic rules of collecting antiques don't get suspended in cyberspace. As with every stage of collecting, research and study result in success. Once you've decided on the items you're interested in buying (hopefully, you've done this by now), you'll need to see who has them online and determine where you want to buy them. Online auction sites such as eBay and Amazon.com are the most active and offer the most variety—eBay, for example, conducts an estimated million auctions every day of the year—but other sites offer such services as well. Many are general auction sites, but a number of sites specialize in certain types and categories of antiques. You'll find a list of them in Appendix E, "Internet Resources," along with several clearinghouse sites where you can search for more.

Always check several different auction sites to see which items they specifically have to offer, or use a service such as AuctionWatch (www.auctionwatch.

com) or BidFind (www.bidfind.com), which will scan for items from a variety of online auction houses for you. Compare the prices you see, both between various sites and to those listed in price guides and auction results. When you've decided where you want to buy, all you have to do is

- Register with the site. You'll be asked to provide a screen name, which will be used to identify you at the site; a password that only you and the system's software will know; contact information including your name, mailing address, and e-mail address; and credit card information. (Companies use the credit card information for security reasons only—you won't be charged for placing online bids). This information becomes the property of the site but isn't generally released unless the company responsible for the site uses it for promotional purposes.

- Read the terms and conditions of sale. Yes, they exist in cyberspace too, albeit in different formats. Amazon.com has a participation agreement and an auctions guarantee. EBay has a user's agreement that is very similar in format to the standard terms and conditions of sale found at live auctions. You'll be asked to agree to these disclosures when you register as a bidder. Don't just click the yes button; read them thoroughly and carefully.

- Read the bidding guidelines. Bidding processes are fairly standard regardless of the site you choose, but there will be some variations from site to site. Be sure you fully understand the ones in place wherever you do business.

Timesaver
Print a copy of the terms and conditions of sale and keep it in a file for quick and easy access should you need to reference it.

■ Glean all the information you can about the
object you're interested in buying. Unlike live
auctions where condition is usually not
included in the description of objects, most
online sellers do give reasonable detail because
they know it's essential to a successful sale.
Such things as cracks and chips, missing hardware, broken glass, warped shelves, and similar
defects are normally pointed out. Many sellers
are also very adept at wielding a camera, so
you'll be able to see pictures on lots of items.
In some cases, more than one image of the
item will be available for you to view, although
you may have to jump to another Web site to
see them. Always e-mail the seller if you need
further information or clarification.

■ Check the seller references. Many sites offer a
rating service on both buyers and sellers where
comments regarding transactions can be
recorded. Don't place all your trust on these
ratings services, however; although online auction houses prohibit it, scammers can rig these
ratings through the use of secondary user ID's
or third parties.

After you've done all this and all questions have
been answered to your satisfaction, it's time to place
your bid.

Types of online auctions

Online auctions operate differently from live auctions. As previously mentioned, they take the form
of mail or catalog auctions, which can last for days or
weeks rather than just a day or two. And, you're fly-
ing a little blind when you participate in them, as
the information you're given on auctions in

progress is fairly minimal. Usually, you'll see the following information and not much more:

- The minimum bid
- The required bid increment
- How many bids have been made
- The seller's identity
- Who the bidders are, but not their bid
  amounts
- When the auction began and when it closes

There are also more types of auctions available
online than there are live. The most common formats include

- Standard, or Yankee auctions. The most common type, these auctions offer a single item or
  a group of items to one high bidder.

- Reserve price auctions. Sellers designate to the
  online auction site the minimum price they're
  willing to accept. Buyers know there is a
  reserve, but not how much it is. They also
  know whether or not the reserve has been
  met. If the reserve isn't met by the end of the
  auction, the seller can merely keep the item or
  accept the highest bid that was received.

- Dutch auctions. In these auctions, bidders
  compete for multiple quantities of a single
  item—five snow globes, for example, or 10 oil
  lamps. Buyers enter bids that indicate both
  how many items they wish to buy and how
  much they want to bid for each. The final per-
  item price is determined by the lowest of the
  winning bids, and the bidder who submits the
  highest of the winning bids is entitled to the
  quantity he or she specified, but at the lower
  per-item price. Remaining quantities of the

item are used to fill other winning bids in order of their bid price.

- Private auctions. The least common type, these auctions conceal the identities of bidders. Only the seller and high bidder are notified of the auction results.

Some online companies also offer restricted access auctions. These auctions pertain to adult-oriented matter—books, videos, and the like—and are restricted from minors and anyone else who hasn't registered for access to these areas. They're not very applicable to antiques so you generally won't see this format used to sell these items, but you will run across the term on a general use Web site like eBay.

Bidding practices

Until you get used to thinking of your computer as a bidding room, online auctions can be just as intimidating and confusing as their live counterparts are. The best advice is to go slow. Read everything about the process. You'll find bidding tips at virtually every auction Web site, answers to frequently asked questions, and an e-mail function where you can ask questions directly of the online company's staff.

Once you're feeling fairly confident about the process, go ahead and test the waters. If you're the cautious type, you may want to participate in an auction for a small, inexpensive item. Find something that you want to buy but can live without (just in case you don't win). A videotape, maybe, or possibly a small collectible—basically, something that won't break the bank if you do end up with it.

As in live auctions, you'll be asked to enter your opening bid. If it doesn't meet the current bid amount, you'll be asked if you want to submit another bid. If this bid is accepted, you're in the

Watch Out!
Never send money to a P.O. box or to anyone unwilling to give you a verifiable home address and telephone number. If the seller refuses, cancel the sale.

running. Unless you use an automatic bid service, or proxy bidding, you'll have to check in at the site on a regular basis to see how your bid is fairing and to update your bid if necessary.

Whenever possible, and especially when you're first starting out as an online bidder, try to monitor the bidding process by following an auction from beginning to end. It's the best way to get a feel for online bidding. Also, don't be too quick to enter a bid when you first locate an item in which you are interested. Sometimes the same product is auctioned over and over again. Learn to follow the product and check different popular auction sites to see if it is being offered repeatedly. If so, you probably want to stay away from it.

Proxy bidding

Some online auction companies offer various systems that will automatically increase your bids until they reach a specified amount. All you have to do is

- Decide how much you want to pay.
- Enter your first bid.
- Give your proxy (the online company) your maximum bid amount, which is kept confidential.

The system then bids on your behalf, both with other proxy bidders and bidders who don't elect to use the system. You're notified if your maximum bid is exceeded by another bidder, and you can either raise your maximum or call it a day at this point. At the end of the auction, all you have to do is check back with the system to see how your proxy did.

Online bidding tips

The general philosophies behind bidding online are like bidding in any other form of auction;

Bright Idea
An easy way to keep track of the items you're bidding on is by bookmarking them. Place each bookmarked item into a special file on your system.

however, a few additional rules pertain specifically to this arena:

- Bid early, and quickly outbid your opponents. Inexperienced bidders are often intimidated by an active bidder who doesn't let them get into the game. Other bidders may get tired of continually being outbid and will pull out of the auction. Another good reason for placing an early bid: Some auction sites, such as Amazon.com, give first bidders on each item a 10 percent discount if they win the auction.

- Use the automatic bid feature if the auction site has one. It makes staying in contention much easier. If you reach your maximum bid amount and are willing to increase your limit, wait until the last possible moment to do so. You may catch your opponents sleeping.

- If bidding is still active, you really want the item, and the bid price is good, strike late and place a final bid before the auction closes. Your opponents may not have time to retaliate. This tactic is also known as sniping and is used by a number of online bidders who like the excitement of swooping down and claiming an auction in the final minutes.

Always set a definite limit on the amount you're willing to spend and stick to it. Auction fever is as prevalent in online bidding as it is at live auctions.

When the auction's over

Buyers are strongly encouraged by online auction companies to keep tabs on the progress of the auctions they're involved in so they know when the auctions are over and if they won or lost. If you're the high bidder when everything is said and done, you can either contact the seller to make payment and shipping arrangements, or the seller will contact you. Be aware that sellers are usually fairly aggressive at this because they want to consummate the sale as quickly as they can.

Many sellers will require that payment be made by means other than personal checks, especially if they're selling expensive items. Some will take credit cards, but most prefer money orders, cashier's checks, wire transfers, traveler's checks, or bank drafts. And they'll require that your payment clears before they send your purchases to you. Understandably, they're concerned that they may not get paid or the check you write will bounce. As a buyer, however, you have similar concerns. Either you may not get what you bought, or you might receive something very different than what you thought you were getting.

If you're dealing with someone who has a positive user profile, the chances of your transaction being anything less than successful will be lower.

Reference checks

To give yourself even more assurance that the person you're buying from is on the level, check the remittance address he or she gives you against telephone directory listings. You can do this online to make sure the information matches—more information on how to do this can be found in Chapter 7, "Antiques on the Internet." If it doesn't, warning flags should go up. Always ask for a phone number, and call it to see if it's a working number. There is nothing wrong with having a chat with the seller to let this person know that you are checking contact information. A legitimate seller will have nothing to hide.

If you are buying from a dealer, ask if he or she is a member of any dealer organizations. Get the

Bright Idea
Pay with a credit card for an extra layer of protection. Some card companies insure their customers against fraud. Virtually all of them offer some sort of investigation and mediation service when transactions go wrong.

name and Web site address for the organization (if they have one) and check the membership rolls. Ask how long this person has been in business and whether the business is listed in the Yellow Pages. Then check the information you receive against the information contained in the Yellow Pages and the White Pages. You can find national directory listings online or at the public library. Call during regular business hours to see if the phone is answered as a business or as a residence. Keep in mind that there are many "Internet dealers" operating out of their garages. They may be as legitimate as the next person. They may also close their garage door tomorrow. If they have a verifiable phone number and address, chances are better of them being viable business concerns.

Right of refusal

If you are buying from a seller that you know and have dealt with before, you can usually ask for and receive the right to refuse and return a purchase after inspection. Reputable sellers have no problem granting this right because they have already made disclosure and, in most cases, you will find the goods to be as represented. It's a good idea, though, to at least confirm this understanding through e-mail or a phone call before the item is shipped. If you're participating in a sale with "all sales are final" terms, your chances of being made whole in a less-than ideal transaction are substantially reduced.

Escrow agents

If you haven't worked with the seller before, or the item is expensive, it's a good idea to use one of the escrow services available to Internet buyers. These companies charge a fee to collect payment and hold it until the buyer has approved the goods. If the buyer is not satisfied, he or she notifies the escrow agent and returns the item to the seller. Once it's back in the hands of the seller the payment is canceled or returned to the buyer. The escrow agent keeps its fee in either event.

Escrow agents typically charge a flat fee plus a percentage of the transaction. The percentage charged is on a sliding scale. A typical example would be a $10 flat fee for purchases under $500 plus a 5 percent commission.

Escrow agents are handy to know about because they also facilitate payment by credit card. This adds an additional layer of protection for the buyer, as you can cancel the transaction if things go wrong and you're not giving a card number to a stranger living halfway across the country.

Even if you know the seller well, it's always a good idea to involve an escrow agent any time a lot of money is at stake. The best sellers, in fact, will insist on it, as it's really the only way to avoid disputes. You'll find contact information for some of the better-known services in Appendix E.

Watch Out!
If a seller with whom you are unacquainted demands certified funds while refusing to use an escrow agent, the best thing to do is walk away from the transaction.

Buyer beware

Internet fraud is, unfortunately, a large problem in the online community. In the first half of 1999, the Federal Trade Commission reported a twenty-fold increase in the number of auction-related fraud complaints, even with stronger security measures being taken and arrests increasing. As discussed above, the largest problem is often nondelivery of merchandise or the receipt of items that bear only a slight resemblance to the objects that were supposedly purchased. The best protection against outright theft is to conduct due diligence when buying antiques over the Internet, but those shady practices themselves can be difficult to spot unless you know what to look for.

Fraudulent activity can happen both during the bidding process and after the auction is over. The following are some of the most common practices to keep an eye out for, and what you can do to avoid them.

Shilling or false bidding

Just as in live auctions, online bids can be driven up by sellers who arrange to have fake bids placed by associates. Some sellers do it themselves by using fake IDs.

This may be the hardest Internet fraud to detect as it's difficult to tell a real bidder from a phony. However, it can be apparent if a flurry of bids are placed at the tail end of an auction. Another red flag is a bid retraction by the highest bidder just before the auction closes. False bidding is much frowned upon, and sellers who use it are generally banned from using the company's services, but getting back online can be as easy as establishing a new screen name and user profile. The only sure method of defeating this scam is knowing what an item's true value is, setting a firm limit on what you're willing to pay, and sticking by it.

Bid shielding

Bid shielding is characterized by a hard-fought battle between two bidders who run up the bid price and suddenly pull out just before the auction ends, leaving the third-place bidder as the winner of the goods. Because the practice is similar to shilling, it can be spotted in much the same way.

Bait and switch

The age-old "bait and switch" scam is a very easy one to perpetrate on the Internet. Photographs don't always match item descriptions, and some items run with no photographs at all. If there is one, make sure it does match the description. Always avoid any items being auctioned that carry such descriptions as "similar to the item shown" or "like the item depicted in the attached photograph." These are good signs of a bait and switch scam.

Selling reproductions and fakes

Selling reproductions and fakes can happen innocently or with the seller's full knowledge. You won't know about it until you actually receive the goods, which is why it's a good idea to know exactly what the terms of sale are. Being able to return what you bought for a refund is the best situation you could be in. Again, dealing with reputable sellers is your best defense.

Lack of full disclosure

Lack of full disclosure is a scam that comes under the heading of *caveat emptor*. Sellers that employ it will misrepresent the condition of the items they're selling. Because such things as chips and scratches can diminish the value of an item, it's important to know if they do exist. Good sellers will disclose them and even point them out on close-up photos.

Misrepresenting condition

Misrepresenting condition differs somewhat from full discloure in that representations are made concerning the item's condition. Where problems arise is in the interpretation of what is being said. What is in "perfect" or "near new" condition to one person may be an entirely different thing to another. Again, this is often an honest mistake made by a seller.

The more buyers, the more con artists will be going there.
—Cleo Manuel, vice president of the National Fraud Information Center

Failure to ship

Sadly, failure to ship happens more often than it should. One eBay seller, in fact, is currently spending 14 months in a federal prison for doing exactly this, having bilked buyers out of approximately $36,000 of money paid for computers and other equipment that was never shipped. Your best defenses against this fraud are to work only with sellers with positive user profiles and to communicate with sellers early and often. Be sure to ask when shipment is made and by what carrier as delivery times can vary depending on who is used. If shipment is supposed to be made by mail, and isn't, this constitutes mail fraud and is punishable by federal law.

When problems arise

If you suspect an online fraud or if you feel you have been taken advantage of during an online transaction, immediately report the problem to the online company where it happened. Also report it to the National Fraud Information Center, which is an arm of the National Consumers League, the nation's oldest nonprofit consumer action group. This organization will forward complaints to more than 150 law enforcement agencies, including the Federal Trade Commission, local sheriff's offices, and other agencies. Contact information for this organization can be found in Appendix E.

Frauds that happen once a sale is complete— even after you've done everything you can to avoid them—are more difficult situations to handle. As discussed earlier, the online companies stay out of these situations as much as they possibly can, so it will fall to you to handle the matter. About all you'll be able to do in this arena is post a negative review on the seller and hope that other buyers are smart enough to stay away from this person.

Give the seller the chance to rectify the situation if at all possible. Honest mistakes do happen, and it's always a good idea to give someone the benefit of the doubt. However, don't cut this person too much slack. If your negotiations drag on for months or the seller stops returning your calls, it's time to take legal action. You may be dealing with a phantom—in other words, a seller who is liable to disappear on you, with your money—before the problem is settled. They can be found, but it takes time and effort to do so. Calling an end to the charade and involving an attorney may be your only solution.

If you made payment by mail, the transaction falls under the supervision of the U.S. Postal Inspector, and you should also bring the problem to the attention of this agency. Mail fraud, even when it involves small dollar amounts, is a serious crime, punishable with fines and prison sentences.

Buying at online auctions can be fun and rewarding. Generally, these transactions take place without a hitch. Still, it's best to take every precaution. Problems typically arise when you least expect them to. Protect yourself every time; the time and effort it takes to do so always pays off.

Bright Idea
When you post a comment about a seller, be sure to include your e-mail address so others can contact you if they have questions about your experience.

Just the facts

- Always research items before bidding online and set firm limits on the amount you are willing to spend. Know what you are looking at and exactly what its current market value is.

- Conduct careful due diligence on sellers before buying online. Use common sense and start with small purchases.

■ Use proxy bidding to stay in the game. Online auctions take place over many days and keeping track of their progress can be time-consuming.

■ On expensive items, or until you have established a reliable relationship with an online seller, use an escrow company to facilitate inspection of goods before payment is released.

Buying from Dealers

Most collectors get started by buying antiques from dealers, and with good reason: Of all the buying venues for antiques, retail settings are the most familiar and the least threatening, especially to new collectors. Antiques shops are also the most accessible and convenient shopping spots for many collectors. If the desire to buy hits, it's much easier to go to your favorite antiques store or mall than to wait months for a show or auction to take place.

In Chapter 4, "Antiques Shops and Malls," you read about the different types of antiques shops that you're likely to find. Now it's time to learn how to negotiate and buy from the people who own and run them. But first, remember that all dealers are business people. Even though negotiating price is more the standard than the exception in this industry, there are times when it's not appropriate. Never assume that all dealers will engage in this practice. And, never assume that you'll ever get better discounts than the standard 10 to 20 percent. Over

Chapter 11

time, as you get friendly with a dealer or two, you may get preferential treatment in the way of access to good pieces, but deeper discounts should not be expected. In fact, assuming that a good relationship with a dealer entitles you to even better pricing is one of the best ways to put your relationship with that person on ice.

66

A bargain means value—not price.
—Harold Sack,
*American
Treasure Hunt*

99

As I mentioned in Chapter 2, "Becoming a Collector," the most important aspect to being a skilled buyer is knowing everything you can about your collecting category. You should have a firm grasp on identifying value and pricing before you attempt to buy from any source. Then, when you see an item that you believe has merit, you will be in a position to judge whether it is priced high, low, or reasonably. The goal is to deal knowledgeably rather than throwing yourself on the mercy of your emotions and your checkbook balance.

Why buy from a dealer?

As the most active buyers in the antiques market themselves, dealers stay abreast of market developments and can be valuable allies when you are trying to locate unique items. Unless you buy through them, you will be competing with their expertise in the race to acquire the best objects. Go to an antiques auction, and you'll be bidding against dealers. Go to an estate sale, and you'll be buying among dealers. Even at antiques shows, dealers often get a head start on collectors by being allowed to browse the various booths before collectors are admitted. Dealers constantly move inventory by buying and selling among themselves. An antique might pass through the hands of many different dealers before it ends up in yours.

The objects you buy from dealers will be some of the most expensive in your collection. For many collectors, however, the convenience of buying from dealers far outweighs the extra expense of doing so. Other reasons for utilizing dealers as a buying source depend on your goals and objectives as well as the type of dealer you're doing business with. They include

- Receiving a reasonable assurance that the piece you're buying is what it's represented to be. Reputable dealers will stand behind their inventory. If they're offering something that they have some questions about, they'll note their uncertainty by charging less than full market value.

- Being able to tap the expertise of a specific dealer. Even longtime collectors often use specialists to help them find very rare or highly desired items.

- Furthering a valuable relationship. If you've relied on a dealer to teach you about antiques during your educational process, you should repay the favor by buying through this person. This individual has taken the time to educate you. It's only fair to compensate this person for his or her efforts.

- Obtaining a particular antique that you really want. If you don't buy it from the person who has it, you just won't land it.

Many collectors also like buying from dealers for the value-added services that are often available, including:

- **Layaway.** Many dealers offer this service and are willing to hold pieces with a small down payment and no interest as long as you make regular payments. It's one of the best ways to buy pieces you want that may be a little beyond your budget. This courtesy is also a good customer relations tool for dealers, which is why they're often willing to extend it.

▪ **Delivery and set-up.** This is a great service if you're buying furniture—especially if you don't have ready access to a truck or van—or antiques that need to be installed, such as wall sconces or chandeliers. Such things as wiring, however, will still be your responsibility.

▪ **Trial period.** Some dealers will let their good customers take items home—especially large pieces of furniture or rugs—to test drive before buying. This is a very nice courtesy especially if there is any doubt as to how an antique will work at home.

▪ **Location services.** As mentioned in Chapter 4, dealers often keep customer want lists that note the specific pieces they've been asked to keep an eye out for. Having dealers call you when they find things you might be interested in is a great timesaver.

▪ **Repair services.** Pieces in need of some tender loving care are often priced accordingly, and they can be great buys if you know how to get them fixed. If you don't, it's something you can ask a dealer to help you with, and it's also a tool that can be used in negotiation.

Always keep the basic rules in mind when buying antiques from anyone. Know what you're buying before you buy it, and always ask questions. Even in the most rarefied of antiques establishments, the questions you ask—especially if they reflect the expertise you've developed as a collector—will establish you as a worthy customer. It can be risky to do business with any dealer who dodges your questions or gives you less-than-satisfactory answers if you're relying on that person to guarantee what you're buying. Your own expertise is a far better guarantee. While you should always do business with people you trust, you can protect yourself from buying mistakes by doing everything you possibly can to assure the authenticity and quality of each and every object before money exchanges hands.

Selecting your dealers

Different types of dealers exist to serve the needs of every level and type of collector. Wealthy connoisseurs of high-end antiques can find shops that sell museum-quality pieces with prices to match. Bargain hunters have a wealth of general merchandise and junk dealers to pick from. Specialists sell only certain categories of antiques. Each offers unique buying opportunities for collectors.

Which antiques dealers will be the right ones for you? Part of the answer depends on the type of antiques that you're collecting. If you're focused on a very specific collecting category, say English sterling silver, your best bets of finding it are going to be dealers who specialize in fine antiques of the nineteenth century. If country-style furniture is to your liking, general antiques dealers in rural settings often have the best quality and quantity to choose from.

Other factors that will influence your choice include

- **Time.** If your time for collecting is truly limited, your best bet will be developing relationships with dealers who specialize in your

Timesaver
Every major city has one or two streets where antiques dealers cluster. Instead of running all over town, save time by finding the antiques "beehive," then get down to shopping.

collecting category. These will be the establishments where your chance of finding what you
want will be the greatest.

■ **Distance.** Beginning collectors often prefer to
work with dealers in close proximity to where
they live. As you continue in your pursuit of
antiques, however, you'll probably end up buying from dealers in other parts of the country
as well. To be a successful collector, you have to
go to where the best antiques are. Limiting
yourself to shopping only at local dealers can
be a limiting factor for your collection as well.

■ **Convenience.** What's easier, driving around
and visiting a bunch of antiques shops or jumping on the Internet and browsing online shops
and auctions? Dealers who have seen the
future are turning their efforts to developing
their Web sites for all the collectors who are
making this shopping method a viable alternative to the traditional retail model.

■ **The amount of negotiating you feel like doing.**
Price negotiation is discouraged in some types
of antiques shops. If you don't like doing it,
these may be venues in which you'll feel more
comfortable. In other shops, it's not only
acceptable, it's expected. You'll find out which
are which later in this chapter.

■ **Whether the dealer offers a guarantee.** Some
collectors distrust this practice as they feel
guarantees are worthless and only unscrupulous dealers offer them. To others, this is
extremely important. You'll find more on this
later in this chapter.

What shouldn't limit your selection is the amount
of money you have to spend. Always remember that

one of the basic tenets for buying antiques is to buy the best you can possibly afford. You might find antiques that fit the bill anywhere you look. Collectors often hesitate to enter antiques shops and galleries on the high end of the scale because they don't feel they can afford the price of admission. This attitude can actually work against them, since even the finest shops carry items in many price ranges.

Dealers understand the value of cultivating new clients by having a few loss-leaders—items that will attract people other than their usual customers—in their standard inventory. The buyer with limited means today could very well turn into tomorrow's millionaire. Be sure to include one or two of these establishments if for no other reason than to view fine quality pieces, with the understanding that they may not yield many pieces in your current price range.

Understanding dealer pricing

As discussed in Chapter 4, dealers have to buy at wholesale or something close to it in order to realize a viable profit from their efforts. They then mark up their cost—the amount they paid for the object—to arrive at their retail price. The average mark-up is double what they paid, or 100 percent of cost. Some pieces will carry an even steeper price if the dealer thinks he or she can get it. Others—especially pieces acquired from other dealers—may have less of a mark-up since they're not purchased at wholesale prices. Dealers usually give other dealers a fairly good discount on the items they buy (anywhere from 30 to 40 percent) but they don't give these items away. However, the retail price on

Watch Out!
Never allow your passion for collecting to open your wallet when your budget says you shouldn't. There will almost always be another chance to buy the object of your desire when your finances will permit you to do so.

these objects will be virtually the same regardless of who you buy them from.

This doesn't mean that you have to pay the sticker price on every object you buy from a dealer. In fact, quite the opposite is true. In virtually every establishment, from the raggiest junk shop to the most opulent specialty gallery, discounts of between 10 and 20 percent are regularly granted to customers who know how to ask for them. You'll find tips on how to do this later in this chapter.

When to buy from dealers

Regardless of the type of dealer you're buying from, there are certain times of the month and year when the buying scenario will be more in your favor. While you'll probably buy antiques fairly regularly throughout the year, focusing your attention on these periods can bring you some extra benefits when it comes to maximizing your buying efforts:

- The end of the month, just before rent and utilities are due.

- Late January or early February. During this period, many dealers are beginning to feel the pinch from dwindling Christmas cash and slower sales due to bad weather. Many antiques shows are held in the spring, and dealers may need to prepare space for new items in their shops by reducing existing inventory.

- Late summer and early fall. As merchants return from the big summer shows and sales, their showrooms get crowded with new merchandise. It's not uncommon to find dealers who hold special sales right before the holiday season to clear out old merchandise that shoppers may recognize from their last seasonal visits.

- During the middle of the week at antiques malls. Since traffic tends to be light at antiques malls during weekdays, this is the best time to shop.

- On the last day of antiques sales. Dealers generally don't want to pack up everything and take it home again.

The worst time to buy: the holiday season, when prices will be higher due to increased store traffic and higher buyer demand. This is also when people who don't know a thing about antiques will buy pieces as presents. Many dealers anticipate this and set their prices accordingly.

Judging good from bad

The best protection from being taken advantage of by any seller, including dealers, is to be a savvy buyer. A good dose of skepticism helps, too. Never assume that a shop is solid and reputable just because it looks like it. Put any antiques shop or gallery you're interested in doing business with through the same scrutiny you would if you were buying at auction or on the Internet. Some specific points to check were discussed in Chapter 4.

Another point you may want to add to your checklist is whether or not the dealer uses a bill of sale. The best dealers will give you one that is very similar to the terms and conditions that auction houses use. In other words, it will specify what the dealer is willing to guarantee about the purchase. Some will also specify the conditions under which the dealer is willing to accept items for return.

Warranties, whether offered by the finest galleries in the world or your local general line antiques dealer, are so carefully worded that they do more to protect the seller than the buyer. Still, it's a

Unofficially...
Although women today occupy a larger share of the collecting pie than men do, this is a fairly recent occurrence. According to Louis H. Hertz, author of *Antique Collecting for Men*, from Roman times through well into the nineteenth century, the greatest collectors, almost without exception, were men.

Unofficially...
Antiques experts warn against placing too much reliance on signatures. Very authentic works of art often carry fake signatures. Artists often don't sign their works; other people will in the interest of gaining a higher price for them.

good idea to get as much as you can in writing. Although these representations can be vague, they'll still stand up better than verbal ones will.

To illustrate how hard it is to enforce a warranty, imagine you want to buy a watch that the dealer assures you was once owned by General Robert E. Lee. Due to this provenance, the dealer has insisted that his lowest price is what you consider a premium figure. The dealer says he will stand by the watch if it turns out to be "wrong" and gives you a receipt that reads, "Civil War-era pocket watch bearing the inscription Robert E. Lee, 1863." So long as the watch is of a make traceable to the 1860s and bears the inscription mentioned, even if you discover that the inscription was added last week, the dealer is free and clear.

A better approach to take is to focus on the quality of the item you are buying, assess its attributes of value, and forget about dealer representations. Approach negotiations with a price already in mind, and always conduct your negotiations with the assumption that the item is not authentic unless you are absolutely assured that it is. Remember, it is very easy to make new items look old, and to increase the value of an item by adding a signature. Even very savvy dealers can be taken by such ruses. You aren't necessarily dealing with unscrupulous people or outright crooks when such situations erupt, but you will have to protect your own interests if they do because the dealer won't do it for you.

Recognizing dealer ploys

Offering useless warranties is just one of the ploys that some dealers will use to get buyers to buy. Here are some of the more obvious squeeze tactics that you could encounter during the buying process:

- "There's been lots of interest in this piece." This kind of statement is intended to pressure you into making a quick decision because it implies that the piece may not be there tomorrow. This is rarely the case.

- "So-and-so (insert the name of a local or national celebrity here) bought something exactly like this a week ago." Celebrity spin is a tactic used by some dealers to put false value on antiques. It's never a reason to buy anything.

- "Absolutely guaranteed to be a good investment." No reputable dealer guarantees an investment. Doing so is far too risky. Any dealer who makes this statement is merely trying to justify the price he or she has placed on the object.

- "You wouldn't be asking that question (or for a discount) if you really knew what you were doing." Another statement meant to dissuade you from challenging the prices the dealer is asking for and anything else about the pieces at hand.

- "This is the latest greatest collecting category, sure to take off." In other words, you should pay an inflated price for it now. Your own expertise should tell you whether it's a category worth investing in.

- "It's a consignment piece and the seller won't take anything less." People who place items on consignment almost always tell the dealer what their bottom dollar is on pricing. Dealers who employ this tactic know full well that there is room for negotiation. They're hoping you don't.

I never tell a collector to buy something from a seller who says it's guaranteed to be a good investment.
—Collector and private dealer Gene Barth

At some time along the way, you may encounter dealers who display their antiques bare—in other words, without prices. These dealers size up customers to determine what they can afford to pay based on how they're dressed. They then set their prices accordingly. It's also a negotiation tool used by some country and home-based dealers, as you'll read later in this chapter.

If you know what you are looking for and the amount you're willing to pay, you'll be able to walk away from this ruse when the price isn't right. Still, it's a fairly questionable business practice, and in some states, such as New York, it's illegal except for pieces used in window displays.

Does this also mean that you should leave the Rolex and diamond ring behind when shopping at antiques dealers? If you want to get the best prices possible, yes. These trappings denote buyers who can afford to pay top dollar. Dealers are more often tempted to stand fast on price when they spot indications that buyers can afford them.

The art of negotiation

Price negotiation is part and parcel of the antiques buying process. Unlike virtually every other retail transaction, you can walk into almost every venue where antiques are sold (or dial them up through the Internet, for that matter) and expect to pay a little less than the asking price...if you know how to do it.

Regardless of the situation, sugar works better than vinegar when it comes to negotiating price. Almost every dealer will tell you that asking someone politely if a stated price is the best that he or she can do has a better chance of resulting in a 10 to 20 percent discount (the industry standard) than if you just state the price that you're willing to pay. An appropriate counteroffer if the price is still too high is to say, "I can offer you X if that would be acceptable to you."

Price negotiations do not need to be lengthy or cumbersome, nor should they take place unless you're serious about buying something. If an object is priced way out of your range, don't assume that you can negotiate the price down to something more affordable. Even if you think the price is really outlandish, keep in mind that it may not be to the dealer with whom you're negotiating. If the price is beyond what your research tells you is a realistic range for the item, you're better off passing it by unless it's something that you absolutely must have.

The pieces dealers offer for sale are priced at the highest point that the dealer thinks the market will bear. However, don't go into every antiques shop with the attitude that you can negotiate to your heart's content because all prices are higher than they should be. Dealers deplore these buyers and will do everything they can to stonewall them. Particularly obnoxious customers may even be asked to leave, and frankly, the dealers have every right to do so in these situations.

Other general pointers to keep in mind include:

- Use discretion. Negotiating should always be handled as discretely as possible. Shouting an offer across the shop at a dealer is the best way to make this person never want to do business with you, especially if he or she is involved with another customer at the time.

- In most cases, don't just offer a set amount based on what you think an object is worth. You're almost always better off asking if a price

Moneysaver
If you see an item priced absurdly high, keep your eye on it. Visit the shop regularly to see if it sells. The dealer may have mistakenly paid too much for the item, and after some time, may be open to offers just to get rid of the mistake.

is firm than stating what you're willing to pay. At flea markets, however, offering a set amount is a commonly accepted practice.

■ Know when no means no. If you're told a price is absolutely firm, it may very well be. Don't push the issue by asking why. As you'll read about later in this chapter, there are ways to keep negotiations open in these situations, but a dealer who says this often means it. Always remember that antiques hold their value. If dealers are in the position to wait for a buyer who will pay the full asking price, they often will.

The ins and outs of negotiating with various dealers follows. Keep in mind that these are general suggestions based on common practices in the antiques industry. No one approach will work in every situation. Your best bet is to be aware of the various negotiation tactics you can use and tailor your approach to meet your needs as warranted. Again, never assume that you're going to get a discount from a dealer. While it's more the rule than the exception, actually getting a discount is a privilege to be bestowed on the best customers, not a right that is extended to anyone who walks through the door.

Buying from generalists

Prices: Reasonable to low

Negotiation Factor: Moderate to high

The people who run general merchandise antiques shops, either as stand-alone enterprises or in antiques malls and co-ops, are often not experts in all categories of antiques, but they do have expertise at selling and merchandising. Since they don't specialize in any one area, their appeal has to be one that will reach a large audience.

For this reason, they tend to be down-to-earth and friendly, and they can be some of the most approachable when it comes to price negotiation. Because the merchandise in these shops is of various levels of quality and condition, these are venues where you're also most likely to be able to get good discounts if you ask for them. If a discount is possible, you'll hear it right away if you've asked nicely. If you're told the price is firm, offer to leave your name and phone number in case the item should be marked down at a later time. If the dealer is willing to take this information, it's a good indication that he or she is at least considering your offer.

When you see an item that you know is priced well below what you think it's worth, inspect it carefully to make sure you have not overlooked a problem or a repair. If there is no apparent reason for the low price, buy it. The good price may reflect nothing more than the fact that the dealer was able to buy the piece reasonably. The dealer will appreciate getting his or her price, and it will be encouragement to work with you in the future.

If an item is priced higher than what your research tells you it should be, ask about the criteria used to arrive at the price. You may be told of factors you overlooked that justify the stated price. You may also find that the price is simply one that the dealer wishes someone would pay. If that's the case, a polite discussion concerning condition and authenticity might result in a reasonable discount.

Parlor games with the tea and crumpet crowd

Prices: On the high end

Negotiation factor: Tough, but doable

> **❝**
> Both sellers and buyers are a lot more sophisticated— it's harder to make a discovery now.
> —George Glazer, dealer of American and European globes, *Elle Décor*, August/ September 1998
> **❞**

Watch Out!
If a dealer bases an inflated price on claims of authenticity and provenance, ask to see exactly what they are and verify them yourself before entering into a firm offer. These claims can be as worthless as the paper they're printed on.

Although these are two different types of shops, I've grouped them together here because they're more alike than different when it comes to buying at them. The dealers who run them are used to customers who place more reliance on a shop's reputation than they do on value, and they generally have a well-defined clientele that does exactly this. They're usually not interested in dealing with buyers who challenge them. The quickest way to get on the bad side of these dealers is to ask for a discount or question the veracity of any representation. Like all shop owners, though, they have to pay their overhead, and they sometimes will deal.

The best tactic with these dealers is to give them every indication that they're dealing with a sophisticated, savvy collector. These are venues where it's possible to score some points by dropping hints related to your collecting prowess. Strike up a conversation with the dealer if the situation lends itself to doing so—this can be one of the best ways to establish a sound trading relationship in any situation. Show your interest in the dealer's merchandise by asking informed, to-the-point questions.

In most situations where price can be negotiated, the negotiations begin with the buyer asking if the marked price is the best that the dealer can do. When negotiating with parlor store proprietors or the tea and crumpet crowd, however, this approach can backfire on you. Oftentimes, the answer will be yes, leaving you in a position to decide whether the item is worth the price or not. If you decide it isn't, you'll probably end up walking out the door empty-handed. These dealers can be very tenacious when it comes to price. If you don't buy it, they figure someone else will.

What you want to do instead is make it seem like a price reduction is the dealer's idea, not yours. You can accomplish this by:

- Saying you'll "think about it." If there's room in the price, you may be asked what needs to happen for you to take the item home today.

- Mentioning that you want to do some more research on the piece before making a final decision. Operating on the "bird in the hand" theory, the dealer may offer a discount to keep you from walking out the door. (This, by the way, is a very valid reason for not buying if you do indeed have questions about a piece.)

- Mentioning that there's an antiques show coming up and you want to see what you can find there. Unless the item you're interested in is very rare, the dealer knows you can find something similar somewhere else. Again, operating on the "bird in the hand" theory, he or she may make an offer that you can't refuse. Many dealers find this practice offensive, but it can work.

Try not to tip your hand with these dealers by showing them that you're extremely interested in anything they have to offer. By maintaining a cool demeanor, you're showing them that you're fully able to walk away from any deal that might be struck. In any case, don't be surprised if your bluff gets called. Of all the dealers in the antiques business, these people are the ones who are most capable of doing it.

Dealers on the Internet

Prices: All

Negotiation Factor: Fair to good

Bright Idea
If you don't hear back from an antiques shop at which you've left a phone number, by all means call or visit the shop to see if the item you're interested in is still available, and at what price.

Antiques dealers who are either mirroring their operations on the Internet or who have moved their base of operations entirely into cyberspace represent extremely valuable buying opportunities for collectors. These individuals can be some of the most convenient to do business with. It's also very much in their best interest to develop a key group of online buyers that they can hold onto with good service and prices to match. The competition is steep online, and if they don't keep their buyers, other online entrepreneurs will snatch them away.

Some collectors find price negotiation to be easier with online dealers as the transactions aren't conducted face-to-face. However, you should still employ the same courtesies you would in live situations. Ask if the stated price is the best the dealer can do and let this individual take it from there.

A key factor in dealing with online dealers is being able to verify their reputation and business practices. The methods for doing so described in Chapter 10, "Buying Online," can and should be employed when establishing a relationship with any of them.

Dealing with pack rats

Prices: Usually very low

Negotiation Factor: Marginal

If you spend much time in shops in this category, or in junk shops, you'll find that the merchandise in them is generally in poor condition and priced accordingly. For this reason, it's often best to just pay the price asked when you see something you want as it's probably more than fair. I've always had a hard time bargaining with these dealers unless I really think they're asking too much. Over time, I've gotten some of my best finds in these shops, and often for a song. These experiences more than balance the rare occasions when I've paid a little more than I'd like.

Dealers at shows

Prices: All

Negotiation Factor: Fair to good

The dealers that you encounter at antiques shows are typical of the general merchandise dealers described above. Deal with these merchants the same as you would with those in shops; take the same precautions and extend the same courtesies.

As mentioned earlier, there is a unique timing aspect of buying at shows that you can definitely use to your advantage. Always shop early to identify items in which you're particularly interested. If they're really things you want, even if they're priced a little high, and you can't afford to gamble on their being available later, snap them up. If not, wait until the end of the show to see if they're still available. By then, dealers will usually allow a steeper discount, especially on large bulky items that are difficult and expensive to transport. Some of the things you saw earlier will have sold. On those pieces that haven't sold, you're likely to get a pretty good discount, perhaps as much as 20 percent or even more.

Timesaver
When shopping shows, bring a notepad and pen with you. Take notes on items you particularly liked and where you found them. When it comes time to buy, you won't waste time trying to remember where you saw them.

Specialty dealers

Prices: All

Negotiation Factor: Little to none

As your skill and knowledge increase within your collecting category, you will identify dealers who specialize in your category. These dealers will play an important part in your collecting activities, both as sources for antiques and as your competitors.

Unlike their general merchandise counterparts, specialty dealers are experts about their inventory. They make it their business to stay abreast of the market, and they use their expertise to track down and purchase the best items. Specialty dealers can be excellent sources for locating unique, hard-to-find items. They can also be real pains because they are constantly trying to beat you to the punch.

Don't expect to find a lot of bargains when buying from specialty dealers; chances are you will end up paying top dollar for the items you buy. You're also paying for a great amount of expertise when you buy from these people. And, unlike some other types of dealers, they're more likely to stand behind the items they sell. Specialty dealers build their reputations on the quality of their inventory. Most of these dealers have loyal customers with whom they transact a lot of business. They have much to lose should word get around that they sold a fake and then refused to rescind the deal.

If you're buying a piece from a specialty dealer's existing inventory, it's acceptable to ask if the price is firm. Be aware, though, that negotiating price with a specialty dealer can be a real battle of wits. It can also test every facet of your collecting expertise. Be prepared for lengthy discussions on authorship, condition, and aesthetics, after which the price will probably still be firm.

If you've asked a specialist to locate a specific item for you, you should be prepared to pay the price he or she quotes for it as long as it's reasonable. By asking this person to do something special for you, you're entering into a tacit commitment to buy. You can limit your liability in these situations by telling the dealer that you won't pay more than a set amount. Then, if he or she comes back with something that's considerably higher, you can refuse it based on your earlier direction. You'll have a better chance of furthering your relationship, however, if you buy the piece. Keep in mind, however, that this is a fairly common retailing practice. A good salesperson will always try to move his or her customers to the next price point. By setting a buying budget and sticking to it, you won't find yourself purchasing at a level you're not comfortable with. Knowing what your limits are always makes it easier to say no as well as yes.

Country and home-based dealers

Prices: Cheap to reasonable

Negotiation Factor: A test of your skills

Many country antiques dealers work from their homes, or from workshops, garages, or barns located on their properties. These dealers often sell antiques in conjunction with a refinishing and repair service. Their shops contain an eclectic blend of items that range from junk to objects that are worthy of display in the finest homes.

They may sometimes look like hayseeds, but these homegrown antiques experts will often surprise you with their depth of knowledge. Before you waltz into a barn expecting a deal that amounts to robbery, think twice. Chances are good that you're the one who will walk away having learned a painful and expensive lesson.

These dealers are often adept at playing the "poor dumb country boy" routine with buyers. Although it may look as though items have been stored forever (raising your hopes, of course, that a hidden treasure is just waiting to be found), this is rarely the case. In fact, dealers in this category usually turn inventory over quickly. They buy two

"
I've learned to make a pretty good living just buying at one auction, fixing things up a little, then selling them at another auction. It's fun. I like the people and the travel.
—David DeMonia, home-based antiques dealer
"

classes of items—those that can be resold immediately (either privately or at local auctions) without much additional investment of time or labor, and objects in need of repair. What you're often seeing are the items that are awaiting repair, not things that have been in the dealer's possession forever.

Country antiques dealers rarely tag items for resale. Rather, they expect buyers to make low-ball offers; in fact, they even encourage it. Ask what the price is and you'll often hear something along the lines of "What will you give me for it?" However, don't expect them to take your offer when you make it. This is usually just the beginning of the negotiation process. What you're likely to hear instead is one or more explanations of why they can't, ranging from "I just have too much invested in it to say yes," to "Mrs. White has been after a piece just like this one for the longest time and I would feel rotten if I didn't offer it to her first." What unsuspecting buyers often do at this point is raise their offer. What they're really doing is bidding themselves up.

These dealers are masters at getting buyers to increase their offers without ever having received a firm counteroffer. If you're not careful, you will end up making two or three offers before the dealer responds with a counter. Usually, you don't realize what happened to you until you're halfway home.

Just as you would when dealing with anyone else, start with a careful examination of an object to satisfy yourself that it's "right." Then, you can make an offer. Stand firm on it. You may get your piece then and there. If not, thank the dealer for his or her time and leave your name and telephone number. If the dealer thinks your offer is in the ballpark and wants to move the merchandise, you'll probably get a call and a counter-offer.

Moneysaver
Get to know your favorite dealers and their buying habits. Try to buy items off the truck as soon as they return from a buying trip. A quick resale for cash is an attractive transaction, especially to a country dealer strapped for cash after a trip.

Flea market dealers

Prices: Low

Negotiation Factor: High

You will find very few fine antiques at flea markets. Why they remain as popular venues is the simple fact that when you do locate an item worth buying, you can usually do so for a lark.

Haggling over prices at these venues is not only accepted, it's expected. This is the only place, in fact, where you can get away with telling dealers what you're willing to pay and using that figure as a basis for negotiation. Still, you don't want to insult the dealer by offering a ridiculous low-ball amount. Be reasonable and you'll have a much better chance of getting what you want.

Just the facts

- There are different types of dealers to meet collectors' different needs. Your ability to negotiate price will vary depending on who they are and how they do business.

- Always negotiate from the perspective that any discount given is a courtesy. While discounting is common, it should never be expected.

- Customers who bargain reasonably with dealers are always more welcome than those who engage in guerrilla tactics. Always treat a dealer as you'd like to be treated.

- If you ask a specialty dealer to locate a certain piece for you, be prepared to pay the price the dealer asks for it. This is another example of a value-added service that can justify a higher price than what you'd pay if you found the piece yourself.

Selling Antiques

GET THE SCOOP ON...

Reasons for selling ▪ Knowing when to sell ▪
Valuing your collection ▪ Expert advice you
should seek ▪ Alternatives to selling

PART V

Becoming a Seller

Chapter 12

U nless you decide to bequeath every single item you ever acquire to your heirs, it's virtually certain that you will sell some—if not all—of your collection at some point in your life.

Building a collection of antiques takes time, patience, and commitment—and the same things are required when it comes to selling one. If you've been a successful buyer, the expertise you've developed while collecting will help you as a seller. You can also look back on the buying opportunities you've had to identify potential selling opportunities. Your experience with dealers, auction houses, trade magazines, collector's clubs, and other individuals will come into play in a major way. The people you have met along the way with interests similar to yours are often the ones who will help you the most when the time comes to sell. Be sure to keep tabs on them as you go.

The information in this chapter will help you sell just a few pieces or your entire collection. Specific sales outlets and how to use them are covered in Chapter 13, "Selling Options."

Why sell?

At various times during your collecting career, you may choose to sell some of the antiques that you've collected for one or more of the following reasons:

- To reduce the number of duplicates in your collection. It's common for a collector to acquire more than one example of the same piece at the beginning of a collection and use the duplicate for trading purposes later as the collection grows in size and depth.

- To refocus your collection. If you decide to change your collecting approach, or focus more heavily on a specific element of a collection, it makes sense to sell pieces that don't add to this focus.

- To elevate the value of your entire collection. In a highly focused collection, having pieces of inferior value can dilute its value. Many collectors get rid of lesser pieces when they buy better ones.

- To raise money for buying other pieces. One piece in a collection can sometimes have such a strong attraction to another collector that he or she will make a great offer for it. Selling the piece may make good sense if doing so paves the way for acquiring other pieces that you want to own.

- To raise money for other reasons. The fast sale of an antique or two is sometimes the easiest way to cover an unforeseen expense or a budgetary shortfall. Antiques are investments that generally hold their value over time. Knowing the value of what you have collected and a few sources where you can liquidate the pieces quickly and at a reasonable price provides a certain level of comfort to many collectors.

- To decrease the size of your collection. Changes in circumstances, such as moving from a large home into a smaller one, sometimes call for culling out a collection. Some collectors go overboard and are forced into selling some of what they've acquired before it overtakes them, their families, and their homes.

- To start an antiques business. Many antiques collectors end up being antiques dealers. It's very common for these individuals to start their businesses by selling a few pieces from their own collections and building from there.

You may also wish to get rid of an entire collection at some point. Some collectors simply get bored with a category and decide they want to cash out and start anew. Collectors who have been buying antiques purely for investment also often reach this point. Economic difficulties can force the sale of a prized collection. The death of a collector almost always results in the liquidation of the estate, and, in turn, the sale of the collection.

The value of planning

Knowing that at some point along the way you'll likely be selling at least a piece or two of your collection will help you be better at it when you do decide to sell. In fact, buying and selling are in many ways two sides of the same coin. Much of what you do when buying can successfully be reversed when it's time to sell.

As I discussed in Chapter 2, "Becoming a Collector," your knowledge is your largest asset as a

Unofficially... Only about 10 percent of all collectors make money at it. —Jack Curtis, *Gannett News Service,* February 27, 1998

66

Prices have gone up and it's posed a little bit of a dilemma. Should I cash in when it's high or wait until retirement? —Collector Dave Cooper, quoted by *Gannett News Service,* February 27, 1998

99

collector. When you're selling, everything you've learned along the way comes into play once again. Just as it's not a good idea to do a great deal of buying before you've thoroughly researched the collecting area you're interested in, it's also not a good idea to sell before doing your homework. With that said, you'd be surprised at how often collectors walk into antiques shops and offer up pieces for sale or consignment without appearing to have given it much thought, perhaps even acting on a whim. I'm not saying that antiques shops aren't good venues for selling your pieces; they can be, depending on the situation. To use them most effectively, however, calls for evaluating their strengths and weaknesses along with those of other selling venues.

Sadly, the majority of collectors give very little thought to selling, and they rarely approach it in an organized fashion. Because of this, they often don't realize the full value of the investment they've made. With just a little planning and some legwork, they could do so much better.

Building a plan for selling your antiques will take some work, but the results can make it more than worth your while. The best collections are valuable because of the time and effort that collectors put into them. Such efforts almost always result in collections with a satisfying level of financial value to them as well. It only makes sense to reap those benefits to their fullest when selling. You can collect what you love and make money when you decide to sell—that is, if you do it wisely. And that means developing a plan. The specifics of a selling plan will vary depending on whether you're selling a few pieces or everything you have. The overall goal—attaining the largest return on your investment—

never changes. Let this be your mantra: Getting there takes time, effort, and lots of research.

Developing a selling plan

A selling plan functions as a road map to guide your efforts. By putting a plan together, you'll be able to identify the best approach or approaches for selling your antiques that will give you the best return on your time and investment.

When you make the decision to sell your collection—either all of it or parts of it—you want a plan that will allow you to do so in the shortest time possible, with the least amount of effort, and at the best price. All the other elements of your plan, from choosing the sales outlets to deciding whether you split up the collection or keep it intact, will be governed by these factors.

You probably won't strike a perfect balance between each factor. Your considerations in one area will outweigh the others and influence them accordingly. If time is your leading factor and you have to sell quickly, you may be forced into a selling scenario that will fit your time constraint but diminish the total dollar amount that you get for your collection. If you don't want to put much effort into the process, you probably won't find the best buyers or get the best prices.

Building the plan

Start with a clear and accurate understanding of your goals. You may find it helpful to write this out and put the rest of your plan on paper so you can track your progress as you go. Be very specific. Why are you selling? Do you want to liquidate your entire collection or just sell a few key pieces in a few months? Review the reasons for selling at the beginning of this chapter and list the ones that most

Bright Idea
Finding one buyer to purchase a collection can take a long time, but the payoff is usually worth it. When you sell the best part of a collection to one or several buyers, you still have to find buyers for the rest of it.

closely fit your situation as well as any others that come to mind.

Next, envision the best possible selling scenario for your collection, the one that will bring the most value for it and allow you to reach your goals. The speed with which you want sell your items will often dictate the direction in which you will move.

Timesaver
As you build your collection, compile a list of the people you meet along the way with interests similar to yours. When it's time to sell, you'll be able to put a contact list together in minutes.

Is time on your side?

The best possible scenario for liquidating an entire collection (and the one that usually delivers the best financial return) is one that allows you to sell when you want and where you want and gives you the best possible return on your investment.

In a perfect world, you'd be able to sell your antiques immediately at the best possible price. However, this almost never happens. Even if you think you've come up with a plan that will allow you to do exactly this, something almost always happens to change it. The economy could take a nosedive. You may need to sell faster than you thought, which may eliminate some of your better selling outlets. The dealer you wanted to consign with may suddenly retire. For these reasons, any plan you develop should be flexible and include more than one selling scenario if at all possible.

Timing is everything

Unlike the collectibles industry, where trends tend to take shape in a fairly definable pattern and prices rise and fall, demand for good antiques tends to stay fairly stable. This isn't to say, however, that trends don't develop in the antiques world. They can and they do. When a celebrity begins collecting Art Deco jewelry (think Barbra Streisand) or a style maven decides to promote her passion for green glass to everyone willing to listen (think Martha Stewart), prices on these in-demand items begin to climb. If you have a nice collection in either category, you definitely may be motivated to sell, especially if you could realize a good profit on your pieces. In general, however, you can't really base your sales plans on trends in the antiques industry because it just isn't as volatile.

In general, you'll get better prices in boom times than in recessions and be able to sell more readily as well. You can find buyers when money is tight, but they may be scarce. When times are good, more people are willing to open their wallets.

Monitoring celebrity spin

A popular movie or television show can kick a category into high gear when you least expect it to, and present a great opportunity for selling. Stay on top of these developments by:

- Reading celebrity lifestyle magazines. It may be a sad commentary on our society, but the celebrities in our midst are most often our greatest style arbiters. Not long ago, several articles appeared in *In Style* that featured the homes of two different celebrities. Coincidentally, each of them had the same vintage lighting fixture in their kitchens. Not soon after, the magazine had to run purchase information on the fixture due to reader requests for it.

- Watching television shows that report on the celebrity scene. All a popular celebrity has to do is show up at a movie premier wearing an antique watch or carrying a vintage beaded purse and there's a run on them soon after. If mention is made of a celebrity's fondness for a particular type of antique, you can bet that the antique will go up in value if it hasn't already. Barbra Streisand blew the prices sky high on Arts & Crafts pieces when it was revealed that she was buying a lot of them. This came after her previous passions for pieces in the Art Nouveau and Art Deco styles.

- Paying attention to women's clothing styles as they are introduced each year. If fashions are trending toward soft and romantic, you can almost bet that Victorian antiques of all types are going to gain in popularity because they'll be used in advertisements to set the mood for the clothing. Ethnic influences, such as the Russian Cossack look that periodically comes into style, can trigger interest in antiques with a similar appeal. Today's more minimalist styles are showcased in modern surroundings, but if you look closely you'll see design elements dating back to the 1920s and '30s.

Popular movies can also have a significant influence on the collecting arena. After the movie *Titanic* scored a big hit, anyone who had collected items even remotely related to the doomed oceanliner stood to profit immensely by them.

It isn't necessary to subscribe to every celebrity rag or watch entertainment television to excess to stay on top of the trends. The more time you spend doing it, however, the better your chances of spotting trends that may affect your desire to keep or sell what you own.

If a trend does develop that causes a surge in prices in your collecting category, you may be very tempted to take advantage of the existing marketing condition and make plans to sell as quickly as you can. This may net you some fast cash, but it may not be your best bet if doing so causes you to sell in a venue that costs you more money than if you sat back and waited for awhile. Remember, antiques hold their value. If something happens to elevate the market, they generally won't go down in price after the trend runs its course.

What's it worth?

Never sell anything until you know what you can get for it. Keep abreast of the prices on individual objects as well as what your collection may be worth as a whole. Some collections can be sold piecemeal and yield a large return to the seller. Very focused collections may often realize their best value if sold as a group to someone who's interested in building the nucleus of a collection quickly or elevating its value by buying many good pieces at once.

You can estimate the value of your antiques by:

- Attending live auctions and tracking auction results. The prices realized at auctions, in fact, can be some of the best indicators of what your collection is really worth. Getting these prices is becoming even easier to do with the growth of the Internet—many auction houses are now including this information on their Web sites.

- Monitoring online auctions. Again, a good and quick way to see what similar items are selling for.

- Checking prices in price guides. Remember, however, that these prices are often based on what the submitters believe items would sell for and not what they actually have brought in the market. Plus, you may never find an item with a description that matches what you have.

Unofficially...
A steadily increasing value on good antiques is such a standard thing that many dealers will buy back from you anything you purchased from them, for the purchase price, but one year later.

■ Reading sales coverage in trade publications.

If you still have questions as to what your collection is worth, you may want to have it appraised by a professional. This should be your last choice rather than your first, for the following reasons:

■ Appraisals are expensive. Anyone worth his or her salt is going to charge a good amount to render an expert opinion. The amount charged by appraisers varies, but it's usually based on an hourly fee plus expenses. Paying several hundred dollars or more for opinions on just a few pieces, or even one, isn't uncommon.

■ In almost every case the expert in the area in which you collect will be a dealer, and that person will often want to buy what you're having appraised. For this reason, you could be given an appraisal that is lower than what your items should actually have.

Bright Idea
Don't forget to revise your insurance coverage when your items are sold. Depending on the dollar amount you had insured and the terms of the policy itself, you could save quite a lot of money.

If you do decide to get appraisals, be sure to tell the appraiser to base his or her opinions on fair market value and not on retail value. As stated earlier, retail values, such as what you'll see in price guides, are usually inflated. You want to see the most accurate valuation possible, and one that truly reflects what the market will bear.

Be realistic about your expectations as you develop your selling plan. Many sellers end up vastly disappointed with their efforts when they simply factor the lists of prices in price guides or given by appraisers and assume they can realize this total, or more, when they go to sell. This is rarely the case; the effort and cost of selling take a bigger bite than you might first expect, and prices gleaned from these sources are often inaccurate.

The specific venues you choose for selling your antiques will have a tremendous bearing on the prices you end up realizing. In Chapter 13, you'll be able to compare the pros and cons in each and decide which are right for you.

Getting help from experts

A complete selling plan also takes into consideration such factors as legal obligations and tax liabilities. If you don't start out on the right foot in both of these areas, you'll soon incur problems. Once they crop up they can be difficult to rectify. It's always wise to seek professional assistance before they do.

If you anticipate deriving a significant amount of money from the pieces you sell, you'll need to make sure that you've considered the legal and tax implications of doing so. If you're selling through an agent—that is, a dealer or an auction house—any sales taxes owed will be collected for you and you will bear no responsibility for doing so. However, if you're selling directly to the public, you'll generally have to apply for a sales tax license and collect the taxes from the buyer if you do it more than once. You may also need a business license. Many of these issues can be addressed by contacting your local and state government. Most entities have packets of information for small businesses that they'll send for free. However, should you have any questions concerning your operations, discuss them with a business attorney.

Another professional you'll need as part of your team is a good accountant. This person can also advise you on your tax liabilities and may be able to suggest ways to ease them. If your collection is small and not particularly valuable, you may not have

Moneysaver
Attorneys issue opinion letters about the applicability of certain laws to your situation. If you rely on the attorney's opinion, this protects you from claims of willfully breaching the law and shifts the responsibility to the attorney's malpractice insurance carrier.

much cause for concern. If it is very valuable, you should consult with an accountant before selling it. An issue such as capital gains, which may arise if you realize a large profit from selling, is best managed through a professional.

Options to selling

Accountants and attorneys can also tell you whether it even makes sense to sell your collection. In certain situations, it may not. If you're very wealthy, disposing of a collection in other ways may have more positive tax consequences for you. A collection that has gained significantly in value can end up costing you a great deal of money to sell when it comes to the tax liabilities it also creates.

Donations

Donating collections to museums or foundations rewards the efforts of the collector in a way few other dispositions can. It's perhaps the best way of assuring that a collection will be maintained intact and will receive the care it deserves. It preserves the ability of the public to access the collection and enjoy it for years to come. For more well-heeled collectors, it can create good tax advantages.

Technically, donations are gifts, not sales, but there are still tax liabilities connected to them. Before you donate a collection, look to your accountant for advice. The rules and regulations that govern donations are complex, so make sure that you handle the transaction carefully, or else you may end up with a problem on your hands. Donations can be made while you are living but are most often built into an estate plan. When gifts of collections are received, the museum or foundation honors the benefactor. The honors will be commensurate with the size and worth of the collection.

Unofficially...
Any noncash contribution, such as artwork, antiques, and other valuables, must have a written appraisal if its value is in excess of $5,000. (Source: *U.S. Master Tax Guide*)

Trading vs. selling

Trading can also be an interesting alternative to selling. Basically, it is an exchange of one or more items between two entities. The transaction is structured so that both parties come out equally, ending up with pieces that are worth about the same as the ones they traded. In some cases money may also change hands to even the score.

Trading is usually done to exchange a few pieces, often among friends. It can be a great way to eliminate duplicates from your collection or elevate the quality of it. It's done less often to liquidate an entire collection, but it can catapult you out of one collecting category and into another almost instantaneously if that's your goal.

If structured correctly, trades should be free of tax liabilities. However, it's a good idea to check with your accountant before you finalize the deal.

Just the facts

- Selling a collection successfully requires careful planning and execution. It seldom happens by accident.

- Timing is the most important aspect of selling. Best results are often realized during periods of high demand in a collecting category.

- Your accountant and attorney should always be consulted before concluding a major sale.

- Take all costs into consideration when researching selling avenues. What may at first seem a good way to sell might end up costing you more than you think.

Bright Idea
Each party in a trade should be able to substantiate current values on the items exchanged, either through appraisals or by checking other sources, such as auction prices.

GET THE SCOOP ON...
Finding an auction house ▪ Expenses of selling
online ▪ Consigning and selling to dealers
▪ Selling it yourself ▪ Selling privately vs.
being a dealer

Selling Options

Chapter 13

A s discussed in Chapter 12, "Becoming a Seller," the methods you choose for selling your collection will largely depend on the type of collection you have and how quickly you want to sell it. Each selling method has its pros and cons, and what will work well for one collection may not for another. The method or methods you choose should ideally give you the best returns on your investment. Some have the potential of delivering very high returns, but they can be costly in terms of price and time.

The most popular selling approaches are detailed in this chapter. The pros and cons of each are listed along with information on what you can expect in each venue. Many collectors end up using more than one selling approach. Whether you follow their lead or decide to use just one, be sure to consider your actions as part of an overall plan. Do not jump into any one approach without researching thoroughly to make sure it's the right one for you.

Watch Out!
Local auction
houses that do
not have access
to a regular flow
of antiques from
regional estate
liquidations buy
antiques for auc-
tion inventory.
Your goods may
not get the
attention they
deserve when
you're competing
against the
auction house.

One final suggestion: Know what your collection is worth and be very confident in your valuation before approaching any of these selling outlets. You'll get the best return on your investment when you are a strong advocate for it.

Selling at auction houses

Pros:

> *Broad exposure*
> *Quick sale*
> *Reasonable return on investment*

Cons:

> *Expensive*
> *Time consuming*
> *Pieces may not sell*
> *Payment may be very slow*

As some of the most popular venues for selling antiques, live auctions owe their appeal partly to the grand tradition of the auction house and the role it plays in bringing together buyers from all walks of life who can openly compete for the lots offered. This open competition creates the possibility of a bidding war among buyers and the realization of extraordinary profit...maybe.

While it's true that auctions can offer great opportunities for huge returns on investment, the reality is that the results gleaned from most auctions often disappoint sellers. Bidding wars that result in extraordinary prices are the exception rather than the rule. Most buyers view auctions as places to pick up top quality goods at bargain basement prices. From the seller's point of view, this isn't such a good thing.

Live auctions, by their nature, are one-time events. Most of the time, everything goes as planned and everyone leaves relatively happy. But things can go wrong, too. If an auction isn't marketed properly or if it's poorly timed, it won't be well attended. An auction audience made up of a few dealers and highly focused collectors is not likely to yield extraordinary profits. If no one shows up, no one can start a bidding war.

Bad weather can even affect the success of an auction. With lots of money already spent on marketing and an auction schedule to satisfy, don't expect the auction house to be sympathetic and reschedule the event. It rarely happens.

Another problem with auctions is their size and complexity. Very few collectors have enough clout to negotiate an auction dedicated solely to their items. While you may have a great collection of porcelain figurines, it may get lost among the hundreds of other items being sold.

Auctions are not all created the same. Some are carefully assembled, widely marketed, and strategically timed. The lots are offered in an order designed to achieve the maximum result. At others, the service pretty much ceases the moment you sign a consignment agreement and deliver your goods. After that, it's a haphazard free-for-all. Local auctions and small regional houses are notorious for conducting frenzied, disorganized auctions.

The cost of doing business

Buyers and sellers both often pay a premium to use the services of auction houses. The amount for sellers varies depending on how much the item sells for, usually between 10 and 20 percent of the final bid amount.

An item doesn't actually have to be sold at an auction for a seller to incur substantial expense. Remember the explanation of the reserve price in Chapter 9, "Buying at Auction"? If an item doesn't

Timesaver
Here's a quick way to calculate the cost of auctioning antiques at a live auction: Figure 25 percent of the median value of the pieces as your cost. If you expect unusually high shipping costs, increase this figure to 30 percent, or even higher.

meet its reserve, the auctioneer will remove it from bidding. When this happens, the seller is still charged a commission. Sotheby's, for example, assesses 5 percent of the reserve price or a set handling fee of $75.

As an illustration, based on commissions quoted by Sotheby's, assume you offer five items for sale at an auction. The catalog lists a price range for each item. Splitting each down the middle gives you a total median price of $15,000. In all, four items sell for a total of $14,000. One item sold for $8,000, and on this piece you are charged 10 percent, or $800. Two sold for $2,500 each. On these the commission is 15 percent, or $750. Another item sold for $1,000, and the last object, with a reserve of $500, didn't sell and was removed from auction. You're charged a $200 commission on the last piece that sold and a handling fee of $75 on the last piece since 5 percent of the reserve price was less than $100. Your total commissions to the auction house would equal $1,825, or 13 percent of your sales price.

Other costs you may incur

If you're contacting auction houses in cities other than yours, you'll have to submit good, clear photos of the items you want to sell. Getting good pictures can be expensive, especially if your antiques are difficult to photograph. Depending on when your items are delivered for the auction, you may have to pay storage fees. Fees for packing, shipping, and insurance may also be assessed. Items that did not sell must be repacked and shipped back to you, usually within 10 days of the auction, and you'll pay for this, too.

Although it is hard to generalize, you should allow for at least 25 percent of the successful bid price to cover your selling expenses at auction. If you anticipate unusually large costs such as shipping heavy items, allow a little more to cover that contingency.

Selecting an auction house

If you've decided to enter this particular venue, the first thing to do is find the auction house that will suit your needs. While it's difficult to make specific statements about the various types of auction houses, many collectors have their greatest success and feel most comfortable with the better-known national and specialty houses. Local auction establishments, unless they're very large and locally prominent, will rarely deliver the best return on investment. The bread and butter for these houses are estate auctions and other types of liquidations. Buyers go to them expecting bargains, and the houses must be able to deliver exactly that. You may not even get one to talk with you unless you're willing to fire sale your pieces and set very low reserves on them. If you don't have enough pieces to fill an entire auction, their interest in doing business with you will also be limited unless they can include your items in other sales.

Such establishments generally don't have the resources to market and sell important collections or even a few noteworthy items, and they usually stay away from doing so unless the pieces are part of an estate. If you have an estate to sell, by all means consider local houses, especially if you need to settle things quickly. Beyond this, they really aren't the best venues for the seller wanting to realize the best prices at auction.

The search process

Begin your search by obtaining information from as many different houses as you feel are appropriate. These may be establishments that you've done

> **❝**
> Of all human activities based on the Compulsion to Own Syndrome, auction has to be the purest form.
> —Helaine Fendelman and Jeri Schwartz, *Money in Your Attic: How to Turn Your Furniture, Antiques, Silver, and Collectibles into Cash*
> **❞**

business with yourself, that your friends have used and recommended, or ones that your research tells you might be good places for you to sell. You should ask for and receive the following:

- General information on the auction house itself—such as its specialties and services to buyers and sellers.

- Terms and conditions related to consignment and selling. Review this thoroughly because it can answer many questions.

- An auction calendar. Even though it may take you up to a year to actually have your items included in an auction (especially at a large national house), you want to see the type of auctions that are scheduled and when.

- A sample catalog. How the information is presented in a catalog can have a significant impact on how well your antiques will do at auction.

Bright Idea
See if you can obtain auction catalogs that contain items similar to what you're considering putting up for sale.

Also ask each house if it will provide you with the names of a few people who have used its services. Auction houses won't put you in contact with dissatisfied sellers, but it's often helpful to talk to people who have used them even if all you get are glowing reports. If you can, try to attend at least one auction at each house under consideration if you haven't done business with them before. It's also a good idea to do this if you're considering a house with which you're familiar but you haven't recently visited. It may have gone downhill since you were last there, but you won't know this unless you see it for yourself or someone else tells you about it.

Checking references

The top auction venues in the United States are so well established that you really don't need to check their sales expertise and credit worthiness. However, you should never skip this step if you have any concerns at all or if you're considering a regional or specialty house with which you haven't done business. Much of this information can be obtained online, especially for larger auction houses like Christie's, Sotheby's, and Butterfield & Butterfield. Some smaller houses have Web sites as well—it's often worth the time to check. If not, contact the houses directly and ask for the following information:

- How long the firm has been in business.

- Who the principals are and how they're trained.

- Credit worthiness. Ask for a bank reference.

If any auction house is reluctant to provide you with this information, or can't provide it, cross it off your list and move onto the next one.

Consign or sell?

A handful of auction houses will offer sellers the option of selling items directly to the house rather than putting them through auction. While this may seem like a conflict of interest, it can benefit sellers who can't wait for the entire auction process to come to a conclusion before they realize any income from the pieces they're selling.

The downside to this scenario is that what the auction house will offer as a cash value is often significantly lower than the prices that the pieces will bring at auction. This option should only be considered after looking at the pros and cons of other selling scenarios as it may net you less money than if you took another approach.

Moneysaver
Improve your chances of reaching the right buyers by searching out specialized auction houses. They target narrowly defined groups of collectors, are more discriminating about the goods they offer for sale, and often produce better sales results than general auctions.

Meeting with the house

Once you've selected one or two houses that you feel will work for you and your collection, call the person in charge of working with potential sellers. This may be a specialist in charge of the type of objects in your collection or a customer service representative. Tell this person that you're interested in selling some antiques at auction and that you'd like this house to represent your interests. You'll probably be asked to provide a general description of your collection and more detailed information on a few pieces. If your information interests the auction house staff, they will want to see what your items look like.

As mentioned earlier, if you're contacting a house in another part of the country, you'll usually be asked to provide a written description of your collection and some pictures of it to the house staff so they can determine if they are interested in it. Here's what you can do to make sure the photos you take are what the auction house can use:

- Make sure the object you're photographing is in focus. Try to use an adjustable focus or auto-focus camera. Automatic cameras with fixed-focus lenses are generally not your best bet in these situations because they often don't deliver crisp images.

- Fill the entire frame with the antique—in other words, shoot it as closely as you can while staying in focus. Background matter can detract from the piece.

- Take as many shots as you feel are necessary to adequately show the antique's attributes. This should include both overall shots to give an idea of size and proportion and close-up shots to show detail.

- Standard 4" × 6" prints are acceptable to most auction houses. Get them in shiny rather than matte finish as detail can be lost in matte prints.

If you're interested in consigning one or two pieces, you may be asked to ship them to the auction house so they can be viewed in person. You will have to pay all expenses for this, including crating, insurance, and transportation. Some houses will send their experts to your home for a fee; however, if you have a very large collection you'll probably end up doing your negotiations via telephone and mail, and the auction house won't see the actual pieces until you agree to consign them.

If the auction house is in your city or town or has a branch located there, it will send a representative to take a look at what you have and discuss what might be done with it at auction.

Ideally these consultations should be evaluations rather than appraisals. As a skilled collector, you should already have a good idea of what your antiques are worth based on auction and sales information. What the specialist tells you should only confirm this.

About a week or so prior to your meeting, gather all the information you have on your collection (if you haven't done so already) and organize it by item in a binder or file. This data should include

- When you bought each piece and how much you paid.
- Current appraisals, if you have them.
- Information regarding provenance and authenticity.

Bright Idea
Jot down a few notes about your collection and several important pieces before calling an auction house. These calls can be a bit disconcerting—having some written notes to work from is often easier than pulling information from your memory.

Also include any special information that you think will help the auction house staff in evaluating your collection. Having pieces chosen for exhibit at a museum or show can say a lot about the value of what you own. If you and your collection have been the subject of a news or feature story, this is important information to tell the auction house representative.

On the day of the meeting, make sure your home looks its best and your antiques are clean, dusted, and polished. If pieces are displayed on shelves or in a display case, make sure that all shelves are dusted and that all lights are working. It's important to give every indication that your collection has been lovingly assembled and taken care of. If you have small children around, have them play somewhere else while the meeting occurs. Clear any pets out of the room as well. Your attention should be focused and undivided.

The best representatives will be very thorough and spend as much time as necessary looking at your antiques. Be prepared for every nook and cranny to be carefully inspected. They'll usually take notes as they go, even if they're looking at just a piece or two.

After the inspection is over, if the house is interested in selling your antiques, the representatives will discuss the following matters with you:

- The anticipated price range for each object. You should already have a good idea of what it would be if you've done your homework. If the numbers you're given are substantially different than what your research tells you they should be, ask for the basis for the variation.

Bright Idea
Be present when your collection is packed and loaded. Check the shipping documentation against your own list to make certain the proper number of items have been packed and accepted for shipping.

- The estimated reserve. Again, this figure will be based on the auction house's knowledge of what the market will bear. It also should correlate with the information you've gathered through your research.

- How your objects might be marketed in relation to the other items being sold. If you have an important collection, the house will discuss special promotional efforts with you. If you're thinking about only consigning a few pieces, the house may want to hold them for a period of time so they can be sold in an auction where they'll best be showcased.

- A general idea of what your expenses will be if you choose to consign the items for auction, including the seller's commission and other costs. You'll find more about what they are later in this chapter.

If you're dealing with a reputable house (and you should be), you will be treated very fairly and the information given to you will be concise and accurate. The sales ranges and reserves given might be lower than what you were hoping for, but they will be what the house's staff believes are realistic estimates of what your pieces will realize at auction. Generally, auction house staff prefer to err on the low side so they don't create false hope in their sellers. The amounts you are given, however, should be within reason.

Be prepared to ask how the auction house staff determined their sales ranges and reserves. If they're not what you expected, and they don't match what your research had led you to believe they would be, talk to another auction house. If you

Unofficially...
Experts advise sellers to get more than one opinion before consigning anything to auction, especially if you don't have a standing relationship with a good auction house. You don't have to drag your things around to each house to do this. Good photographs and descriptions sent to different houses will provide you with ballpark estimates.

get the same information from the next one, however, it's an indication that they know something you don't know. You may have to go with the experts and revise your expectations accordingly.

It's not always the best idea to consign with the highest estimator. Sales estimates that are too high may scare bidders away. When bidders smell a bargain, however, they're more likely to start bidding and keep on bidding. If you do decide to set reserves on your antiques, be sure to set them no higher than the lowest bid you would ever accept. Your best chance for the highest bid is the first time the piece is offered. Most auction houses know this and they try to get buyers to accept reasonable estimates and reserves. Pieces that fail to sell the first time can be offered again, but most houses will let at least one or two similar auctions take place before they'll do it again. Even then, if buyers recognize the piece as one that didn't sell before, they'll often pass it by.

Signing, sealing, and delivering

If you and the auction house can agree on acceptable parameters for selling your collection, you'll be given a consignment contract to sign that specifies the following:

- The auction house's responsibilities and liabilities
- Your obligations, such as shipping and buyer's fees, and when you'll be expected to fulfill them
- Catalog range prices and reserves for each item
- Payment terms following the auction

Be sure to read and review this document thoroughly before signing it. Have a clear understanding of what it contains. Also review all the specified fees, including the following:

- Penalties for withdrawing items before they sell. Auction houses frown heavily on this, and they will charge a fee to buyers who do it.

- Insurance costs.

- Photographs. Some houses charge the seller for illustrating items in their catalogs.

The costs of selling at auction can quickly mount. If, for example, the house decides that restoration work is necessary on a consigned piece, you'll be charged for it, either as a deduction to the final amount for which the piece was sold or directly to you. Gemological tests conducted on jewelry are also often paid for by the seller.

You will be asked to deliver the pieces you're selling to the auction house by a specific date. This may be as much as six months before the auction takes place. Most auction houses have packing and shipping companies with whom they do business on a regular basis and they'll usually provide this information to sellers.

Be prepared to pay handsomely for packing or crating because you'll be charged for both materials and time. If you're tempted to save some money by trying to do it yourself, be sure to check with the shipper first. Some of them won't take pieces unless they're prepared for shipping by a professional. If they do agree to transport such items, they'll generally limit their liabilities regarding loss or damage.

Moneysaver
Moving companies often will grant a 10 percent discount for shipments that are associated with certain companies. Be sure to ask your auction house if they have a discount arrangement with any shippers.

If the auction house you choose doesn't give you packing and shipping information, you can find companies that do this through the Yellow Pages. Dealers often can recommend people they've used and trust. Listings for companies that specialize in packing and transporting antiques can also be found in the trade newspapers listed in Chapter 2.

If possible, make arrangements to review the information on your antiques that will be printed in the auction catalog. You should see the following:

■ Accurate descriptions on each item

■ Photos corresponding with descriptions

■ The price ranges you agreed to

Auction houses are careful to be accurate, so the chances are good that you won't see anything wrong. If you do, notify the house immediately so corrections can be made if possible.

While the auction house will do a fair amount of promotion on the auction itself, it may not promote your pieces individually if they don't comprise a major part of the sale. There's nothing against your promoting them on your own, especially if you think it will help you realize a better price at auction. These efforts could include

■ Posting information about the auction on your Web site, if you have one.

■ Providing information on the auction and your pieces to your collecting club's magazine or newsletter.

■ Contacting the lifestyles editor at your local newspaper. Many papers run features on interesting collectors and collections, especially when the items are unusual or of broad interest to readers.

Remember, you're merely trying to give your collection an extra boost at auction, not trying to sell pieces before the auction takes place. Once you've made the decision to consign your pieces, it's best to live with it. The fees for removing pieces from a scheduled auction can be steep.

Going to the show

Many sellers can't resist being present on the day of the auction. They enjoy the experience and like to be on hand to answer any questions that may arise. Others would just as soon not see their items sold— their attachment to them ended when they decided to sell. There is no right or wrong approach to this. Don't feel that you have to go, but keep in mind that it can be a nice touch if you do. Buyers often like to talk to sellers and you may have an interesting story or two that could make them even happier about the pieces they bought.

Once your items have been sold, the auction house will settle its accounts with you and the buyer. You'll be given a detailed statement on the items that sold and their hammer price. If you have outstanding fees with the house, these will be deducted from the final amount owed to you. These monies will be sent to you in accordance with the terms of the contract you signed. Depending on these terms, it can be a few weeks or a few months before you receive full payment.

Selling online

Pros:

> *Inexpensive*
> *Reasonably fast*
> *Convenient*
> *Good return on investment*

Unofficially...
The world won't end if there are errors in your item listings in an auction catalog. Mistakes can happen, even in the best houses. Auction houses frequently make corrections and updates to listings on auction day.

Cons:

> *Competition*
>
> *Arms-length transactions*
>
> *Problems with buyers*
>
> *One bad apple can spoil it for all*

Although still in its formative stages, the world of online auctions is an exciting new venue for sellers. The costs of doing business in this arena are very low, literally a fraction of what you'll pay at a live auction. This is a major consideration if you have many pieces to sell. For example, a $2,000 item can rack up $500 or more in auction house fees and expenses. If it were sold online, the selling cost could be anywhere from about $150 to around $250, depending on the service used and how fancy the advertising was.

It takes little effort to list an item in an online auction, another reason why this arena is becoming so popular. However, as discussed in Chapter 10, "Buying Online," the actual transfer of goods and money can involve significant risks. And with so many items being listed for sale every day—eBay estimates 2.5 million pieces at its site alone—the competition to get your items seen can be steep unless you're willing to pay additional fees to give your pieces more visibility.

Bright Idea
If you're a first-time seller, spend some time looking for items similar to yours to get an idea of how the sellers described them.

As a seller, you must determine whether you want to set reserves on the items you sell (it isn't required, but it can be a good idea), and what the reserve amounts should be. You can determine them by checking the final hammer prices on the items sold at online auctions. Compare these against prices found in recent sales reports and price guides, and set your reserve accordingly. However, as with live auctions, a reserve amount that is too high may result in your item not selling. Should you choose to relist it, you'll pay a relisting fee and it may not sell again.

You'll also have to come up with an item description that will entice buyers to place bids. Having a good photo or two that you can display at the auction site is almost a necessity these days. Buyers like to see what they're bidding on even if they can't reach out and touch it.

Becoming an Internet seller

As is the case with live auctions, look for the site that is most appropriate for the items you have to sell. Most sellers prefer general sites like eBay and Amazon.com for their ease of use. It's also difficult to beat the sheer volume of action at these sites, but this factor may lead you to looking elsewhere. If you're offering items in a high-volume category, such as glass, they may get lost among thousands of listings, or you'll have to pay more to have them stand out. A site with lower volume or one that specializes in your category may give you better exposure among buyers who are more likely to put their money down.

Once you've found the site you want to sell through, you'll be asked to register as a user, which means filling out some basic identification data. Usually you are given the option of volunteering additional information (like a driver's license number) that can be independently verified by third parties. Doing so adds to your credibility as a seller, so it's a good idea to provide this information. Once your basic data is entered, an account is established for you. Next, the software program will ask you if you are a buyer or a seller. After identifying yourself as a seller, you enter in the details of your sale. These include

- The type of auction, such as standard, Dutch, or private.

- The category you want to sell in, such as antiques, collectibles, art glass, or pottery.

- When the auction will begin and how long it will last.

- The reserve price, if you're setting one.

- The starting bid; that is, the lowest price you'll accept for the item.

- A several word description of the item. Like a headline in a newspaper, this will let buyers know immediately if the item is something they want to look at. Good descriptions contain information that succinctly describes the item and its condition—for example, Lalique perfume bottle, early 1900s, good condition.

- A description of the item, including details on its condition. Be as objective about condition as you can, and always include any factors that may detract from the value of the piece. For the Lalique perfume bottle mentioned above, such information may include "scratches on bottom of the base," or "small chip on neck of bottle." The best sellers even post photos of those flaws so buyers can see them for themselves.

- Payment terms, delivery information, and other pertinent data.

If you have photographs (and it's highly suggested that you do), add them to this information as well. They can be scanned into your computer, uploaded from a digital camera, captured from a video camera or taken off of a photo CD. Both Amazon.com and eBay have information at their sites on how to do this and the digital formats that they prefer using.

The software will notify you when the auction begins and ends. Your credit card will be billed for the cost of the auction and it is up to you and the seller to work out delivery in accordance with the terms you dictated.

The cost of doing business

Internet auctions are much cheaper than live auctions. Fees are broken down into three categories:

- Insertion fees: This is the cost related to listing your items for sale. These fees are based on the reserve price and are generally very low. On eBay, for example, the insertion fee is 25 cents for items under $10, 50 cents for items from $10 to $24.99, $1 for items from $25 to $49.99, and $2 for items valued at $50 or more. Amazon.com charges fees from 25 cents to $2 dollars as well.

- Listing option fees: Want to promote your listing and make it stand out? Options here range from displaying your item in bold type ($2 on eBay) to listing it in the featured auction section ($99.95 on eBay). Again, these fees are similar on Amazon.com.

- Final value or completion fees: This fee is calculated based on the final sale price of each item. Again, using eBay as an example, it is calculated by factoring 5 percent of the first $25 of the item's value (if the item sold for $25 or less, this is the final value fee). If the final value was more than $25, an additional 2.5 percent is factored on this amount up to $1,000. For items selling over $1,000, 1.25 percent is

Moneysaver
Listing option fees can add up quickly. Try to sell buyers through punchy descriptions of the items you list rather than relying on these options if at all possible.

calculated on the remaining amount.
Amazon.com uses the same fee schedule.

To illustrate, let's say you decide to sell a Roseville vase on eBay. You've valued the piece at $450 and you've decided to set a reserve price at $300. Your insertion fee would be $2. After browsing through the other items in this category, you decide that bold type would help your piece stand out. You elect this option and are charged another $2. Your auction is successful and you end up with a high bid of $500. You pay $1.25 on the first $25 of value, and $11.88 on the additional amount. Your total auction fee is $17.13, or about 3.5 percent of the total amount that you received for the item. As a comparison, the same item may cost you $120 or more to sell through a traditional live auction after all your costs are factored in.

If the item didn't meet its reserve, you would still owe the insertion fee, which is nonrefundable. You may also owe an additional reserve price auction fee (in the above example, it would be $1). Online auction companies also charge a final value fee if the auction is successfully completed but the sale isn't consummated with the buyer. This fee can be returned to the seller if

- Attempts to contact the high bidder fail. Sellers and buyers are encouraged to contact each other as soon as possible after the conclusion of an auction. Sellers are further encouraged to give buyers a reasonable amount of time to respond, generally within three to seven days.

- The high bidder backs out.

- Funds do not clear (i.e., check bounces or a stop payment is placed on it).

- Bidder returns the item and a refund is issued.

- High bidder decides that the terms of the sale are unacceptable.

- High bidder couldn't complete the auction due to an unforeseen financial or family emergency.

Part of the fee is returned if the sale price ends up being lower than the highest bid. This can happen if a high bidder backs out and the seller is able to sell the item to another bidder at a lower price.

Selling through dealers

Pros:

  Convenient

  Easy

  Can give a good return on investment

Cons:

  Can take too much time

  Consignment fees may be high

  Payment can be slow

Timesaver
If an item fails to sell over the Internet, you don't have to worry about having it repacked and shipped because it never leaves your hands until it's sold.

Having dealers sell your antiques for you scores high on the convenience scale. Once you find someone who is willing to take your pieces, all you really have to do is sit back and wait until they're sold. If you're looking for a fast sale, however, you're taking your chances here; items can sit for months, especially if you choose a dealer with low foot traffic.

Selling through a dealer is best if you have just a few pieces you want to get rid of and you don't have the time to find a buyer for them on your own. Many dealers won't consider a consignment of more than just a few pieces, especially if the pieces are large. Unless they think they can turn the consignment quickly, or they have a specific buyer in mind who will take a number of pieces, they'll want to devote their selling space to items on which they can make more money.

Shopping for a dealer

Ideally, you should try to place your antiques with dealers you know and trust. You also should find someone with strong knowledge in your collecting area who can use this knowledge to the best advantage when selling your antiques. A dealer who specializes in what you're selling can often get you far more than the highest realized auction price. People you have bought items from can be some of your best selling sources, especially if they have a strong reputation in your collecting category and a loyal following.

Other methods for finding a dealer to consign with include:

- Referrals from friends. Word of mouth is always a good way to go. Your friends aren't going to recommend someone they don't like or trust.

- Ads in industry newspapers and magazines. Dealers will often note if they're accepting consignments and what they'll take. If they're running display ads that highlight certain pieces in their shop, you'll be able to get an idea of what they carry and if your items will fit in.

- Local antiques shows and sales. Visit booths that have antiques similar to yours and talk to the dealers there. If you hit it off well with a few of them, ask them if they'd be interested in a consignment. If so, take their cards and call them after the show.

If you're asked to bring your items to the show, do so if you feel like it. However, you should never consummate a deal at this point unless you've had time to research the dealer. All businesses can fall on hard times. An under-financed dealer can suddenly close up shop and disappear. This can be a real disaster if your collection is on the premises. Creditors, and especially landlords, often try to place liens against consigned property. If they're successful, the items will not be released until the liens are. Although many states have passed laws to protect artists in these situations, the laws do not always apply to other consignment arrangements. At a minimum, ask to see the portion of the dealer's lease that speaks to the landlord's right to make claims against abandoned property. Make these provisions an attachment to the consignment agreement so that you can defend against unscrupulous landlords.

Always research any dealer you're thinking of working with, even those who have the trappings of success and who you know have been in business for years. Ask for a bank reference, speak with the Better Business Bureau, and contact any professional associations with whom the dealer is associated.

Consignment costs

Dealer's commissions can vary greatly. Most will charge at least 20 percent of the final sales price to take pieces on consignment; however, it's not uncommon for commissions to range as high as 40 percent, especially if the dealer is also going to arrange for such services as packing and shipping. While this seems expensive, remember that the dealer is doing all the work for you. Once you deliver the items to the dealer you've chosen, your responsibilities are virtually over beyond maybe answering a phone call or two from a prospective

Moneysaver
Dealers will often quote a high commission right off the bat. Since there are no standard commissions in the business, you have nothing to lose by asking for a lower amount.

buyer. If an entire collection or a significant portion of it can be sold fairly quickly at a good price, it's probably worth the expense.

Setting prices

Most dealers will ask consignors what they want to get for their pieces and will set prices from there. Collectors are often surprised when the final prices are higher than what they expected, and dismayed when they're lower. If you've selected a reputable dealer who has been in business for awhile, you can be fairly well assured that the prices that are set are a good indication of what the dealer believes the items will sell for. If you have a significant disagreement on price, ask for specifics on how they were calculated. If you have information that you feel would impact them, be prepared to show it. It may be enough to justify an increase or a decrease.

Since negotiation and haggling is common at antiques shops, always tell the dealer the lowest amount you're willing to accept on each item consigned. Hagglers often stick to a fairly standard discount amount, usually between 10 and 20 percent. Your bottom dollar amount shouldn't be any lower than this unless getting rid of the piece means more to you than getting a decent return on your investment.

Making things legal

Most dealers have consignment agreements with their sellers. They come in many standard forms but should include the following:

- Key terms of the agreement, such as commissions and consignment period.
- The dealer's limits of liability.
- Descriptions of the items consigned and prices.

- Payment terms. Some dealers will cut a check monthly for items that sold during this period of time. Others don't pay until the end of the consignment period.

Consignment agreements come in many different forms; there really is no single standard. If you see something you don't like, there's usually room for negotiation.

Selling to dealers

Pros:

> *Convenient*
>
> *Can be quick*

Cons:

> *May not be the best return on investment*
>
> *Can take time to find someone who's interested*

Like auction houses, some dealers will offer to buy items outright. Many, in fact, prefer to do this over accepting pieces on consignment. There is less paperwork to keep track of, they don't have to keep in touch with consignors, and they can set their own prices. Consider this very carefully should a dealer make you an outright offer to buy. They have to buy at good prices in order to realize a decent markup, so what you'll be offered will often be less than if you consigned your items. However, it will usually be somewhat more than what you'd get at auction, especially after you factor in your selling costs.

If you need money right away and you're looking for a convenient way to sell, this may be your best bet. You can enhance your returns by searching for dealers who specialize in your collecting area, and by selling to dealers that you've bought from. Many will buy back pieces you've bought from them for about the same price or a little better.

Watch Out!
Be sure you fully understand the elements of your consignment agreement. This is a legally binding contract and it's an important piece of protection should something happen to the store, the dealer, or you.

Selling at local shows and antiques markets

Pros:

> *Fast—you could sell everything in one weekend*
> *Good return on investment*
> *Can be fun*

Cons:

> *Can be expensive*
> *Time consuming, at least during the show*
> *May need sales licenses*

If you have a large collection, selling at a local show or a weekend antiques market can be a viable approach and a lot of fun. Selling at these locations gives you a great deal of control over the situation. You can price your items exactly as you want and decide the price you wish to take for them. You can strike a deal for multiple pieces with someone or just say no. The decision is completely up to you.

The first negative—expense—is a big consideration. Shows and antiques markets charge for sales spaces, and these fees can be steep. Other costs can include

- Fees for display materials at shows if you don't have your own.

- Buying tables, signs, and other items needed to exhibit at flea markets.

- Packing and transporting items.

- Sales license (required in some cities and states). The show or market at which you sell will tell you if you need one.

There's a significant time element involved in selling this way as well. If you don't like the idea of losing large chunks of your weekend, these places aren't for you.

If nothing else, selling at shows and markets will settle any questions you have about going into the antiques business if you've been thinking about it. If you don't enjoy yourself as a seller in these venues, you probably won't like doing it in a shop or out of your home, either. If you're the sort of person to whom the adage "Time is money" means a lot, selling this way may frustrate you, as it requires hours of standing around, many of which are not all that productive. You can close up shop when you want to at an antiques market, but most shows will require you to open and close on a specific schedule and stay open through the entire run of the show.

If you don't like getting up early, these sales venues are definitely not for you. Antiques markets often open at the crack of dawn, and it can take hours to travel to and set up at a show.

Watch Out!
There is a big difference between antiques markets and flea markets. Avoid selling at the latter unless you have pieces that you're trying to unload for not much money. Shoppers go to flea markets expecting deals. They're not good places to sell quality antiques.

Selling at antiques malls and co-ops

Pros:

    Good return on investment

    Relatively inexpensive

Cons:

    Can be time consuming

    Shrinkage

    Lost sales

Some collectors with more collection than space open small spots at antiques malls or share space with friends at a co-op. These situations afford sellers many of the advantages of a retail operation without the costs, and they can work out well for the occasional seller because of this. Many malls and co-ops will allow sellers to operate seasonally or sign short-term leases if they're not ready to make a long-term commitment.

The time you spend selling at these venues can vary. If your time is limited, malls are often your best bet because they're staffed by paid employees. You can spend time at your spot—or not—as you choose. In co-op situations, sellers usually work a few shifts per month to satisfy their obligation to the group. Theft can be a problem in these venues, especially if staffing is short on any given day. If you're not actively working your spot, you can lose sales to someone who is.

Selling at garage sales

Pros:

Easy

Inexpensive

Quick cash

Cons:

Poor return on investment

May need a sales license

Rain and snow

Selling your antiques at a garage sale is very easy and relatively inexpensive. All you have to do is put up some flyers or run a few ads, display and arrange the items you want to sell, and open your garage door when it's time to start the sale. However, this approach is only a good idea if you're willing to take a deep discount on the pieces you're selling. Garage sales will never attract your best buyers, only those looking for bargains. If your antiques don't bear fire sale prices and you're not willing to haggle, you won't sell them. Bad weather can not only hurt your sales, it may force you into canceling your sale and rescheduling for another time, which means incurring the expenses for advertising all over again.

Selling privately

Pros:

> *Control, control, control!*

> *High return on investment*

Cons:

> *Time consuming*

> *Expensive*

> *May need to acquire sales and business licenses*

Many collectors, once they've pondered all their options, decide they'll realize the greatest value for their antiques by selling them directly to other collectors. It's the same approach a private dealer takes with one significant difference: You're going to be doing it for only as long as it takes to sell what you want to get rid of. In other words, it's not an ongoing effort.

If you continue your actions beyond this and begin to acquire pieces with the intention of selling them, you're technically a dealer. You'll need business and sales tax licenses in order to keep going. A one-time sale between collectors is usually exempt from all this.

This can be one of the most satisfying sales approaches if you have the time and talent it takes to be successful at it. Not only does this approach take planning and patience, it also calls for a good amount of sales and promotional talent. You could have the greatest collection going in your category. If no one knows about it, however, it will be yours for a very long time. You have to be willing to actively market your pieces and work your connections in order to be successful at this.

Collections that can be acquired between individuals can be purchased more cheaply than when a dealer or auction is involved. With no buying premiums or selling commissions to pay, buyers can be extremely motivated to do business with you, especially if they can secure desired objects quietly and at a fair price.

If you're thinking this approach is for you, ask yourself the following questions:

QUESTION	MUCH LIKE ME	A LITTLE LIKE ME	NOT ME AT ALL
1. I am enthusiastic about my collection and love talking about it to others.			
2. I always follow up with anyone I meet who expresses an interest in my collection and wants to learn more.			
3. Calling people and talking to them about my antiques is no problem for me.			
4. I keep a list of the people I've bought antiques from and other collectors in my collecting category.			
5. I have no trouble setting a firm price on something I own and holding to it.			
6. I keep a close eye on the antiques industry and on developments that can affect the value of my collection.			
7. I set aside a certain number of hours a week for working on my collection.			

8. My family is either involved in my collect-ing pursuits or supports them.

9. I have a set budget for my collecting activities and I am able to stick to it.

10. While I enjoy collect-ing, I have no deep emotional or sentimental attachment to the pieces I own.

Give yourself 3 points for every answer in the first column, 2 points for every answer in the second column, and 1 point for every answer in the third column.

What Your Score Means:

30 points: What are you waiting for? You have a good level of enthusiasm for what you're doing and you like to talk to others about it. You're aggressive and confident enough to actively market your antiques to others. You already spend a good amount of time keeping track of the industry and working on your collection, and your family sup-ports your efforts.

20–29 points: You enjoy your collecting efforts but you may have a lower comfort level in switching from buying to selling, especially when it comes to marketing directly to others. This doesn't mean that you can't be successful, but you'll have to be aware of your weaknesses and rise above them.

10–19 points: While you enjoy collecting, there are factors in your life that may work against you as a direct seller. Try to identify what your biggest obstacles are and see if they present permanent roadblocks to this selling method. For example, if

Watch Out!
Fees to the seller at auction houses can add up quickly. Always estimate what your worst case scenario is before making the final decision to consign to one of them.

your time for collecting is limited and your family doesn't support your efforts, you may be setting yourself up for trouble because selling can take a lot of time. A better approach might be utilizing another sales outlet until your other obligations are lighter. If you're not a natural networker, you'll have to train yourself to become one, but this isn't that difficult to do. Shyness is a real hurdle, but it too can be overcome. Remember, the world won't beat a path to your door. You have to beat a path to it.

If you decide to take the direct sales approach, keep in mind that having items or a collection worth selling is only half the battle. You also have to effectively market and sell it. If you have a talent for selling, this isn't difficult to learn. In fact, all you really have to do is watch how others go about it. Pay attention to how ads are worded. Listen to the pitches that dealers make to buyers at shows. Keep your eyes and ears open at all times and glean all you can. Reading a few books on the subject can also be very helpful. Several that specifically address selling antiques are listed in Appendix C.

Private selling approaches

As a private dealer, you can choose a number of approaches to selling. The following are the most commonly used.

Direct contact

You've read about the need to keep good records on the people who have expressed an interest in your collection. This is when you'll use them. You can either prioritize your list, target the people you think are your best chances, and contact them each individually, or throw it open to everyone and send out a blanket communication to all of them at the same time via telephone, mail, or even e-mail. If you're looking for one key buyer for your entire collection, the first method is your best bet.

Advertising

Classified ads in trade periodicals and local or national newspapers may also help you reach buyers. Often as not, however, you'll attract a lot of dealer inquiries. This isn't necessarily bad, but remember that dealers will not pay your asking price unless they feel they can tack enough onto it to cover their interests.

Post classified ads first at Internet sites on collecting and in specialty trade magazines and newspapers. You'll have a better chance of reaching buyers interested in your collecting category through these outlets. If this approach doesn't yield the results you're seeking, then put an ad or two in your local paper.

Be careful to protect your identity when advertising your collection. Use a separate screen name from your usual one for inquiries. Screen anyone who might come to your home by asking for information that you can use to positively identify them. Even if they don't have a listed telephone number, their name and address can be checked against a city directory. Make it clear that you will need to see positive identification that verifies the information that you have already received before you will allow entry into your home.

Be upfront about your sensitivity to security. Most thieves will shy away from anyone who makes it clear that they are security conscious. Honest buyers will understand.

Holding a private sale

Another selling option is the home or "tag" sale. Essentially, they're like estate sales but limited to

Watch Out!
Thieves commonly watch the newspaper looking for opportunities to "case" a potential target. Before you let anyone in your house, ask several questions that only someone you've previously talked to could answer, and make sure you get positive ID, such as a driver's license.

only the items you're selling, not the contents of your entire home. If you're going to hold this kind of sale, it's best to confine it to one room of your home—preferably, one that you can close off from other parts of the house—in order to avoid any confusion over what it is that you're selling. Doing so will also keep security issues to a minimum.

Home sales should be promoted to specific audiences. If you decide to run classified ads, make sure to specify that you're having a one-time sale of an antiques collection. Such terms as "serious buyers only" or "qualified buyers only" will help keep the garage salers away from your door. Other things to mention in your ad include

Bright Idea
Consider holding a house sale with a friend who also collects. You can share the expenses and the time it takes to organize and hold your sale.

- When the sale will begin and end. Your best bet will be to run the sale for one day only.

- Payment methods. Specify cash only if this is all you'll take. Other options include traveler's checks or cashier's checks.

- Whether dealers are welcome. If you don't want them, say so.

A description of your collection, or at least of some of the key objects in it, should also be included. Don't go into too much detail; such general descriptions as "good variety of Victorian antiques" or "extensive collection of English sterling silver" should be enough.

Just the facts

- Read all sales contracts thoroughly. There's a lot of detail in the fine print, and you don't want to be taken by surprise.

- The sales outlet you once thought was best may fall from favor when you factor in all your costs. Be sure to take everything into consideration before you make a final decision.

■ Selling through dealers can be a viable method if you have just a few pieces to sell and you don't have time to do it yourself.

■ Know the local regulations before you decide to sell your items yourself, either at an antiques market or at home. The expenses and hassles involved in getting sales tax and business licenses can negate the gains from sales in these venues.

Displaying, Managing,
and Caring for Antiques

PART VI

Decorating with Antiques

A primary reason for collecting antiques is the aesthetic and visual pleasure that owning such objects can bring. You would think, then, that collectors would take every opportunity to surround themselves with these items and display them proudly to the people who enter their homes; quite often, however, the opposite is true. Collectors regularly put their cherished objects completely out of sight, move them to the periphery of a home far from any real or perceived danger, or display them so poorly that they are not shown off to their best advantage. I've actually seen beautiful antiques stashed away in warehouses and storage rooms because the owners were leery of using them.

Of course, there are times when you must move cherished items out of harm's way, such as when you have young children. But I'm a firm believer in making the things we collect an integral part of our lives whenever possible. Since so many of these objects began as decorative items, it seems a shame to remove them from their original purpose. It saddens me when I meet people who let the cost of the items they have acquired deter them from using these pieces in their daily lives.

It's no secret that antiques suffer from stereotypes. They're seen as too expensive to use on a daily basis, or they're believed to be too old-fashioned for today's decors. Some people think they're hard to mix with new furniture. There's a kernel of truth to all of this. But there's hardly a room where an antique—even the most fragile or old-fashioned item—can't be used in some fashion. All it takes is knowing how to do so, which is what this chapter is all about.

Living with antiques

Collectors tend to fall into two categories when it comes to the role that their collections play in their lives. The first includes people who use antiques as an integral element of the decor of their homes. Many of these individuals grew up with antiques and feel comfortable with them, which is one of the reasons they decided to decorate with them. They may have inherited antique furniture or other items from their parents or grandparents, which made it easy for them to build a design theme around them.

The second category of collectors consists of people who are less comfortable about using their collections in decorating their homes. In many cases, these individuals did not grow up with antiques or had little appreciation of them when they were younger, which makes them think of antiques differently than the other items that surround them. They often segregate their collected

66
The whole point of collecting is surrounding yourself with objects that make you happy.
—Dianne Pilgrim, *Elle Décor*
99

objects from less valuable pieces and display small items in cases or grouped on shelves away from everyday objects. They tend to showcase furniture and larger pieces rather than integrate them into the look of a room as a whole.

The goal for both types of collectors when it comes to decorating with antiques is the same: the creation of a beautiful home that reflects the personality of its inhabitants. This can present a challenge for any collector, regardless of type. Feeling comfortable around antiques doesn't always go hand in hand with a great sense of interior design; in fact, it's often the people who have been around antiques the longest who need the most help. Experts say there's always room for improvement. Making those improvements can range from adding an accent piece or two to a room (or eliminating them, for that matter) to redoing an entire home with the objects you love.

Interior views

Your personal style and the kinds of things you like to collect will largely determine how they're used in your home. If you're collecting large pieces of furniture, regardless of style, they're going to play a greater role in your decor than will small objects, which can fit in just about anywhere. If you prefer modern design to more traditional styles, there's a good chance you won't be collecting ornate Victorian pieces.

There is really no right or wrong way of using antiques in the home. The key is finding what works best for you and your particular situation. If you have young children, rare and delicate items absolutely should be placed out of harm's way. If you have a lovely Victorian sofa that isn't comfortable to

Unofficially...
The two most
widespread
design styles in
the U.S. are con-
temporary and
country. (Source:
The American
Society of
Interior
Designers)

sit in, it shouldn't be placed in a room where people gather and need to be comfortable.

While there isn't one specific approach to take when decorating with antiques, most collectors find that their design efforts are more successful when they encompass a specific style, such as one of the following:

- **Traditional.** Traditionalists tend toward the elegant and the formal. They like rich colors, rich fabrics, and rich-looking wood, generally darker rather than lighter. Traditional decors are often based on eighteenth and nineteenth century antiques. In the past, a specific style or period was emphasized, such as Victorian, Queen Anne, Chippendale, or French Provincial. Today, the tendency is toward mixing periods by choosing pieces that have similar lines, styles, and colors. Accent pieces can range from oriental rugs to English porcelain. Fabrics often are flowered, and similar patterns commonly are combined in a room. Windows are almost never left unadorned; window dressing plays an important role in the overall ambiance of a room.

- **Contemporary.** Contemporary decors are characterized by clean, simple lines and an emphasis on pieces created by modern technology. They can range from casual to formal; casual rooms often contain softer, less hard-edged furniture than do the more formal rooms, but the lines are always clean and elegant. Antique furniture is almost never seen in these well-edited decors, although an occasional accent piece, such as a single table or chair, can be used if the color and line of the piece blends well with the room. Neutral colors are preferred throughout; bright "pops" of color may be used sparingly as an accent. If a patterned fabric is used, the pattern will be subtle, often tone-on-tone or a muted stripe or check. In these decors, antiques generally take a background role and are used as accessory pieces displayed along the periphery of a room, such as in cases or on shelves. It's more common to see one perfectly selected antique piece, such as an unusual vase, highlighted as a piece of art than many pieces grouped together.

▪ **Eclectic.** This free-wheeling style has evolved into one of the most popular interior decors thanks to its universal appeal and warmth, which is created by combining pieces from various periods and styles that share common elements such as color, pattern, or personality. It's not unusual to see German Bauhaus chairs used around an American primitive table and to have an oriental rug underneath it all, or a collection of chairs of different ages and styles used in various seating areas. Furniture and accessories share the spotlight in eclectic interiors, and they often carry the strongest colors in the room. Walls, window treatments and floor coverings (aside from accent rugs) are kept simple and are unified through the use of neutral colors such as taupe, greenish-gray, various shades of tan, and even violet or amethyst, which may vary in intensity from room to room and even wall to wall.

▪ **Country.** This is another of today's most popular styles. While it's always been a strong design theme, it gained in popularity in the early

1990s at the same time that the interest in collecting antiques also surged. This is by no means coincidental, as the pieces that were readily available to these new collectors, such as American primitives, had the "back to basics" look and feel that appealed strongly to baby boomers trying to create a simpler lifestyle. Country used to be a lot like traditional in that it typically emphasized one specific furniture style, often from a particular region of the United States. Today's country interiors have more in common with their eclectic cousins in that they generally combine a variety of styles that, once again, are united by color, line, and feel. Other characteristics of older country interiors, such as the strong use of primary colors and fabrics with small, busy prints, have also been updated through more subdued colors (although still in the primary range) and fabrics with larger, bolder designs. Walls are often painted in various shades of white to showcase the texture and color of the furniture and accessories.

66

Contemporary classics and timeless antiques also make good bedfellows.
—Mary Emmerling, *Mary Emmerling's New Country Collecting*

99

Chances are you already have a decor in one of these styles, as they are the most prevalent in today's design world. If so, you're probably less concerned with learning how to create a look from scratch than you are in maximizing all the existing elements for the best effect, which I'll address in more detail later on in this chapter.

If you feel like your home's decor falls somewhere in between all of these categories, take another look at your surroundings. While it's possible to have a home that really does reflect them all, most interiors fall into a specific category. If yours doesn't, it's time to create one that does.

Assessing your interiors

The assessment process is a great way to bring logic and sense to an interior that lacks definition. Once you go through this process, you'll have a better idea of how and where your cherished objects can be used and placed. Even if you have a defined interior style in your home, it's not uncommon to have to refine it from time to time.

The process starts by taking an inventory of your home's current interior style. Consider the entire house from a general perspective and ask yourself the following questions:

- Is there a unifying element to your home? Even houses with a hodgepodge of interior decors often have something that can be used to create a more harmonious feeling, such as a particular color that is used throughout the house or the use of one floor covering. If there isn't one, how difficult would it be to create?

- How does your home make you feel? Elegant and gracious? Warm and comfortable? Each interior style has its own ambiance. If you don't get a strong sense of it when you first enter your home, or the sense you get isn't what you'd like, it's time to make some changes.

- Is the interior style of your home compatible with its exterior? While it's possible to separate the exterior and interior styles to a certain extent, greater harmony is created when they are linked in some fashion, such as through color or the use of similar architectural elements.

Next, walk through your entire house and look critically at every interior space. Are you using each space well? Is there room for improvement? Do you have any rooms that have outlived their purpose?

Other factors to ponder as you're doing your assessment include

- Your overall decorating or design goal. Do you have a complete renovation of your home in mind, or are you simply looking for a better or different way to display a collection?

- Your future objectives as a collector. Are you planning to build on what you have now or might you consolidate your collection as you get older? Is there a particular type or style of antique that you aren't collecting now but can see yourself collecting in the future?

- Your lifestyle. Take into consideration such things as small children, animals, and your housekeeping style. The amount of time that you're willing to spend maintaining a collection can impact how you showcase it; for example, keeping small objects in an enclosed display case can minimize the amount of time spent dusting them.

- Available resources. Money is a big factor here, but other resources are important too. Can you achieve what you want to do by yourself, or will you need to hire outside help? Do you have a good friend who is willing to help you move furniture and pictures around as you explore various layouts, or do you need the help of an interior designer? Do you have access to a library with a good collection of books on design and decoration? Do you live near design centers and stores where you can actually go see furniture, floor coverings, and other items, or are you going to have to order by mail?

▪ Your own design or decorating abilities. While collectors as a group tend to be highly visually oriented, this trait alone doesn't always translate into envisioning how a built-in bookcase, for example, will work in a particular area. Some people, frankly, just have an inherent knack for pulling together a room and making it look right. Others lack this particular ability.

Don't allow less-than-positive answers in any area to deter you from going forward with your efforts. Nor should indecisiveness hinder you; if you don't know where your collection is headed, make plans based on where you are now. You can always revise them in the future. If you don't feel secure in your abilities to design or decorate, there are ways to boost your abilities in this area, and there are experts to whom you can turn for help.

Bright Idea
If you have antiques that you want kept off limits from your pets, consider putting an invisible barrier around them. The same technology used to invisibly corral pets outdoors can be installed indoors around furniture, rugs, and anything else you want to keep away from Friskers and Fluffy.

Developing a decorating eye

Like any artistic endeavor, decorating calls for a certain ability to see things as you'd like them to be, not necessarily as they are. This means knowing how to add things to a blank canvas, as well as knowing how and when to remove things that shouldn't be there.

When artists face blank canvases, they don't just see empty space; they visualize what they'll create to fill that space. Your goal when decorating is to do the same thing. Regardless of whether you're redoing an entire room or devising a way to better display a collection in a cabinet, the idea is to envision what you want the overall image to be, and what you need to do to get there.

Sources of inspiration

As human beings, we're constantly taking note of the world around us, whether we're aware of it or not. When you take on a decorating project, however, this ongoing process needs to become much more focused. Here are some ways to do it:

- Look through home decorating magazines that catch your eye and suit your individual style. Seeing how others approach decorating obstacles and challenges is one of the best ways to learn how to do it yourself. If, for example, you just can't figure out how to use the old antelope skull that your husband insists on keeping (and displaying), there's a good chance that someone else before you has faced the same problem and come up with a good solution.

- Study books on decorating and interior design. If you have a specific style and look in mind, search for titles along those lines. If not, there are plenty of general design and decorating books that present a broad variety of styles so you can compare different looks. You'll find some suggestions in Appendix C, "Further Reading".

- Visit antiques stores and galleries in your area and pay particular attention to how items are displayed. Some store owners (especially ones with very successful shops) have a real gift for knowing how to show off items to their best advantage. Their techniques can be used at home as well.

- Museums and house museums often have rooms set up as beautiful examples of how to decorate.

- If you have friends whose homes you particularly admire, take note of specific interior design elements, such as color, texture, light, and balance, the next time you visit. Be discreet about it, though. Some people are flattered by the attention. Others may find it disconcerting.

■ High-end furniture stores and showrooms also can be good places to research design and layout ideas, especially if they feature specific areas that showcase various design styles.

■ Designer show homes or home tours sponsored by various clubs and organizations are often great sources of inspiration. Even if the overall style of the home doesn't appeal to you, there are many lessons to be learned in the details.

Seeing how others tackle decorating projects will help you develop an eye for what is or isn't pleasing to you and expand your awareness of good design. And, it can expose you to ways of doing things that you may not have considered on your own, especially if you're looking for ways to incorporate your antiques in an existing design scheme. "Books and magazines are great sources of inspiration," says Julie Ann Johnson, an interior designer based in Minneapolis, Minn. "As a designer, I'm constantly looking at how others in the business create interiors. No one person knows it all. A fresh eye can bring a lot to the table.

"If you're like most people when it comes to pulling together a room, you'll have moderate to good success in doing it," Johnson adds. "However, all it takes is one inspired idea to turn a so-so plan into something really brilliant. Even something as simple as how a collection of items is grouped on a tabletop and how the pictures are hung behind it can make the difference between a good design scheme and a great one."

Timesaver
If you see a room layout in a book or magazine that you particularly like, preserve it by clipping it or making a color copy of it. Put all your favorites in a folder or binder for a quick reference book that you can take wherever you go.

Mining the fine points

As you look at various interiors, whether on the printed page or when visiting homes and shops, pay special attention to the following:

- **Focal points.** You'll notice that the most pleasing rooms have one specific focal point, or primary function, upon which the room's decor and design are based. If the room has a fireplace, this is often the focal point. Other popular focal points are large windows (especially bay windows), display cabinets (great places to showcase small items or very valuable ones), and wall units that are designed to conceal such things as stereos and televisions when not in use. A collection can define a room's focal point. One specific piece, such as an antique cupboard or wardrobe, can serve this purpose as well.

- **The specific elements of the room.** Note particularly how furniture, color, light, pattern, and accessories are used to highlight the room's good points and diminish its weak areas. For example, a mirror along a wall is often used to widen and brighten a narrow space. Many older homes where rooms have been divided suffer from ceilings that are too high in proportion to the room. Painting them in a darker color makes them appear lower. A particularly beautiful ceiling arch or other decorative accent may be enhanced by strategically placed lighting. An ugly radiator can hide behind a cozy vignette composed of a table and a lamp with a picture or two on the wall. A brightly patterned pillow can showcase a prized sofa or draw attention away from a piece that needs reupholstering.

- **How furniture is placed and grouped.** It can be difficult to achieve a pleasing placement, especially if you're accustomed to a specific furniture layout and tend to leave your pieces in this format rather than changing them around. However, it's often necessary to move pieces around quite a bit in order to come up with a layout that fits the use of the room and makes it as comfortable as possible. Grouping furniture in the right way also adds a certain rhythm to a room that makes it feel orderly and balanced.

- **How accessories are used.** A room can have all the right elements but look empty and unbalanced if it lacks the necessary finishing touches. The best rooms have an artful interplay of accessorizing objects, such as pictures, lamps, rugs, window coverings and other items that both complete and personalize it. This is an area in which using antiques is a natural.

The main goal when designing and decorating a home is to create harmony through the basic elements of design: balance, order, symmetry, and scale. By increasing your awareness of such elements, you'll be better able to see how they can be used to create a home that welcomes you every time you set foot in it.

Getting out the red pencil

After you've spent some time culling ideas and determining what you do and don't like, it's time to tackle your own home. First, review all the ideas

Bright Idea
Sometimes an antique that's been moved from one residence to another is the wrong size for the new location. Rather than struggling to fit it into a design scheme where it may never look right, consider selling it and using the money to find something that works better.

you've gathered. If they reflect your home's current interior style, focus on the following:

- Using your antiques to create or improve the focal point in each room. Fireplaces and windows are superb areas for displaying many different kinds of antiques: boxes, pictures, baskets, candelabras, you name it. Treat each area as a vignette. Ask yourself which items could be added or removed to make it great. If the room lacks a strong architectural focus point, think about how your antiques could be used to create one. Do you have a collection that could be displayed as a group? Could a favorite piece of furniture serve as a visual anchor?

- Using space effectively and attractively to display smaller antiques. Could a closet be converted into a display area by removing its door? Can a closed display cabinet be opened in order to better showcase the items it contains? If you removed that floor lamp in the corner, could you then create a pleasant seating area with your prized antique pen collection gathered on a small table? Would rearranging the furniture allow you to add a pleasing accent, such as a quilt artfully draped over the back of a sofa? Collector Sherry Heller says it was the desire to make better use of the space around a fireplace that motivated her to build a display case for her Czech glass over it. "I didn't have a good place to put my collection," she says. "And I hated the fireplace."

Even if you generally like the way your house looks and feels, you might be ready for a change. Something as simple as painting the walls can brighten and update your interiors and showcase

Bright Idea
Computer-based interior design programs are great for trying out different room configurations before moving heavy furniture. Kits with graph paper and tiny cutouts of furniture and accessories, available at many art supply stores, also achieve the same results.

your antiques more effectively. Choose your colors based on the style of your home's interiors. Traditional decors generally employ stronger colors that tie into the fabrics used in each room. In contemporary and eclectic designs, walls are kept neutral and tend to blend seamlessly from room to room, although there may be variations in the intensity of color used. In country decors, where the colors, patterns, and textures of furniture and accessories are emphasized, a warm white will make these elements stand out.

Success is in the details

In all matters of life, it is often the small things that make the biggest difference. The creation of beautiful interiors is no exception. Knowing how to maximize the effects of the little things—the details—can elevate a good room to a great one. Here are some ways to do it:

- When grouping furniture, choose pieces of similar quality, color, and texture, but vary their size and shape. If everything looks too similar, you'll lose visual impact.

- Small items, such as boxes, do well when displayed on tabletops. Lots of little objects look best grouped together by size, shape, color, or theme.

- Don't be afraid to move things around. Just a slight shift in the position of an item can make all the difference in the world.

- Less is usually best in small spaces. A few large pieces often work better than lots of little ones.

- Create visual interest and depth when displaying items on shelves by placing smaller pieces in front of larger ones.

Moneysaver
If you're using custom-colored paint, make sure you love the color before buying the quantity you need to complete the job. Standard colors can be returned. Custom paint usually can't be unless it was mixed incorrectly.

- Items displayed in cases almost always look better on glass rather than wood shelves. Think about highlighting really special pieces by installing a mirror in the back of the case.

- Mantelpiece arrangements don't need to be exactly symmetrical. Having two of everything is fine, but the sides don't have to match as long as you end up with a balanced feel.

- Unify artwork and photographs by frame style, theme, and color. They'll look better when hung together.

- Pictures and paintings look best when hung in odd numbers. Larger pieces should be flanked by smaller ones.

- A photograph or painting displayed by itself is generally at the right height if its center is at eye level.

If you are making changes throughout your home, balance your efforts as much as possible. Working room by room is acceptable, especially if your time or resources are limited, but try to finish one area or room completely before moving to another if you take this approach. Having lots of incomplete areas can be very unsettling, as I found out when a painting project in my home went unfinished for several months. It didn't bother me much at first, but as time went on it really irritated me. I couldn't wait to get it done. Focus your efforts on the part of your home that needs it the most if time and resources are very limited. If you have doubts about being able to finish a project, make small changes first and leave the big ones for later.

66

There isn't a house or apartment in the world that wouldn't allow you to indulge in a little oriental monkey business.
—Mark Hampton, *Mark Hampton on Decorating*

99

Turning to the experts

If the images you selected during your assessment process don't reflect your home's current style, you have a greater challenge ahead of you. Looking for ways to incorporate antiques into an existing decor is something most people can tackle on their own. A complete reworking of a home's interiors may call for enlisting the advice of an expert, such as an interior designer or decorator.

If you've never worked with an interior designer or decorator before, the thought of doing so can seem awkward or intimidating. You may even be embarrassed to admit that you need help. Don't let any of these feelings deter you from exploring this option. Doing so can eliminate much frustration and heartache, and it can save you money in the long run.

The talent search

Working with a designer is a more personal experience than you may think. In order to do a good job, this person needs to know a lot about you and your family. For this reason, it's important to find someone you like and trust. It also doesn't hurt to work with someone whose taste is similar to yours. Finding such a person can be challenging, but not impossible. Here are a few tried and true ways to do it:

- **Referrals.** If you know someone who has used a designer and you like the results, ask if he or she wouldn't mind passing along the name. Some people don't like to divulge the fact that they've had help, but many others appreciate the compliment. If there is a design center where you live, ask if they have a designer referral service.

Unofficially...
The difference between a decorator and an interior designer is that decorators usually have skills related to creating home decors within existing spaces. Designers generally have broader skills and knowledge in such areas as local building code requirements and architectural standards and specifications, and can tackle more complex jobs.

- **Designer show homes.** These are popular fund-raisers for various nonprofit associations. If there's one where you live, by all means visit it. They often showcase the work of a variety of designers with different styles.

- **Resource directories.** Designer yearbooks or sourcebooks, which display the work of various designers and design firms, are often published in larger metropolitan areas.

- **Local lifestyle magazines.** Most of them regularly feature articles on various interior design projects.

- **Furniture stores and galleries.** Many offer free design service if you buy products through them. Keep in mind, however, that such services may be limited.

- **If all else fails,** get a list of designers in your area from the American Society of Interior Designers. Contact the nearest ASID office, or call their designer referral service at 800-775-ASID.

It may take you a few months to come up with a list of people to call. Don't get discouraged. It pays to take your time with this, especially if you have a large project ahead of you. You're going to spend time with this person. Do everything you can on the front end to make sure it's a good fit.

The selection process

Interview more than one designer if at all possible. Everyone has a different approach, and you'll want to compare a few of them to get a feel for what will work best for you. On the other hand, it isn't a good idea to talk to more than two or three people. Too many opinions can throw you off track.

Watch Out!
Don't hire your best friend to help you redo your home, even if he or she is very talented. The adage "Familiarity breeds contempt" often applies to friendships that turn into business relationships, especially when matters of individual taste are concerned.

Your first conversation with a designer candidate can be over the phone. If you like what you hear, invite that person to your home to see it. Before you do, make sure you know the answers to the following questions, which are just some of the ones that any good designer will ask:

- **The scope of the project.** Are your needs as simple as developing a new color scheme and a different look for your window treatments, or are you looking at making structural changes?

- **Your budget.** Be sure you know how much you can and want to spend on both design and anything you buy. Don't be afraid to specify a certain dollar amount. Most designers are accustomed to working with products in various price ranges. It will be easier for both you and the designer to know where the price ceilings are before the process starts.

- **Timeline.** Are you making changes because of a specific event—an in-home wedding, let's say—or can you take a more leisurely approach to your decorating project? Again, it helps designers know how much time they have when working on various projects, as shorter deadlines might rule out the use of custom-order fabrics or custom-covered furniture, for example.

Be very honest about what you want to do and what your expectations are. Don't feel like you're belaboring the point or wasting time by asking for every detail to be spelled out. Doing so can avoid misunderstandings down the road.

> **"**
> Don't overdecorate. The secret of success is knowing when to stop.
> —*Better Homes and Gardens New Decorating Book*
> **"**

Money matters

One of the most important details to discuss with the designers you interview is how they'll be paid. The following scenarios are most common:

- **Hourly rate.** You pay the designer based on the total number of hours he or she works for you. Hourly rates vary across the country so it's hard to give specific figures for this; however, rates from $75 to $150 per hour are fairly common. You may pay more or less depending on where you live. Monthly billings are common with hourly rate contracts. In some cases, especially on very large projects, designers will ask for a retainer before they begin and will bill their hours against it. In either case, you should ask for (and receive) a monthly statement detailing the number of hours the designer spent on the project and any purchases that were made.

- **Flat fee.** The designer estimates the number of hours in a particular project and sets a fee based on that estimate. This method works well if your needs are very specific (say, you want help in developing an overall style for your home or you need a display case designed). A common billing procedure in these situations is to split the fee into halves or thirds so the designer receives some money at the start of the project.

- **Mark-up.** The designer buys furniture, wall coverings, carpeting, window treatments, and other materials at wholesale, or a price close to wholesale, and marks up the price to the customer. The difference between the two amounts is the designer's compensation.

Although once common, this method is not widely employed by designers today; when it is, it's generally used in conjunction with one of the other compensation methods discussed above.

Unofficially...
The first meeting between a designer and potential client is usually free.

If you do end up buying custom-ordered or custom-covered items such as furniture through a designer, you can expect to pay for at least half of your purchases in advance. You can also expect to pay in advance for such things as window and floor coverings or countertops. If this is the case, see if you can pay for installation separately.

Making things legal

Once you've decided on who you're going to use and how you're going to pay this individual (or individuals), make an agreement in writing. Most designers have a standard contract or letter of agreement that they have their clients sign before work is begun. Before you sign such a document, make sure it says exactly what you want it to say. If you need to make any changes, do so in writing. Don't expect a verbal change to be binding, because it isn't.

Be sure to follow the same approach as long as your contract is in place. Put your requests in writing. If they constitute major changes to your original agreement, your designer may have you sign addendums or change orders that specify exactly what the changes are and how much they'll cost.

The amount of involvement you have in your interior design project is mostly up to you. Some people prefer having their designers present interior schemes that they have developed after an interview or two; others like to be intimately involved throughout the process and enjoy visiting

showrooms and design centers with their designers
to select such things as window and floor coverings,
fabrics, lighting fixtures and other interior elements.

This is another point to discuss with your design
candidates as they too have work styles they prefer.
However, most designers like a good level of involvement from their clients and, in fact, encourage it. In
the best scenarios, design projects are true collabo-
rations between client and designer. The more you
bring to the table in terms of the looks and styles
that you like, the more successful your project is
likely to be.

Just the facts

- Use your antiques whenever possible. Don't
  just display them.

- Even the oldest and most ornate antiques can
  find a home in most home decors.

- Creating beautiful rooms is like painting beautiful pictures. Treat every setting as an empty
  canvas that needs to be filled.

- Never stop working on your rooms. Improvements can always be made.

- If you're having trouble decorating on your
  own, don't hesitate to call in an expert. Just a
  few hours spent with a good designer can make
  all the difference in the world.

GET THE SCOOP ON...
The main enemies of all antiques
▪ Cleaning methods ▪ Storing antiques
▪ Restoring vs. refinishing

Caring for Antiques

Chapter 15

L ike anything of value, antiques must be cared for properly. If you're buying pieces of good quality, your motivation for doing so will be quite high. This is the first component of a well-planned preservation and conservation program. The second component consists of knowing exactly how to preserve and protect, and even mend when appropriate or necessary.

Your antiques will have already lived a long life by the time you acquire them, which means that things have happened to them or have been done to them that are out of your control. Rarely do you come across a piece of art glass that isn't a little scuffed up on the bottom from being moved around on various surfaces, or a table whose legs haven't been banged up by something crashing into them. While these preexisting dings and scratches often add the unique character to an object that makes it a cherished item, new blemishes generally add nothing to the value of old objects.

When antiques enter into your care, your chief goal is to help them continue to grow old gracefully by preventing any further damage to them and by preserving their condition. Doing so can not only protect your investment in them but also enhance their value. At the very minimum, maintaining their condition will make it possible for their value to increase with inflation. This chapter will help you build a plan for taking care of your collection.

The frontline enemies

Light, temperature, humidity (or the lack of it), dust, and dirt...these forces can change the structure of any object and alter its appearance. Fortunately, you can control most of them and minimize their negative effects.

> **"**
> It is sad to grow old, but nice to ripen.
> —Brigitte Bardot
> **"**

Every preservation and conservation effort begins by understanding how these elements affect antiques and what you can do to avoid the problems that they cause. Although it's not necessary to be obsessive about it, taking the time to ensure a positive environment for all of your belongings can minimize problems along the way.

Light

Both natural and artificial light can be damaging to many antiques, especially those made of organic fibers such as wood, paper, wool, canvas, or cotton. The most harmful aspect of light is the ultraviolet (UV) radiation received from the sun, which can cause chemical changes at the molecular level. Artificial light from halogen and some fluorescent fixtures can also be extremely damaging. Even the soft glow of incandescent bulbs can have a cumulative damaging effect, especially if they're of high wattage and focused closely on an object. All cause materials to dry out and colors to fade or change over time.

Most homes are lit from a combination of sources, which means that you must take steps to protect valuable objects from all of them. Although you should never display valuable objects in strong light, avoiding it isn't always feasible, or, for that matter, practical. You can protect them as much as possible in one of the following manners:

- Shielding them from the sun. Curtains, blinds, shades, and ultraviolet film can protect valuable objects from the harsh effects of natural light. Of these materials, ultraviolet film is the only permanent shield against the sun. It's expensive and it will alter your view to the outside, but it's worth considering, especially if you have large picture windows that you are loathe to cover. Ultraviolet film comes in various strengths and can block out up to 99 percent of harmful rays while reducing heat levels also caused by the sun. Even with it, however, you will get some fading over time. Curtains and drapes, if they're heavy, can be very effective for screening out light, but opening and closing them on a regular schedule can be a chore. Sheers, blinds, and shades will screen out some light, but they are most effective when used with another screening element.

- Rotating antiques and artwork on a regular basis. This helps to even out light damage.

- Purchasing fluorescent bulbs with low UV output and using UV filters on halogen lights.

- Turning or rotating rugs. Again, doing so can minimize light damage and even out the fading that takes place.

- Periodically rearranging your furniture. Not only can this help rugs fade more evenly, it will

Watch Out!
Avoid putting very valuable antique rugs in direct sunlight whenever possible. They will fade and the light will weaken their fibers.

help protect the finish on furniture from crazing or cracking and the fabric on upholstered pieces from fading.

Some things should never be displayed where they'll be constantly exposed to the sun, regardless of how much filtering you can provide. They include

- Works of art on paper and canvas. Regardless of where they're hung, you should still rotate them occasionally to protect them from damage from other light sources. Even light reflected from outside of your home can affect such pieces.

- Photographs. Light causes the paper they're printed on to turn brown (called "light burn") and weaken. Mounting them under UV-resistant plexiglass can minimize damage.

- Pieces made of linen, lace, or silk. Even a brief amount of time in the sun can scorch and fade fine fabrics, and it can cause lace to literally disintegrate. Burn marks can be treated on some fabrics, but the treatment itself can ruin very delicate or fragile pieces even more. It's best to avoid the problem completely rather than to risk such damage to a prized piece.

Temperature

Temperatures that are too low or too high can damage many antiques, especially when combined with humidity, the next culprit on the enemies list. The ideal temperature for most antiques—about 65°F—is cooler than most of us keep our homes, but it's a good idea to come as close to this temperature as possible. More importantly, maintain a consistent temperature. If you can keep your interiors at about 72°F, a temperature that feels comfortable to most people, chances are your antiques will be fine.

As much as possible, avoid wide variations in interior temperatures, which, when combined with fluctuations in humidity, can wreak havoc on wood, textiles, and fabrics over a period of time. Heat is more of an issue than cold in most homes, so the idea is to moderate its effect by

- Keeping antiques away from heat sources such as radiators, fireplaces, furnace vents, and stoves.

- Storing antiques in temperature-controlled storage facilities. Never store pieces that are vulnerable to changes in temperature in the attic. Basements are often a better choice if other elements, such as humidity levels, are favorable.

- Installing and using a setback thermometer for your heating and cooling system. These devices are often used to conserve energy by automatically decreasing interior temperatures at night when everyone's asleep. However, they're also great for keeping rooms at an even temperature at all times of the day.

- Servicing your furnace and air conditioner annually. Doing so can assure that all systems are running efficiently and avert problems before they happen.

- Displaying fragile or sensitive pieces in cooler parts of the house. Heat rises, so rooms on the lower level of your home will naturally stay a little cooler than those that are higher. Window areas are usually warmer as well.

If you have a number of very valuable pieces, you may want to consider having a temperature sensor installed as part of a home security system. These

Bright Idea
If you must put an antique near a floor vent, divert the air from the vent away from the antique by using a plastic air director, available at most hardware stores and home centers.

devices alert you to extremes in temperature caused by fire or the failure of heating and cooling systems.

Humidity

As previously mentioned, temperature causes the most problems when combined with its partner in crime, humidity. Anything comprised of organic materials contains moisture, and these objects maintain their moisture levels by taking up or releasing moisture from their environment. If they're placed in too dry an environment, they will lose too much moisture. Too much humidity can cause them to retain excessive levels of their own moisture.

High humidity can cause as many problems as air that is overly dry. When combined with unfavorable temperatures, the following problems can erupt:

- Cracks in furniture and paintings. These can be caused by extremes in both temperature and humidity, or rapid changes in either condition.

- Crazing or cracking of the finish on furniture. This is caused by too much or too little humidity in temperatures of all ranges.

- Mold and mildew growth. This usually takes place when temperatures are low and humidity is high, and can affect all items made of organic materials. On paper items, it causes "foxing," the eruption of reddish-brown spots when mold reacts with iron salts in the paper.

- Metal corrosion. Low temperatures and high humidity also create favorable environments for this type of damage.

- Insect infestations. High temperatures coupled with high humidity levels create prime breeding grounds for all sorts of bugs.

Watch Out!
Never display antiques made of paper near console humidifiers. The stream of moisture that these systems emit can buckle or ripple paper and cause it to mildew.

- Rapid tarnishing of metals, especially sterling silver.

The temperature of the air influences the water content of air, which is why humidity is correctly referred to as "relative humidity." The ideal level of relative humidity for the health of antiques is about 50 percent, which is also a comfortable level for most people. Maintaining this level calls for balancing both temperature and moisture content, as cooler air will retain moisture better than warm air does.

It can be a real challenge—not to mention somewhat expensive—to raise the level of relative humidity in homes that are kept too warm or that are located in arid parts of the country. If you live in the Southwest, for example, achieving ideal humidity levels usually calls for adding moisture to the air. Residents in more humid areas have the opposite problem and need to find ways to remove moisture from the air at certain times of the year. If you live in the Midwest, you probably face both challenges— too much humidity in the summer, too little when the heat comes on in the fall and winter.

You can maintain a consistent level of relative humidity by

- Avoiding fluctuations in the temperature of your home. Large changes in temperature, as mentioned previously, affect relative humidity. If your home gets too warm, which is generally the problem, it will take some effort to get humidity levels up to where they should be.

- Using humidifiers to add moisture to rooms that are too dry. The best are built right into your heating system as they deliver moisture to your entire home when the heat is on. Console humidifiers are effective as long as their output matches the size of the area.

- Running dehumidifiers in rooms that are too damp. These devices pull moisture out of the air and are often used in rooms that are below grade, such as basements or cellars.

Bright Idea
Buy a portable hygrometer/ temperature gauge so you can measure the levels in each room.

If you are concerned about the humidity levels in your home, install a humidity gauge, or hygrometer, which measures relative humidity. These often come in conjunction with a temperature gauge, which makes it easy to see the correlation between these measurements. Most hardware or home stores have basic ones. If you want something fancier, try a department store or a specialty gadget store. Retailers that carry sauna supplies also have these items.

You get what you pay for with hygrometers. Very cheap ones can be very inaccurate and give you readings that are too high or too low, which defeats the whole purpose. Good gauges can be had for around $25 to $30 and up. Many are designed as part of home weather meters that also include thermometers and barometers.

Creating a better environment

If your home needs temperature and humidity adjustments in its interior environment, make these changes gradually. The pieces you have in your home have adapted to their environment as it is. Making drastic changes could harm them as much as keeping them in a less-than-ideal state.

Start by moderating the temperature of your home; not only will this be the lowest costing option, but it may also solve minor humidity problems. After you make adjustments to the temperature, take humidity readings for several days to see if you have enough of an improvement. If not, explore one of the methods for adding or subtracting moisture discussed above.

Controlling dust and dirt

Dust and dirt exist in every home, no matter how immaculately kept. Besides being unsightly, dirt can actually damage rugs if the particles work their way deep enough into the fibers. Try to minimize the amount of each that finds its way into your home. Having a balanced interior climate helps to keep dust levels down. Other control methods include:

- Making sure doors and windows fit correctly. Any gaps to the outside are conduits for dust and dirt. Check them all annually and repair any cracks or gaps around them.

- Changing the filters on your heating and cooling system regularly, usually every 90 days. Also, consider using high efficiency filters. They're more expensive, but they do a better job of filtering particulates.

- Installing electrostatic air filtering systems on your heating and cooling system. These devices, which can remove more than 90 percent of airborne particulates, can be expensive both to install and to operate; to be most effective, the fan on your system must stay on at all times, even when you aren't heating or cooling your home. A less-costly alternative is to replace standard air filters with electrostatic ones. These filters are also very effective at controlling dust levels. Both remove other particulates from the air, such as pollen, which can be a big boon for allergy sufferers.

- Leaving dust and dirt at the door by taking your shoes off as you enter the house. This

Timesaver
Avoid extra trips to the hardware store by buying a box of furnace filters once a year. Tape a calendar to the box or the furnace to remind you when it's time to change them.

Japanese custom is one of the most effective ways of keeping outside elements where they should be.

▪ Using portable air filtration systems. If you're going to go with this approach, buy one that is large enough to effectively clean the area in which it will be used.

▪ Rotating any rugs that are in a major traffic pattern in your home. Again, the idea is to balance the wear and tear on these items that dust and dirt will cause.

▪ Installing a central vacuum system. Even the most efficient vacuums still emit a certain amount of dust back into the air when you use them. A central vacuum collects all the dust and dirt into one canister that is located away from living areas, usually in a garage or utility room. When you empty the canister, any emissions into the air are confined to this area. These systems also do a better job of cleaning than most vacuums due to their higher suction capacity.

▪ Installing a central air conditioner. If you're cooling your house by leaving windows open, you're bringing in dust with that cool air.

Many of the most effective methods for controlling dust and dirt are expensive. As with temperature and humidity control devices, try the simpler, less costly methods first. If they don't yield the results you're looking for, then it's time to consider some of the others.

Cleaning antiques

Caring properly for antiques includes knowing how to keep them clean. This may seem academic, but you might be amazed at the damage that has been done to valuable pieces by well-meaning people with the wrong cleaning tools. An overly aggressive cleaning program can literally ruin rugs and fine textiles and can damage the finish on furniture.

In your first level of effort, keep pieces dusted and vacuumed as part of your regular housekeeping schedule. Using the following items can make your job easier, especially if you have pieces with lots of detail:

- Artist's brushes and make-up brushes. These soft-bristled brushes are great for fragile antiques. Buy brushes made of sable, if possible, as they're softer and will last longer. Big, fluffy brushes work well for overall dusting. Smaller brushes are better for getting into nooks and crannies.

- Cotton-tipped swabs. These are good for accessing hard-to-reach spots. You can find swabs with longer than normal shafts at craft stores and some hardware stores.

- Canned air. These items can make short work of cleaning delicate pieces and blowing dust out of hard-to-reach areas. Most office supply stores carry them as they're also used to clean computers and other electronic equipment.

- Photographers' air brushes. These are good for dusting very fragile or delicate pieces, as they don't deliver the blast of air that canned air devices do.

The first rule of thumb when cleaning antiques is to tread lightly. You'll never go wrong if you keep pieces dusted and vacuumed, and this is the basic level of care that should be provided to all items. Never use dusters, cloths, or brushes that have been

Moneysaver
You can prolong the life of dusting brushes by cleaning them periodically with a mild soap such as Ivory or Dove. Rinse thoroughly and dry them flat, away from light.

treated with a cleaning agent. The chemicals in these products could damage the finish on some pieces. Additional efforts vary as to the type of antique being cleaned. The cleaning methods detailed below are appropriate for the vast majority of pieces in each category. If you're ever concerned about cleaning a specific item, your best bet is to do nothing. Consult conservation specialists or experts in your particular collecting category first.

Furniture

Most antique furniture does well with regular dusting and little else. Use a soft cloth, slightly dampened, and dust with the grain of the wood. Avoid using dusting or polishing sprays because they can leave a deposit that builds up over time. If polishing is necessary, do it only occasionally. Apply a thin layer of paste wax and buff it with a soft cloth. The wax of choice is a product called Butcher's Wax, which protects the surface but doesn't penetrate it.

Silver and silver plate

Keep silver clean of tarnish as much as possible because it will leave pits in the metal when you finally remove it. Any commercial polish can be used; anti-tarnish or tarnish-retarding products can extend the time between polishings. Always use the smallest amount of polish you can and be sure to dry silver thoroughly when cleaning because water also will tarnish it. You can use a hairdryer to blow the water out of the nooks and crannies of ornate silver. Never use harsh abrasives such as scouring powder or steel wool. Toothpaste, which is often suggested as a quick fix in the absence of silver polish, is also not a good idea. Depending on the brand, it can contain elements that also can scratch silver.

Unofficially...
Wood does not need to be "fed." Treatments made for this spurious purpose are almost always oily; they only momentarily make the surface look slicker, and they attract dust and eventually darken the surface.

Pottery and porcelain

Dusting is generally all it takes to keep these pieces in good shape. If more extensive cleaning is necessary, proceed with care. Start by wiping with a damp cloth. If this doesn't remove the grime, add a small amount of mild liquid detergent, such as Ivory Liquid or Joy. Avoid immersing items in water if at all possible, although porcelain, which is not porous, can be immersed if necessary to remove dirt and grime. Pottery is porous and more likely to become stained. You can try removing stains with regular laundry bleach if the other methods detailed above are ineffective.

Books

Dust books regularly, and treat leather-bound books with leather dressing every two years or so. If they are musty smelling, try placing them in a large container, such as a plastic garbage pail, in which you've placed about a half a small bag of kitty litter (the old-fashioned, clumping type is best) or about the same amount of deactivated charcoal, such as what you would use when potting cactus. Make sure to keep the books from touching either substance. Suspending them from the top of the container in a webbed bag, such as a grocery or laundry bag, works well. Leave them in the container for several days, then open it and check the progress. If you still detect a musty smell, put in fresh kitty litter or charcoal and put the books back in for another round of treatment. Removing the smell can take up to a week, so be patient.

Always display books completely upright or flat. Placing them at an angle can damage their bindings. Don't place them too tightly on shelves; it's

Watch Out!
Never use window cleaner on porcelain that is gilded. It won't affect the paint, which is under the glaze, but will remove the gilding, which is laid on over the glaze.

possible to rip the head of the binding when removing books that are shelved too snugly.

Brass, copper, and pewter

Dust these items with a soft-bristled brush, feather duster or soft towel. Brass and copper both develop a patina or tarnish over the years from exposure to the elements that most collectors feel adds to the value of these pieces. If it becomes extremely dark or unpleasing, it can be polished off, but be aware that such efforts may make the piece less valuable. If the patina is very dark, it's best to have it evaluated by a restoration specialist.

If you do decide to polish brass or copper, use as light a hand as possible when polishing and always polish in a circular motion. Remove all traces of polish and water or they will corrode these pieces. A soft toothbrush or toothpick are good tools for removing cleaner or polish from crevices.

Pewter also develops a patina that is best left intact. It also will corrode if exposed to moisture. Trying to remove it usually damages the piece further, so it's best to leave it alone and prevent further corrosion from occurring. If you wash pewter, make sure you dry it immediately. Usually, periodic dusting or wiping down is all it needs. Polishing pewter will remove its patina.

Watch Out!
Never polish bronze, as doing so will damage its patina.

Bronze

Bronze, a very tough metal, doesn't need much care beyond dusting and an occasional rubbing. Never wash it with water, as it can corrode the piece. You may make a brief swipe with a dampened cloth to clean it as long as you dry the piece immediately.

Leather

Clean antiques made of leather, such as saddles and boots, periodically with saddle soap if the leather is in good condition—that is, not flaking or crumbling away. Follow the cleaning with an application of a leather preservative or oil to prevent drying out the piece. Both products are available through many shoe repair shops or saddle shops. Apply all products with a soft cloth to prevent scratching, and work them in well; any residue that's left will attract dust and become grimy.

You may also use glycerin-based facial soaps for cleaning leather. If you do this, you won't have to apply the leather preservative because the glycerin in the soap will protect the leather. Buy clear bars that have nothing added to them; if you see a brand-name soap line that offers soaps with many different purposes, choose the basic cleansing bar.

It's best not to do anything to leather items that are damaged because any action may injure them further. Proceed with caution when cleaning leather trim on items such as swords or trunks. If you do clean the trim on these items, keep the cleaning materials away from the non-leather parts in order to avoid damage.

Rattan and wicker

Wicker or rattan baskets and furniture need moisture to keep them from becoming dry and brittle. Wipe them down occasionally—every few months or so, more often in dryer climates—with a damp rag or sponge after they've been dusted, or give them a light spray of water periodically with a plant mister. To help them retain their moisture, you can spray them with a light furniture oil, or wipe them with a solution of 40 percent castor oil and 60 percent alcohol. Don't do this frequently; once every year or two is sufficient. Keep these pieces away from direct sunlight and heat so they don't dry out. Repairs on these items can be very expensive,

Bright Idea
Silica gel packs placed in display cases with metal objects will draw moisture away from such items and keep them from tarnishing.

so always buy these pieces in as good of shape as possible.

Paper

Paper antiques are some of the most fragile and sensitive items in the antiques world. Rarely is it necessary to actually clean these items, so the main concern is to prevent them from being damaged. Framing is often the best protection for them.

Any paper item you frame should be mounted with acid-free products. An acid-free mat should always be used in order to create a space between the item and the glass that goes over it. If glass lies flat on paper, anything that is on the paper may transfer to the glass and damage the piece. If you have pieces that are already framed and you aren't sure that an acid-free backing, mat, and adhesives have been used, it's worth the cost to have them remounted. Any non-acid-free materials that come into contact with paper items will cause a chemical reaction with the acids contained in the paper and will discolor and deteriorate them. The best thing is to take these objects to a framer who does museum quality framing.

The backs of mounted items should be sealed to keep them dust-free and to keep mold spores and moisture away. Plain cardboard or wood should not be used as backing materials as they, too, will damage paper.

Never handle a paper item by anything other than its edges if it's unframed. The oils in your skin can damage the paper. If it ever is necessary to clean a paper antique, take it to a conservationist or restoration expert. Never attempt cleaning or repair on these objects yourself, as doing so will usually cause more damage.

Watch Out!
Never use a glass cleaner directly on the glass over a framed print, as the fluid may seep through a corner of the frame. Spray the cleaner on a cleaning cloth first.

Paintings

Antique paintings can be some of the most beautiful items collected. Because they are created with a mixture of media—paint, canvas, and wood—they can also be the most challenging to keep in good shape. Protect them from extremes in temperature and humidity as much as possible. Too much moisture can make canvas stretch and sag, which then also damages the paint.

Oil paintings bought while traveling may need restretching after they acclimate to their new surroundings, especially if they were bought in a humid climate and their new home is arid. The wood on the stretcher will shrink in a dry climate and cause the canvas to sag.

Oil paintings should be carefully dusted because dust can build up into a film on the canvas and alter the appearance of the piece. A soft sable brush is best for this. Don't neglect the frame as you dust. The lower edge, where dust is most likely to accumulate, will need particular attention. Also dust the back of the picture.

Jewelry

Always make sure that you know what the jewelry is made of—both settings and stones—before cleaning it; using the wrong cleaning products can cause damage. Start by wiping pieces with a soft cloth. Check for loose settings as you do; if you find any, take the piece to a jeweler for repair. Rinsing gemstones set in gold or sterling silver in water will remove surface dust. Be sure to dry them thoroughly, especially sterling silver settings, as they will tarnish. A rouge cloth can be used to remove tarnish and polish both silver and gold pieces. Don't rub too hard; you're removing small amounts of the metal when you polish it and you don't want to take away too much. If necessary, you can clean pieces further by washing them in a weak solution of ammonia. A toothbrush or toothpick is helpful for removing accumulated dirt and body oils from settings and crevices. Do not scrub soft gemstones or you may scratch them.

Never wash pearls; doing so can damage their luster and weaken their knots if they're strung. If absolutely necessary, wipe them with a barely moistened cloth. Using soap on opals also is not recommended. Never use ultrasonic cleaners on antique pieces set with opal, emerald, pearl, lapis, coral, amber, turquoise, and malachite, as doing so will expose them to internal stress and cause them to crack or shatter.

Water can tarnish the foil backing on rhinestones used in costume jewelry and cause them to darken. It can also loosen glued-in stones. Clean these pieces with a cotton swab dipped in rubbing alcohol and rub metal surfaces clean with a soft cloth.

Watches and clocks should be taken to an expert every two to five years for cleaning.

Textiles

Antiques made of fabric are the only items that benefit from regular cleaning, as accumulated dirt can do more damage than the cleaning process does. Most of the time, vacuuming is all that should be attempted. If deeper dirt or stain removal is needed, treat all fabric antiques as delicate textiles. Most will do best if they are hand washed in cool or tepid water with a pH-balanced or nondetergent soap. Spot-test colored items first by wetting an inconspicuous corner of the item. Place a white towel behind

Watch Out!
Do not attempt to clean silk, most 18th-century fabrics, and most 19th-century fabrics, as they are too delicate to stand up to even the gentlest techniques.

the spot to see if any of the dye has bled through. Be sure to rinse thoroughly because any soap that remains can also damage the piece. Dry flat and away from heat and light. Ironing is generally not a good idea because the heat can damage delicate fibers. Never iron a dirty piece.

You can usually remove brown stains on linens and other non-woolen pieces by dampening the piece and rubbing in a paste made of laundry detergent and color-safe bleach. Place the fabric in the sun for a few hours and wash it by hand. Scorch marks will lighten when rubbed with white vinegar. Ink stains can sometimes be removed by rubbing with toothpaste.

Rugs

Antique rugs should remain in good condition if they are swept or vacuumed on a regular basis and rotated to even out light damage. Cleaning them occasionally generally is fine for them as well. Small carpets can be shaken out but never "snapped," as doing so can damage them.

Toys

The care given to toys depends on the materials the toy is made of. The guidelines above will apply to most items.

Storing antiques

Antiques that are not in use should be carefully stored in order to prevent them from being damaged while they're packed away. It is important to have the proper materials with which to pack your antiques. You'll find a list of sources for these items in Appendix B, "Resource List".

In general, make sure all items are dusted or clean before packing. Check to make sure they're

Bright Idea
Keep the tissue from gifts and clothing purchases for wrapping and packing small antiques.

free from moisture as well if you've just cleaned them.

Small items (porcelain, pottery, glass, crystal)

Wrap pieces in tissue or paper to protect them. Fill spaces around items with crumpled pieces of packing material to keep them from shifting. If you need to stack boxes, don't stack them too high as the weight may damage pieces in lower boxes.

Textiles

Quilts, curtains, coverlets, and other textile items should be packed with a minimum number of folds. Pad each fold with unbleached muslin or acid-free tissue. If you have enough room, roll them around acid-free cardboard tubes instead of folding them. Place muslin or acid-free tissue on top on the item before rolling to protect the layers.

Store any items made of wool with cedar wood or mothballs.

Sterling silver

Wrap silver in tarnish-retarding cloths before storing. Some people use mothballs to prevent tarnishing when they store their silver. If you do, make sure that the mothballs don't come into direct contact with your pieces because this will damage them. You may also be able to find anti-tarnish strips, which contain activated charcoal and work by removing the harmful chemicals from the air that tarnish silver.

Never wrap sterling in plastic or bubble wrap because it can melt on the sterling and cause damage that can't be erased. Some experts maintain that you don't need to remove tarnish from pieces prior to storage, as doing so will expose fresh sterling to the elements. Store individual silver objects inside polyethylene bags (wrap each piece first in anti-tarnish cloths or acid-free paper).

Other metals

Like sterling, they should be stored in acid-free boxes. Wrap each piece in acid-free paper or pieces of clean linen or cotton. Don't use newspapers or bubble wrap, and don't secure them with rubber bands. Never wrap them in plastic.

Paper items

These antiques are best stored flat. Put a piece of acid-free paper between each and place them in an artist's portfolio to keep them dust-free. If they must be rolled, try to do so as loosely as possible. Tie the roll with string. Never use tape or rubber bands as the chemicals in these pieces can damage the paper. Place acid free paper on the surface prior to rolling.

If you're storing framed pieces, try to stand them straight up against a solid support such as a wall. Place a piece of foam core board or cardboard between them to protect their surfaces from rubbing against each other. If you're moving framed pieces, it's best to have them packed professionally.

Paintings

Paintings should also be stored upright if possible. Laying them flat can cause canvases to sag and they're more vulnerable to damage should something fall on them. Cover them with acid-free paper or unbleached muslin to keep them clean, and, again, place Foam Core board or cardboard between them. Unmounted canvas paintings should never be rolled.

Furniture

Furniture should be lightly draped with dustcloths to keep it from becoming too dusty and grimy while it's not being used. If you're storing these objects away from home, try to find a climate-controlled storage facility to protect the furniture from damaging

Bright Idea
Crisscross strips of masking tape on the top of the glass on framed objects that are being packed for moving. If the glass should break, the tape will make it easier to remove the shards without damaging the artwork.

extremes in temperature and humidity. Raise pieces off the floor to protect them from water damage by placing them on masonry blocks.

Jewelry

Always store pieces of fine and costume jewelry separately to prevent them from scratching and chipping each other if jumbled together in a drawer. Put them in separate padded compartments or wrap them in soft, lint-free cloths.

Repairing, restoring, and refinishing antiques

Many repair or restoration efforts can diminish the value in an antique. If you're collecting more for aesthetic reasons than for investment, you have more leeway in what you can do with and to your antiques. If you are a more serious antiquer with an eye toward collecting for investment, tread cautiously when entertaining the possibilities of repair and restoration. In either case, be sure to know your collecting area extremely well before attempting any sort of repair or restoration with any antique. Repairing a piece of furniture, for example, can seriously diminish the value of the piece unless it is very old and rare, in which case some repairs are acceptable. Refinishing these pieces almost always destroys their value. Overzealous restoration of paintings can ruin them.

Even if you never plan to sell the antiques in your possession, it's always a good idea to have them repaired and restored by a professional unless you feel very confident that the job you can do will be just as good. If you ever have a change of heart and decide to sell a piece, it's better to have repairs done right the first time than to redo a haphazard effort in the future—that is, if it even can be redone.

Buying high-quality antiques will keep these issues to a minimum to begin with as any necessary repair, restoration, or refinishing will already be done. If you're taking some chances and buying pieces that need work, knowing your collecting area well, once again, will guide you to pieces that are worth your effort and will tell you if such efforts are worthwhile at all. If they aren't, you better be buying such pieces merely because you love them, as they won't increase in value unless they are very rare.

Since I believe that any action taken with an antique should be mounted with an eye to preserving its value, the recommendations below are on the conservative side. Where appropriate, I've noted repairs and conservation efforts that can be undertaken by a collector without diminishing the value of the piece. If you feel called to a more aggressive approach, Appendix C, "Further Reading," lists several books that will guide you.

Furniture

Most antique furniture needs minor repair work from time to time. Repairs such as tightening the pulls on a chest of drawers can certainly be performed by just about anyone. Other efforts that are within the ability of most collectors include

- Gluing down loose veneer. Use a hot iron over a cloth placed on the lifted veneer. It will melt the glue and reaffix the veneer. Be careful with this and check your progress often as the heat from the iron can also melt the finish. If this doesn't work, take the piece to a restorer.

- Erasing scratches and grooves. Surface scratches often disappear with a good coating of wax. If the scratch is through the stain, a stain pen (available at hardware or

> 66
> I don't do any restoration and I certainly do not buy anything that requires it. I suggest you avoid it too.
> —Milan Vesely, *Money from Antiques*
> 99

woodworking stores) can be stroked over scratches to disguise them. These tools come in various colors, so be sure to match the pen with the stain you need to fix. Deeper scratches and gouges can be filled in with wax sticks (also available at hardware in woodworking colors). If the area of damage isn't too deep, rubbing the stick over it will fill it. If this doesn't do the trick, melt the end with a match and let the wax drip into the mark. After using either product, wax the piece of furniture. If the area you filled with wax is a little higher than the rest of the piece, take a rag with just a bit of mineral spirits to the spot to dissolve the excess wax. If you go too far, you can rewax the area.

■ Unsticking stuck drawers. Apply soap or wax to the runners or slides or around the front edges of the drawer.

66

The debate over refinishing really divides antiquers into two opposing camps—to refinish or not to refinish. There is no definite answer.
—Frank Farmer Loomis IV, *Is It Antique Yet?*

99

Anything beyond these repairs is best left to an expert, as attempting it may diminish the value of the piece. Even if you feel competent, check with an expert first. The curatorial staff at public museums can be good sources of information. Other resources to check include club magazines and newsletters and Internet antiques sites. Contact information for several sources of conservation and restoration assistance is listed in Appendix B.

Antique furniture generally loses a great deal of value when it is refinished. This still happens more frequently than it should, and it's sad when it does because the refinished piece will never be worth as much as it once was, nor will it ever look like it once did. If you're a fan of the *Antiques Roadshow*, you've seen these points illustrated more than once. One of the more dramatic examples involved a Queen Anne highboy that had been stripped of its original reddish stain. In its original condition, it could have fetched more than $50,000 at auction. Since it had been refinished, it was only worth around $10,000.

Many antiques dealers and collectors, especially the older, more traditional ones, believe that original finishes should always be left intact even if they are severely damaged. I tend to side with this school of thought. To me, the patina of the original finish is what gives an object its strongest degree of character. If I am not attracted to the finish, no matter how much I like the piece in other ways, I won't buy it. However, there are things that can be done to improve the finish without stripping it off and starting all over again. Polishing or waxing the crazed finish on a piece of furniture can bring a great deal of life back to it. Restoring the finish by cleaning it and removing such damage as mildew, water or ink stains makes great sense as well, and even these restorative measures will not damage the characteristic patina of the piece.

Many people find it enjoyable to restore or refinish furniture. Doing this well takes years of practice and experience. If you're new to the business and are considering such efforts, consult with an expert before doing anything. You want to make sure that your efforts won't diminish the value of the piece.

Painted furniture should never be stripped; if you don't like the look of painted pieces, don't buy them to begin with. Painted furniture in very bad condition can be repaired by a restoration expert much as a painting would be.

Books

Repairing and restoring books ranges from re-attaching covers on leather-bound books to rebinding them, which should be avoided if at all possible as it will reduce their value. Torn pages should be left as they are as well unless the book is very valuable, in which case pages should be repaired by a skilled restorer.

Glass

Even a slight chip will cause a significant drop in the value of a piece, so always buy glass in the best condition possible. Minor chips can be ground down and even filled, but doing so will further diminish the value. Most pieces should be left as is.

Unofficially... Although the terms are often used interchangably, restoration is in fact only part of the conservation process, which includes examination, analysis and research to determine the original structure, materials, and extent of loss, and structural and environmental treatment to retard future deterioration.

Paintings

All repair or restoration work on paintings should be done by a conservationist or a restoration expert. Be sure you find a good one, as it is very easy to damage these pieces by overcleaning or overrestoring them. Museums will sometimes recommend restorers and conservators that they have used.

Porcelain and pottery

If pieces are very rare, it may pay to repair chips or cracks. If they aren't, doing so will decrease their value even more than the imperfections will.

Textiles

Textiles should generally be left in original condition. Any repairs should be done by an expert unless you aren't concerned about the value of the piece.

Rugs

Repair work on rugs is almost always done by experts because most collectors don't have the materials or the tools necessary to do this sort of work. A simple repair, such as tacking a binding back into place, is acceptable to do on your own since it can be easily redone if you decide to sell the rug. It's also a good idea to do this if the rug is being used; otherwise, leaving it loose could cause further damage.

Jewelry

Loose settings on all pieces of jewelry should always be taken to a jeweler and tightened to avoid losing stones. If it's necessary to replace a missing gemstone, try to do so with an old stone to get the best match. When it comes to rhinestones, the age of the replacement stone doesn't matter all that much; just make sure the stone matches in size, shape and color. Discolored rhinestones should always be replaced. You can do this yourself by gluing the stone into place with Epoxy 330 (available in craft shops and bead stores), or by taking the piece to a jeweler.

Toys

Never attempt to repair or restore toys by yourself, especially dolls or teddy bears, unless you really know what you're doing. Repainting or restoring the paint on metal or iron toys, for example, destroys the value of these pieces. Badly damaged teddy bears, especially if they're rare, have much more value to collectors than do repaired bears. Dolls that are in their original condition, even if the condition isn't that good, are very often more valuable than those that have been repaired.

Just the facts

- The best way to preserve the value of antiques is to take good care of them once they're in your possession.

- A good balance of temperature and moisture is essential to keep antiques in good condition.

- Dust and dirt are enemies of all antiques. Keep them clean and dusted at all times.

- Proceed cautiously with anything beyond basic cleaning and care, especially when it comes to

furniture, porcelain, glass, and other fragile
antiques. Restoring or repairing such items can
diminish their value.

■ It's always best to check with experts if you
have any concerns about caring for your
antiques.

GET THE SCOOP ON...
Home security systems ▪ Fire and
water protection ▪ Insurance for
collectors ▪ Inventory systems

Protecting Your Collection (and Your Investment)

Chapter 16

Whether you've amassed a collection worth hundreds of thousands of dollars, or one that is worth a few hundred, you must protect it from the perils that the world holds. In Chapter 15, "Caring for Antiques," you read about protection as it relates to cleaning, preserving, and storing your old treasures. In this chapter, I'll discuss the other aspects of protection that you should also consider, such as from theft, fire, flood, and attack from other elements.

Who hasn't worried from time to time about protecting themselves, their loved ones, and their possessions from all sorts of disasters, natural or not? Such concerns are almost inevitable, so much are these occurrences a part of the times we live in. While you can't always prevent bad things from happening, you can control many factors that will minimize your risk. Preventing problems before they occur can also be a less costly approach than waiting until problems arise.

When it comes to ensuring the safety of a collection, some people go overboard to such an extreme that you almost expect to see an armed guard when you go to their homes. Others are surprisingly lax. The best approach is to protect your collection in much the same manner as you would when protecting your home and your loved ones from harm. It doesn't need to be difficult or expensive; in fact, there are many simple actions that you can and should take as a matter of route regardless of how much you collect and what it is worth. The easiest and sanest approach consists of three steps: Use common sense, take appropriate precautions, and document your collection in case of a loss.

Home security

Would it surprise you to learn that most people's homes fall far short of being truly safe and sound? Chances are pretty good that you're in this group as well, especially if you are one of the millions of Americans who rely on nothing more than basic protective devices such as window and door locks to secure their homes from intruders. In 1997, there were 2.43 million burglaries and 489,000 robberies (both residential and commercial) in the United States. It's somewhat sad, as homes are often one of the largest financial assets people have to protect; but the truth is that most people don't get serious about home security until something happens that forces them into it.

Obviously, if you live in a low-crime area, you don't need the kind of complex security system that those living in high-crime areas feel safest

Bright Idea
If you don't know what your neighborhood's crime record is, check with your local police department to see if they keep crime statistics broken down by neighborhood or specific areas of your town or city.

with. But random acts of burglary and theft can happen anywhere and at any time, and one of the best ways to prevent such incidents from happening to you is to construct as many barriers to it as you can.

If it's been awhile since you've taken a careful assessment of your home's security level, or you've never done it before, take the time to do it now. It will help you spot problem areas that can be easily fixed, such as loose door locks or a gate that needs repairing, and it also will help you decide if you need a higher level of protection than what you currently have.

The basics

The following list details the basic things to look at as you evaluate your home's exterior appearance. As you do your assessment, keep a pad and pencil handy to note any areas of concern:

- The condition of your home in general. Does it give the image of being safe and secure? Houses that look a little run down invite burglary, as they are easier to enter, especially if screens are torn or have holes, or door locks appear to be loose.

- If you have a fenced yard, is the fence in good shape? Are gates kept closed and locked?

- The status of garage doors and windows. Are they kept open or closed during the day? How about at night?

- The condition and level of exterior lighting.

- The size and condition of shrubs near the home.

- The type and condition of doors and windows.

Unofficially...
Many break-ins—an estimated 23 percent—happen through first-floor windows, especially the side and rear windows of homes, which are often obstructed from view by trees, fences, and shrubs.

Quick fixes

Once you've completed your evaluation, you can start improving your home's security level. These are some of the quickest and easiest things you can do:

- Replace all burned-out exterior light bulbs. Lights not on motion detectors should be turned on at dusk and turned off at dawn, or placed on timers or photoelectric cells that will do this.

- Trim shrubs to below the level of your main floor windows.

- Keep the garage door closed and locked. According to the National Burglar & Fire Alarm Association, nine percent of all residential intrusions happen through the garage. People with young children sometimes leave their garage doors up if their children are playing in the yard or in the driveway, but this isn't a good idea. Even if you have nothing inside the garage besides cars, keep the door down. You don't want to give any clues about what your house contains to anyone who might be driving by. If your garage is designed with a side access door, encourage your kids to use it instead, and keep it locked when not in use. Eliminating free access to the garage will take some getting used to for you and your kids, but it's worth the effort in the long run.

- Fix all torn screens or screens that have holes in them.

- Tighten any loose doorknobs.

- If windowpanes are cracked or loose, replace them. Also replace or repair any broken window locks.

Bright Idea
Be sure to get estimates from more than one home security company. Compare cost and coverage before deciding on a specific system.

Not-so-quick fixes

The fixes listed below will take more time, effort, and money, but they're well worth considering:

- If your doors don't have deadbolt locks, have them installed in addition to your existing doorknobs and locks. Choose locks with a one-inch or longer hardened steel shaft for the greatest protection.

- Add window stops or wood or metal bars to your windows to prevent them from being opened from the outside.

- If yours is an older home with overgrown evergreens or junipers planted near it, consider having them removed. They can obstruct your view to the street and provide hiding places for burglars.

- If you have an extensive and highly valuable collection, and you live in a high-crime area, consider having metal grilles installed over your windows. If your doors are made of glass and wood, think about replacing them with security doors, which are constructed of steel and wood and are difficult to kick in. Glass doors, while aesthetically beautiful, are vulnerable to break-ins, sliding glass doors especially so.

- If your exterior lighting consists of front and back porch lights and little else, it's highly advisable to add more. Floodlights with photoelectric cells or motion detectors are relatively inexpensive to install. Other exterior lights to consider are walkway lights and garden lights. Accent lighting such as wallwashers, which illuminate the walls of your home, and uplights,

Moneysaver
Improving your exterior lighting doesn't have to be expensive. Low-voltage garden lights are economical and easy to install, and they'll make a big difference in how your home looks at night.

used to highlight shrubs and trees, also can be strong deterrents to burglars.

These are just some of the things you can do to improve the existing condition of your home while increasing its security. However, the best security programs, experts say, consist of layers of different types of protection, the theory being that if one is ineffective in stopping an intruder, another one will do the job. The next layer of protection for most people, and one that you may find yourself considering as well, is electronic security.

Home security systems

Electronic home alarm systems, also called home security systems, used to be rather scarce and quite expensive, but they're not so today. Because they can be so effective at preventing trouble from happening, more and more homeowners have found these systems to be well worth their expense—by the end of 1998, an estimated one in five homes was electronically protected. Increased demand for services and technological improvements have also made these systems less costly than they once were, with the average price dropping from $1,509 in 1990 to $1,200 in 1998.

Although hard statistics on the number of burglaries that security systems prevent are not available, most police departments believe that alarms deter burglary attempts. In 1994, the International Association of Chiefs of Police passed a board resolution stating that professionally installed and monitored alarm systems are useful in deterring crime and providing peace of mind.

Security systems range from fairly simple to quite complex, and come with prices to match. Depending on the size of the systems and their features, they can range from several hundred dollars to $5,000 and more, especially if they include such advanced technology as fingerprint recognition. They all consist of three basic elements:

- A control unit, which functions as the brain of the system.

- Sensors that detect problems, such as smoke or an open window or door, which are installed on doors and windows and inside the home. The sensors mounted on doors and windows are designed to protect the perimeter of the home by sensing breaks in the system (that is, a window or door being opened). Interior sensors are primarily designed to detect motion or fire and generally consist of photo relay sensors, or photoelectric eyes; passive infrared sensors, which detect both movement and the heat given off by the human body; and smoke sensors. Sensors that detect drastic changes in temperature are also common; so, too, are strategically placed panic buttons that can be pressed during an emergency.

- A warning device, such as a bell or siren. Strobe lights are sometimes used, and are a good idea if the alarm system is in the home of a hearing-impaired individual.

- A touchpad, used to tell the system what to do.

These elements can exist as parts of a system installed in a home or apartment, or they can be contained in one portable unit that you can take with you wherever you go. For complete home security, individual component systems are the most prevalent and the most effective because they can be adapted to a wide variety of needs and can be expanded if necessary. However, you shouldn't

Moneysaver
Many insurance companies offer reduced rates to policy holders with security systems. Be sure to check if yours does.

entirely dismiss the thought of a portable unit. If you're living in an apartment, they're really the only option that makes sense since most buildings don't allow the installation of component systems. And they're great to take along when you're traveling if you have expensive items with you.

It is possible to install security systems yourself, and this option is growing in favor with many homeowners, thanks to new wireless technology that makes them easier to install than the older hardwired systems. However, doing it yourself also means that you have to deal with such issues as permits and compliance with any local regulations that may be in place regarding the use of residential security systems. For this reason, some people still prefer to have home security companies do it for them.

Hiring an expert

When you have a home security company do the work for you, you're getting the benefit of an entity with years of experience in this particular field. Not only are these companies extremely knowledgeable when it comes to knowing how to protect homes and loved ones, they're also extremely adept at custom tailoring security systems to meet individual needs.

One of the best places to find such companies is your local edition of the Yellow Pages. Chances are good that you'll find both locally owned and operated companies and national service providers listed. While national companies tend to be better known, don't immediately eliminate the others from your consideration. Some people feel they get better service from smaller local companies than they do from large national concerns.

What to expect

Generally, any company you call will set a time for a service representative to come to your home to assess your security needs and design a system to match them. Most often you'll be asked to pay separately for installation and equipment costs and to sign a monitoring agreement for service. Multiyear agreements are often required; their length will vary depending on the individual company. Most companies bill quarterly for the service.

Be extremely careful to read the fine print on any contracts you sign, and make sure you understand all the terms and conditions of your agreement. A particular point to note is whether you're purchasing or leasing the equipment. Many companies offer both. Leasing can be preferable to buying a system outright since you're only paying for the use of the equipment, but it also can be more problematic, especially if you cancel your contract for any reason before it expires. Security companies make their money on monitoring, not on equipment, and they will do all they can to protect their investment, including removal of the leased equipment and suing the homeowner for the balance of the unexpired contract.

Another important point to clarify is the monitoring that will be provided. Most security systems are monitored by central stations, where staff will respond to a tripped alarm in about 30 to 60 seconds, and notify the numbers designated by the homeowner if the alarm is not false. These numbers usually include the local police station.

In the past, security systems were wired into the home; however, wireless systems are now available that transmit their signals by radio waves rather than

Moneysaver
Many security
companies will
give you some
sort of discount
on longer-term
service contracts
(for example,
one month free
for every year of
the agreement).

electronically. These systems, which operate on the same 900 MHz frequency as do newer cordless phones, are more expensive than the traditional wired systems; be prepared to spend about double what you normally would. The cost is enough to deter many people from considering them, but for many homes without crawl spaces or attics, they are the only option. They also appeal to people who don't want their walls, floors, or ceilings drilled into for installation purposes.

Having a security system is one of the most foolproof methods of protecting your home, your family, and your belongings, but its effectiveness is diminished if you don't use it properly or if you do not adhere to other security measures. The following tips will help you maximize your system's value and effectiveness:

- Get into the habit of using it regularly. It takes some time to adjust to having a security system, and you'll speed up the adjustment if you use it from the beginning. Experts recommend using security systems on a daily basis, even if you're at home, rather than just when you're away from the house or on vacation.

- Learn how to use all the features of your system. If you've purchased a system with all the bells and whistles, don't diminish your investment by not using them. If you're having trouble learning or remembering them all, ask your security company to come out and instruct you again. Along these lines, make sure you're not the only person in your family who knows how to use the system. Basic functions should be taught to all members of the house who are old enough to understand the

features, especially those who are old enough
to stay home alone.

- If you assign a temporary security code to
  allow someone access to your home on a limited basis, be sure to erase the code once the
  access period is over.

Remember, a security system is just one part of
your overall protection plan. Don't get lax about
other protective efforts just because you have one.
It's always a good idea to do such things as placing
very valuable objects away from where they could
easily be seen from the street and keeping shades
and drapes drawn at night and while you're away.
Other security measures to keep in mind include

- Checking the identity of service people entering your home. Many companies now use sub-
  contractors to assist them, and these people
  may or may not have clear physical identification in the way of emblems on uniforms or sig-
  nage on trucks. However, they should always
  have some form of picture identification as
  well as a work order from the company that
  hired them. If you have any concerns, don't
  hesitate to call the company directly.

- If for any reason your collection is going to be
  photographed in your home, ask that your
  identity and address remain anonymous.

- If you're going on vacation or will be away
  from home for an extended period of time,
  make your residence look like it's being lived
  in. Lights should be on variable timers so they
  don't go on and off at the same time every day,
  grass should be mowed and flowers watered.
  Although the advice used to be to stop mail

> **"**
> You have to love
> the things you
> collect, but they
> can't ever be so
> precious that
> they take over
> your life.
> — Marjorie Reed
> Gordon, *Elle
> Décor*
> **"**

and newspaper delivery, experts now say it's better to have a trusted neighbor or friend pick up these items when they're delivered to your home and keep them until you return.

Add-ons to consider

When you meet with a security company consultant, you may be presented with some options that add increased functionality to your security system but are not essential to the basic operation of the system. They may or may not be worth considering, depending on their cost and what you wish to achieve with your security system. Here are a few that I would recommend taking a second look at if your budget permits:

- Closed-circuit camera. I thought this was a fairly silly device to have until I moved into a home with a long, narrow hallway that didn't allow me to see who was ringing my doorbell until I got up to the door. Now, all I have to do is flip on my television—the camera transmits its signal to an unused channel—and I can see exactly who's there. This also is a great device to have if you own a larger home or if your office is in your home, as it can save you from responding to a lot of unwanted callers.

- Intercom system. If the thought of putting your front door under video surveillance isn't your cup of tea, think about installing an intercom there instead. It's not my preference, as it forces you into establishing voice contact with whomever is at your door, but some people like them better than cameras.

- Wireless remote controllers. This is an expense that I feel is well worth the money, and they're generally not all that expensive. These devices,

Unofficially...
Statistics show that 80 percent of all break-ins are through a door. Doors with low visibility from the street and neighbors are particularly vulnerable.

which usually look like the keyring controllers used to lock and unlock a car or arm and disarm a car alarm from a distance, let you operate your security system from outside of your home. For example, you can pull up to your garage and disarm the system before you enter your house, or you can turn lights on from the front of your driveway before reaching your home. A console version also can be placed inside your home to allow you to turn on and off any lights or appliances that are equipped with a receiver module. I have used both types of controllers and really liked them.

Protecting against fire and other disasters

Burglars are not the only unwanted visitors that can enter your home. So can water, fire, and non-human pests. A home security plan really isn't complete unless you address these concerns as well.

Eliminating fire hazards

Fire is one of the most devastating things that can happen in a home, but it's also one of the disasters easiest to prevent. Start by surveying your property regularly to spot any obvious hazards, such as flammable materials in the home or garage or frayed electrical cords. If you have flammable materials around, such as rags soaked in turpentine, paint thinner, or other flammable liquids, either throw them away or store them in a fireproof box.

These items can ignite by spontaneous combustion, which means that you should never throw them in the washer or dryer; this also goes for rags used to polish cars because car polish usually contains flammable chemicals. Replace any electrical cords that are in less than optimal condition.

Bright Idea
Insurance companies and fire departments are good sources of information on ways to protect your home from fire and other disasters.

Bright Idea
If your smoke detectors are battery-operated (not hardwired into your home security system), their batteries will need to be replaced twice a year. An easy way to remember to do it is to change them when daylight savings time begins and ends.

Other precautionary measures to take include

- Regularly checking furnaces, boilers, and stoves to make sure they work properly. Change the filters on them frequently.

- Cleaning chimneys on woodburning fireplaces or stoves annually. It's a good idea even if you don't use them very often. Built-up creosote can cause a fire or explosion.

- Installing smoke detectors. If you don't have them installed as part of a security system, you can put up battery-operated stand-alone devices. They should be placed in every room of your home, or, in the case of a bathroom, a few feet outside of the door. Be sure to use the exhaust fan when you take a shower to prevent excessive steam build-up near these detectors, which can trigger a false alarm and shorten the life of the batteries in them. Keeping the bathroom door shut when taking a steamy shower helps, too.

- Having at least one fire extinguisher in your home. This is the bare minimum; a better idea is locating one on each floor of your home, or in each primary living area if your house is on one level. If you're going with only one, the best place to put it is in or near the kitchen.

Water damage

If you live in an area prone to flooding, you are probably already paying for flood insurance in addition to your homeowner's insurance. However, even in areas where heavy rain and flooding are uncommon, both can happen in a flash if the conditions are right. While you can't prevent either from taking place, you can guard your valuables from damage caused by minor flooding by taking a few easy steps:

■ Keep your gutters clean. An especially heavy rain can overflow even a clear gutter if it doesn't have the capacity to handle the water. If your gutters are clogged with leaves and branches, water can back up behind your gutters and under your roof flashing, where it can then enter your home.

■ Don't leave windows open in rooms where rain is most likely to come in. Even if you're home when a storm hits, you may not get around to closing them before damage is done.

■ Don't store valuables in the basement. Even the driest basements can sometimes get water in them. If you must use your basement for storage, raise your valuables off the floor by putting them on inexpensive plastic or metal racks. Furniture can be placed on cement blocks covered with mover's mats, old towels, bedspreads, whatever. Just make sure these items aren't touching the ground as they can pick up any moisture that's there.

Along these lines, attics aren't the greatest storage places, either. As with basements, even the soundest roof can leak if the conditions are right. If you must store pieces up there or in the rafters of a garage, try to give them some protection from the elements by draping them with plastic. Don't wrap them in it; you want to allow enough room for air to circulate freely around these objects.

Pest damage

I recently went out to my very secure garage (so I thought) to retrieve one of my old saddles for its annual cleaning and conditioning. As I lifted one of the flaps to clean the girth straps under it, I discovered that several had nearly been nibbled away. This saddle had been stored properly in a heavy canvas bag and in a trunk, away, I thought, from anything that would harm it. But sure enough, some sort of pest had worked its way into the trunk and eaten through the canvas cover right to the leather.

Antiques made of paper, canvas, fiber, and wood are especially vulnerable to insects and pests; leather is a favorite munchie for mice, rats, and squirrels. For these reasons, regular pest inspections are another "to-do" item to add to your home survey list.

Be sure to check both the exterior and interior of your house, garage, and any other spaces where you may be storing your valuables. If you see any obvious gaps in walls, floors, and ceilings, make sure you get them plugged with the appropriate material. Even a slight gap should be sealed; rats, for example, can literally collapse their skeletons, which allows them to squeeze into places that you would swear they couldn't reach. Remove any nests you see. Also, be sure to check anything you have stored for any signs of damage. It's a good idea to do this at least twice a year; quarterly is even better.

Another clue to vermin infestation is droppings, which you may find even if you don't see any other visual signs of rats or mice making their homes amongst your belongings. Don't assume that it's a one-time deal if you do see droppings; chances are pretty good that the pests are not just coming in from the rain. Either put out rat poison yourself, taking great care to keep it away from children or pets, or call a professional exterminator to do the job for you.

Also, make sure your house is kept clean and picked up at all times. Don't do anything that would give pests a chance to nest in your home. Years ago, I knew a couple in Washington, D.C., who were finishing part of their basement as a playroom for their young son. The carpenters were leaving a large pile of wood scraps and sawdust in a corner of the basement that wasn't being worked on, with the intention of cleaning it up when they were done. A family of mice took up residence there before the workmen removed it. Their presence was discovered before too much damage was done, but the situation shouldn't have developed in the first place.

If bugs are your problem, your best bet is to call an exterminator. Retail sprays and baits are effective, but these professionals really know how to get to the root of the problem. Rarely is it possible to eradicate such problems entirely, so you may get to know your extermination company quite well. If this is the case, it's often a good idea to sign an annual service contract rather than calling on someone to come out when you spot signs of a problem.

The bugs that most often cause problems are moths, mites, carpet beetles, wood-boring beetles, and silverfish.

When the earth moves

If you live near a major faultline, there's a good chance that you're already aware of it. But there are also many underground faults that we don't know about, which means that an earthquake could occur just about anyplace.

Again, there's really nothing you can do to avoid the occurrence of the event, and, frankly, if you're living in an area that is not prone to earthquakes, you'll probably want to just take your chances that

Watch Out!
Always ask for references and credentials of any company you hire to perform a service for you. Checking with the Better Business Bureau isn't a bad idea either, but they will only report whether or not a particular company has had any complaints filed against it.

one won't occur. However, if you are in earthquake territory, here are some actions you can take to protect your valuables from damage:

- Firmly attach all display cases, bookcases, and other storage units to the wall. Yes, doing so will cut down on your decorating flexibility, but it's much better to work around an immovable bookcase than it is to find that bookcase lying prone on the floor with your collection of art glass cracked to pieces underneath it.

- Install shelves with raised lips along the front and sides. While they won't prevent items from crashing to the floor during large shocks, they can keep objects from tipping off the edges during minor tremors.

- Anchor pieces on shelves with museum wax or putty. These products, which are available under such brand names as Anchor Wax, Stickum, Quake Hold!, and Collector's Hold!, have just enough stickiness to secure objects in place but allow them to easily be picked up and moved when necessary. It's available at craft stores and at some department or hardware stores. Antiques shops and malls sometimes stock it as well. It also can be ordered from companies that sell conservation materials. You'll find a list in Appendix B, "Resource List".

- Make sure shelves are securely fastened inside cabinets. Again, this might cut down on your decorating options a little, but it's better to have shelves bolted securely in place than to rest them on the adjustable pegs that many shelving and storage units come with. The shocks from an earthquake can cause shelves

Timesaver
If you're out of museum wax and you need to secure an item, check to see if you have any wax earplugs around. They are sticky enough to hold small items in place. Modeling clay will work in a pinch as well.

to come unseated from these pegs and make them crash down on anything below them.

These precautions can also help save valuable treasures during hurricanes and tornadoes, but only to a certain extent. Little really can be done if your home is in the path of either of them, especially if they're very severe. When it comes to hurricanes, there's usually enough warning given so you can take the necessary precautions—fastening down shutters and boarding up windows, for example—and you may even have time to gather some of your possessions to take with you if you're advised to move to storm shelters. However, you should never endanger your life for your antiques; if time is short, leave them behind. In cases like this, your best protection is adequate insurance.

The ultimate protection: insurance

Insurance is good protection to have for your valuables. It can be expensive, especially when collections are extensive and costly, but many collectors believe that it's much better to pay the premiums necessary to insure adequate coverage than to be caught short if something happens to their treasures.

If you're just starting out as an antiques collector, or the value of your collection isn't that high, your existing homeowner's policy might provide enough coverage without the use of additional schedules or riders. However, the acquisition of just one piece can be enough to exceed the limits of a standard policy, especially if it's a significant item, or you may find that your policy doesn't cover issues specific to fine items. Theft, for example, may be covered, while breakage or loss is not.

It's a good idea to start with your current insurer and the policy you have in place to see if your

Unofficially...
If the total value for any one type of item exceeds $1,000, you may not be adequately covered.

coverage is adequate. If it should be increased, your current company may be able to provide you with a new policy that is specially tailored for covering art and other valuable possessions. If not, you'll need to shop for one that can. If you have a full-service insurance agent, start with this person. If not, look for insurance companies that offer such things as art and valuable possession coverage.

Whichever company you choose should schedule a time for a representative to meet with you and design an insurance package tailored to your needs. Desirable features of such policies include

- Automatic coverage for new acquisitions. This gives you a period of time—a month, in most cases—to get new purchases listed on your policy. It's a great feature to have if you're on an extended trip and you're acquiring antiques along the way.

- Worldwide coverage. You're protected no matter where you are.

- Low or no deductible. A deductible will limit the amount you recover. Most collectors prefer to pay a higher price for their insurance coverage and recover the full amount of an object should loss or damage occur.

- Automatic value adjustment. This feature automatically factors in appreciation and adjusts the values of your possessions without your having to have new appraisals done.

- Individual coverage for each item. This allows you to list and insure each item for a specific amount. However, some people prefer the convenience of blanket coverage, which lets you select a total amount of coverage for each category of your belongings rather than listing each item separately.

- Flexible loss recovery. This feature lets you replace an item if you choose to do so and if you can, or you can take a cash settlement and do what you want with it. When it comes to antiques, the latter usually is preferred as it allows more flexibility in replacing lost or damaged items.

If the cost of the insurance is too high, ask about insuring some pieces instead of the entire collection.

Each insurance company has its own way of providing coverage, and it's a good idea to talk to several to see what they offer and what they require of you as a client. In most cases, you'll be asked to provide appraisals for items over a certain dollar amount. For other items, you'll probably only be asked for a good description of each object and its estimated value.

Record Keeping

If you purchase fine arts or collectible coverage, your insurance company will keep detailed records of your belongings as part of the service they provide to you, but you'll have to start the process off on the right foot by providing them good information to work with. Both you and your insurer will find it easiest to work with records that are in order. If you have a large collection, you'll also want to inventory it.

Documenting your collection can take time that you'd rather spend doing something else, but you'll find that it's worth the effort in the long run. Such documentation should include the following:

- What the object is; for example, a Mission-style chair or a Rookwood vase.

- A description of the object. Be very specific. Note the maker or the artist, if you know who it is. Also note the object's size, age, color, material of manufacture, its identifying marks, and anything else that could be used to identify the piece.

- A clear photograph of the object. If your photo processor doesn't automatically put the date on the back of the prints, do it yourself so you and the insurance company know when the shots were taken.

- The object's condition. Again, be very specific. Make note of every little scratch and ding.

- The date you acquired it, from whom, and where.

- How much you paid. Keep the original receipt or a photocopy with your records for documentation purposes. If you don't have a receipt, a canceled check will work. If you don't have a canceled check, you'll need to create some sort of written record detailing what the object's purchase price was.

- Its appraisal or current market value.

- Anything else you know about the piece that could add to its value.

Your inventory can be kept in a notebook or binder, or you can use a computer program that has been developed especially for this purpose (you'll find some of them listed in Appendix B). Both methods have their advantages and disadvantages. Paper-based systems, for example, are more flexible than computer-based programs, as you can basically set them up as you wish, although most computer-based programs also allow for some customization. If you decide to use a computer-based program, it will streamline record keeping somewhat, but you'll still have to keep some files for such things as receipts and appraisals.

If you have a digital camera, storing your information on a computer makes a great deal of sense, as you can store digital images of your collection on the computer as well. However, you'll want to make sure that you have a back-up copy of this information in case your system crashes or your computer is stolen.

While I like the convenience that computerized inventory systems can afford, I still prefer my old paper-based system. I like browsing through my binders (although my current collections are small enough to be contained in one large binder, I've kept the others for a variety of reasons). And, after many years of trial and error, I've finally developed a system that works well. Here's what it looks like:

- Choose a binder large enough to allow for some expansion, but not so large that you can't handle it easily. I like the two- or three-inch D-ring binders that you can get at any office supply store. The D-ring, in my opinion, allows pages to be moved back and forth a little easier than the standard round ring binder does.

- Group each category being collected behind a different tabbed divider. I also insert a manila envelope in each division (with holes punched on its side) for storing receipts, appraisals, and other papers that I don't want to punch holes in, such as pertinent magazine articles, newspaper clippings, and other information.

Bright Idea
Always keep two copies of your inventory. Keep one in a safe deposit box at the bank or in another secure location. If your inventory is stored on disk, make sure you have a printout of it as well.

You also can use a manila pocket for this purpose, but you then run the risk of items falling out of it.

■ Give every object its own page. I start by putting the name of the object at the top of the page, followed by a photo of the object and various informational items about it. For the best preservation of the information on each page, either use acid-free paper or slip each sheet into a plastic sheet protector. If you choose the plastic protector route, buy the best ones you can afford. They'll last longer and they're less likely to stick to photographs and each other.

■ Although I generally start by keeping alphabetical track of the pieces in my collections, my binders usually end up in chronological order by purchase. Either way is perfectly valid; however, the chronological order seems to make the most sense.

Be sure to add each piece you acquire to your inventory as soon as you can. Also, update your inventory at least once a year to reflect current market prices or any new appraisals you may have received. Provide your insurance company with these updates as well to make sure that your coverage is maintained at an appropriate level.

Just the facts

■ The security in and around most homes can and should be improved.

■ An annual or semi-annual inspection of the interior and exterior of your home and garage will help you spot potential problems before they erupt.

- The presence of one intruding bug or animal usually means there are others lurking. Hire an expert to control them.

- Keeping complete records of your collection is one of the best ways to protect against loss in any situation.

Glossary

Absentee bid A bidding method for those who cannot or do not wish to attend an auction in person. Also known as order bid.

Adapted An older, sometimes period piece that has been altered for modern use.

Altered A piece that has been substantially changed in appearance.

Antiques Objects of substantial age, usually 100 years or more, that are prized for their beauty, age, condition, rarity, workmanship, and design.

Antiques malls Medium to large buildings that house a number of individual antiques dealers.

Antiquities Handmade items manufactured prior to 1830.

Appraisal The determination of the approximate monetary worth of an item or collection.

Appraiser An individual considered to be expert in the technique of determining the monetary value of an item.

Art Deco (1918–1935) A French furniture style that uses veneers and lacquer to create a sleek, streamlined look. A distinctive element of Art Deco design is the bleached or light-colored wood used to create most of these pieces.

Art Nouveau (1895–1915) A French furniture style characterized by whiplash curves and organic ornamentation.

Arts and Crafts Movement (1850–1900) A design movement that emphasized simple, hand-made objects of good workmanship and quality materials.

As is A legal term designating that the property is being sold without any representations or warranties.

Assembled A set whose pieces are similar in appearance but do not match. In England, they are referred to as Harlequin sets.

Auction A method of selling objects where each item is placed before an audience and competitive bids are solicited.

Auction catalogs Booklets or brochures published in advance of an auction containing written descriptions, photographs of lots being offered for sale, the terms and conditions of the sale, a glossary of terms related to the description of lots, etc.

Auction houses Establishments that sell merchandise at public auction.

Auctioneer The individual who conducts an auction.

Authenticity The determination of whether an item is real or fake.

Authorship The identity of the creator, period, culture, source, or origin of an object.

Automatic bid A service provided by Internet auction companies that automatically increases bids according to predetermined parameters established between the buyer and auction company. Also known as proxy bidding.

Bait and switch A fraudulent scheme where a purchaser is enticed into paying for an item only to be delivered another item in its place.

Baroque A furniture style emphasizing a grand scale and heavy embellishment. Popular during the 1600s and early 1700s.

Bears a signature, bears a date, or bears an inscription Someone has added information to an object that it didn't originally bear.

Beauty The aesthetic appeal of an object.

Bidding guidelines The processes and procedures established by auction companies to facilitate the bidding process.

Boot sales The European equivalent of the modern American flea market, where sellers drive in, open the trunks (boots) of their cars, and start hawking products.

Bought in A lot at auction that has no bids or does not meet its reserve. Also referred to as pass in or unsold.

Buyer's premium An amount added by auction houses to the winning bid on a lot.

Catalog or mail auctions Auctions conducted over the telephone or by mail, offering special merchandise geared to a well-defined collecting audience.

Caveat emptor A Latin phrase meaning Let the buyer beware.

Charity auctions Auctions conducted to raise funds for charitable organizations.

Chippendale (1755–1780) Named after the English cabinetmaker Thomas Chippendale. Distinguishing elements of Chippendale style include claw-and-ball feet at the ends of cabriole legs and the open back splat on chairs.

Circa At or around a specified date.

Collectibles Objects other than antiques that are sought after and accumulated by collectors.

Collecting category An established group of objects that are sought after and accumulated by collectors.

Collection An accumulation of like objects that represents a distinct interest in an artistic style or subject.

Collectors People who acquire and assemble antiques and other desirable objects.

Colonial Revival (1875–1910) A Victorian-era furniture style inspired by Colonial America.

Complete or in entirety Everything is being offered for sale. Used at estate sales and auctions.

Condition An object's state of being.

Conditions of sale The specific legal terms that control a sale.

Conservation The process of preserving the condition of antiques.

Consignee An entity that accepts the property of another for the purpose of selling it to a third party.

Consignment Placing property with an agent for sale to a third party, or the property that is consigned.

Consignment shops Antiques shops that sell items owned by others for a fee or commission.

Consignor The owner of a consigned item.

Contemporary A decorating style characterized by clean, simple lines, emphasizing modern technology.

Copy An exact reproduction of a piece.

Country auctions Auctions conducted on-site at a house or farm.

Country A decorating style emphasizing a back-to-basics look and feel reminiscent of farm living.

Cranberry glass A transparent, cherry-red glass made in England in the nineteenth century and later in America.

Cyberspace A colloquial term used to describe the electronic communications universe.

Discount A lowered price offered to a seller to entice a purchase.

Divorce An item that has been split apart to create two or more new pieces.

Dutch auctions Auctions where multiple identical objects are sold to a number of bidders at one price. Typically used in Internet auctions.

Eastlake Style (1872–1890) Pieces inspired by the design ideals of Charles Lock Eastlake, who advocated the reform of furniture design, calling for a return to high-quality craftsmanship, an honest use of materials, and the integration of form and function.

Eclectic A free-wheeling decorating style that combines pieces from various periods and styles that share common elements such as color, pattern, or personality.

E-commerce Business transacted on the Internet.

E-mail   A short term for electronic mail, used to communicate in writing on the Internet.

Empire (1820–1840)   A furniture style popular during Napoleon's time in both Europe and America. Sometimes called Late Federal.

Ephemera   Antiques made of paper, such as autographs, letters, and other documents.

Escrow agents   Individuals or companies who facilitate business transactions between buyers and sellers.

Estate auctions   Auctions held to liquidate an estate.

Estate sales   Sales held to liquidate an estate.

Execution   The quality of manufacture of a work of art.

Fair market value   The price an object is likely to achieve if offered for sale at an auction.

Fair warning   A term used by auctioneers that gives buyers a final chance to bid before a lot is sold.

False bidding   Entering bids to drive up the price of items at auction.

Fantasy   A form that didn't exist when the original items were manufactured.

Federal (1780–1820)   A furniture style influenced by the revival of classical design elements that comprised Neoclassicism, which swept through Europe after the ancient Roman ruins of Herculaneum and Pompeii were excavated in 1738 and 1748. It is distinguished by straight lines rather than curved, and classical decorative devices such as the Greek key and the urn.

Final value fees   Fees assessed to online sellers based on the final sale price of each item.

Flea markets Bazaars that feature second-hand articles.

Fraud A deceptive act perpetrated for financial gain.

Gavel The hammer used by an auctioneer to signal the beginning and end of an auction.

Glossary of terms An explanation of the terms used to describe antiques at an auction. It defines the portion of the description, if any, that the auction house is prepared to warrant.

Gothic Revival (1825–1865) A design style that incorporated Gothic arches, quatrefoils, and trefoils to lend a medieval feeling to pieces. It was more popular in England than America and was used more in American architecture than furniture.

Hammer price The amount of the final bid for an object sold at auction.

Highlights only An estate auction term meaning that only selected pieces of the estate will be sold.

Historical significance The existence of an identifiable connection to a historical person or event.

Increment The amount by which bidding is increased at auction.

In-home shops Antiques shops operated from a home, barn, or garage, often in conjunction with a furniture refinishing or antiques restoration business.

Insertion fees The fees charged to list items for sale at an online auction.

Internet The worldwide communications network that allows computer users to access other users and databases around the world.

Internet cookies   A software device used by many Internet sites to collect information on the people who visit them.

Internet portals   Connections to the Internet offered through services such as America Online and Prodigy.

Internet service providers   Companies that facilitate connection to the Internet through a telephone or a coaxial cable.

Jacobean   King James I (1603–1625) was the ruling monarch when the earliest American colonies were founded. Furniture from this period is called Jacobean in his honor.

Junk shops   Retail establishments that feature second- or third-hand merchandise often in poor condition and needing repair.

Knocked down   An auction house term signifying the sale of an object. When an item is knocked down, it is considered sold to the highest bidder.

Limited warranty   A warranty that guarantees certain aspects of an item while excluding others.

Listing option fees   Costs related to various options that sellers can use to highlight items in an Internet auction.

Live auction   The most common form of auctions, these events bring buyers and sellers together in a single room for a specific period of time.

Markup   The amount added to the wholesale price of an object to obtain a retail price.

Marriage   Two separate pieces that have been joined together to form one.

Medium   The materials used to create a work of art.

Mission The defining style of the Arts and Crafts Movement, furniture in this style had a functional "mission," hence the name. Pieces in the Mission style are distinguished by their boxiness and solid appearance.

Newsgroups Internet sites dedicated to a specific interest.

Online antiques malls Internet Web sites that list multiple antiques dealers.

Online auctions Auctions held on the Internet.

Online chat rooms Web sites where users can conduct real-time conversations by typing messages that instantly appear on screen.

Online communities Subject-specific Web sites that combine bulletin boards and newsgroups with other content.

Pack-rat shops Dirty, poorly lit antiques shops that are crammed with merchandise.

Paddle The implement used to signal the entry of a bid for a lot at an auction.

Parlor shops Antiques stores that feature an eclectic blend of ornate furniture and decorative pieces.

Partial contents An estate auction term indicating that only a portion of an estate is being sold.

Partial listing or in part An advertising term indicating that more items are available than what are listed in an ad.

Period Indicates pieces that were made during the original time frame for the design.

Pickers Freelance buying and selling agents.

Presale estimate The price range that an object is expected to sell in at auction.

Preservation Actions taken to preserve the condition of an antique.

Preview The opportunity given to prospective bidders to examine objects that are to be offered for sale at an auction.

Price guides Books that list approximate market values of items in established collecting categories.

Price list Published by auction houses, these lists detail the final prices of items that have been sold.

Price realized The successful bid price of an item sold at auction.

Private auctions Auctions where the identities of bidders are concealed.

Provenance The history of an object's ownership.

Proxy bidding A form of bidding that grants an entity the authority to enter bids for an absentee bidder.

Queen Anne (1725–1755) A furniture style with simple and graceful lines, characterized by scrolls and sinuous "s" curves.

Rarity An item not commonly found.

Reconstructed A piece that fell apart and was put back together.

Refinished An item that has had its earlier finish removed and replaced.

Renaissance Revival (1860–1885) Pieces in the Renaissance Revival style are characterized by straight, rectangular forms rather that the curved and flowing lines of Rococo. Decoration was heavy and showy, with lots of medallions and trim. Many pieces incorporate bronze, porcelain, or mother of pearl plaques.

Replaced   A new part substituted for a period or older part.

Reproduction   Something that is produced as a copy of a style rather than a copy of an exact piece.

Reserve or reserve price   The confidential minimum price for sale established by agreement between a seller and auction house.

Reserve price auctions   Internet auctions that include items with reserve prices.

Restored   A piece that has been returned to what is believed to be its original appearance. Often used derogatorily.

Re-strike   A new item made from an original mold or pattern.

Revivalism   A general design influence that extended through the nineteenth century. As its name implies, it borrowed, or "revived" design elements from styles popular in earlier times.

Rococo Revival (1845–1900)   A Victorian furniture style that featured fanciful carvings, curved surfaces, and scrollwork in both "s" and "c" forms.

Rummage sales   Events where donated items such as clothing, books, small household items, and children's toys are sold to raise money for a charity or nonprofit organization.

Salting an auction   Including items in an auction from a dealer's existing inventory that have not been specifically consigned for the auction.

Scarcity   A measure of the relative abundance of a specific item.

Screen name   A name created by an Internet user to mask his or her true identity.

Search agent Special software that facilitates searches of many information indexes on the Internet.

Search engines Software that allows Internet information searches by key words or phrases.

Shaker A furniture style created by the Shakers, a religious sect that came to America from England in 1774. It is simple and functional but by no means plain.

Signed and dated The named artist inscribed and signed the work with his or her own hand.

Site See Web site.

Specialty shops Retail locations that offer a specific type of antiques.

Standard auctions Sales that offer a single item or group of items to one high bidder.

Style A specific or characteristic manner of expression, execution, construction, or design, as in "rococo style." Also used to denote a piece that is made in the fashion or nature of an earlier period but at a later time.

Subject matter The content or subject of a work of art. Examples are people, cities, animals, flowers, and landscapes.

Successful bid price The winning bid accepted by an auctioneer at an auction sale.

Surge protectors Devices installed between computers and power sources to protect against electrical surges.

Tea and crumpet shops Retail establishments operated by owners that specialize in silver, china, linens, textiles, and similar decorative objects.

Thrift shops Retail establishments that sell donated items.

Title A legal term denoting rightful ownership.

Trade periodicals Newspapers or magazines published on a regular schedule (weekly or monthly) and dedicated to a particular subject.

Traditional A decorating style that utilizes elegant and formal decor.

Ultraviolet (UV) radiation Light outside the visible spectrum that can cause damage through discoloration and drying.

Unique Used to describe an item that is believed to be the only one of its kind.

Uniqueness The peculiar qualities of an object that make it distinctive.

Unreserved or without reserve Items offered at an auction without a preset minimum price.

Usefulness The utilitarian quality of an object.

Victorian (1837–1901) The time period during which Queen Victoria reigned. Also used to describe the styles and mannerisms that evolved during this era.

Vintage An object of considerable age but not yet considered antique purely from an age perspective.

Warranty The guarantee by the seller given on an object or on various aspects of an object.

Web browser Software used to navigate the Web.

Web site The information stored at a specified electronic address on the Internet.

William and Mary (1700–1725) An eighteenth-century English style named after the Dutch king and queen who ruled England near the end of the century. Distinguishing features include elaborate lathe-turned legs, deep carvings, strong curves, contrasting colors created by lacquering, and a tapering scroll foot.

Windsor　An English chair style instantly recognized by its construction: Pieces made in this fashion have a plank seat to which stick legs and spindles are attached.

World Wide Web　Developed in the early 1990s, this technological advance added graphics and sound to the Internet and opened the door for much broader applications.

Resource List

Appraisal associations

American Society of Appraisers
P.O. Box 17265
Washington, DC 20041
1-800-272-8258
703-742-8471 Fax

Antique Appraisers Association of America
11361 Garden Grove Blvd.
Garden Grove, CA 92643
714-530-7090

Appraiser Association of America
386 Park Ave., Suite 2000
New York, NY 10016
212-889-5404

Appraisers National Association
120 S. Bradford Ave.
Placentia, CA 92670
714-579-1082

Art Dealers Association of America
575 Madison Ave.
New York, NY 10022
212-940-8590

International Society of Appraisers
16040 Christensen Rd., Suite 320
Seattle, WA 98188
206-241-0359

Mid-Am Antique Appraisers Association
P.O. Box 9681
Springfield, MO 65801
415-865-7269

Professional associations

American Association of Museums
1225 I St. NW
Washington, DC 20005
202-289-1818

Art and Antique Dealers League of America
353 E. 79th St.
New York, NY 10021
212-879-7558

Antiques Dealers Association of America
Box 335
Greens Farms, CT 06436
203-259-3844

Antiques Dealers Association of California
3232 Sacramento St.
San Francisco, CA 94115
415-567-9898

Connecticut Antique Dealers Association
104 Shepard's Knoll Dr.
Hamden, CT 06514
203-288-4356

Maine Antique Dealers Association
105 Mighty St.
Gorham, ME 04038
207-839-4855

National Antique and Art Dealers Association
of America
15 E. 57th St.
New York, NY 10022
212-826-9707

New Hampshire Antiques Dealers Association
RFD 1, Box 305C
Tilton, NH 03276
603-286-4908

Vermont Antique Dealers Association
55 Allen St.
Rutland, VT 05701
802-773-8630

Repair and Conservation Resources

American Institute for Conservation of Historic
and Artistic Works
1717 K St. NW, Suite 301
Washington, DC 20006
202-452-9328
202-452-9328 (fax)

Institute of Metal Repair
1558 S. Redwood
Escondido, CA 92025
619-747-5978

International Fabric Care Institute
12251 Tech. Rd.
Silver Springs, MD 20904
301-622-1900

National Institute for the Conservation of
Cultural Property
3299 K St. NW, #602
Washington, DC 20007
202-625-1495

Society of American Silversmiths
P.O. Box 3599
Cranston, RI 02910
401-461-3156

Silver Information Center
295 Madison Ave.
New York, NY 10017
201-891-7193

Sterling Silversmiths Guild of America
312A Wyndhurst Ave.
Baltimore, MD 21210
410-532-7062

Textile Conservation Center
Museum of American Textile History
800 N. Massachusetts Ave.
North Andover, MD 08145
508-686-0191

Professional Picture Framers Association
P.O. Box 7655
4305 Sarellen Rd.
Richmond, VA 23231
804-226-0430

Society of Gilders, Inc.
P.O. Box 50179
Washington, DC 20091
202-347-1171

Williamstown Regional Art Conservation
Laboratory, Inc.
225 South St.
Williamstown, MA 01267
413-458-5741
413-458-2314 (fax)

Intermuseum Laboratory
83 N. Main St.
Allen Art Bldg.
Oberlin, OH 44074
216-775-7331
216-774-3431 (fax)

Old World Restorations, Inc.
Cincinnati Art Conservation Center
347 Stanley Ave.
Cincinnati, OH 45226
800-878-1911
513-321-1911 (fax)

SPNEA Conservation Center
185 Lyman St.
Waltham, MA 02154
617-891-1985
617-893-7832 (fax)

Strong Museum
One Manhattan Sq.
Rochester, NY 14607
716-263-2700
716-263-2493 (fax)

Conservation, storage, and packing supply sources

Abatron, Inc.
33 Center Dr.
Gilberts, IL 60136
708-426-2200
Wood restoration products.

Albert Constantine and Sons, Inc.
2050 Eastchester Rd.
Bronx, NY 10461
1-800-223-8087
Wood, cane, and mother-of-pearl products.

Allied Resin Corp.
Weymouth Industrial Park
East Weymouth, MA 02189
617-337-6070
Resins and epoxies.

Antiques and Collectibles Restoration Services
1417 Third St.
Webster City, IA 50595
1-800-832-3828
Porcelain and glass restoration materials.

Andrews/Nelson/Whitehead
31-10 48th Ave.
Long Island City, NY 11101
718-937-7100
Complete line of restoration products.

Art Essentials of New York Ltd.
3 Cross St.
Suffern, NY 10901
914-368-1100
Gold-leaf supplies.

Brodart Company
500 Arch St.
Williamsport, PA 17705
1-800-233-8467
Complete line of refinishing products.

Broadnax Refinishing Products, Inc.
112 Carolina Forest
Chapel Hill, NC 27516
919-967-1011
Wood care products.

Colophon Book Arts Supplies
3046 Hoburn Bay Rd. NE
Olympia, WA 98155
206-3655-1188
Bookbinding and restoration supplies.

Competition Chemicals, Inc.
P.O. Box 820
Iowa Falls, IA 50126
515-648-5121
Metal restoration supplies.

Conservation Materials, Ltd.
1275 Kleppe Lane
Sparks, NV 89431
702-331-0582
A complete line of conservation products.

Conservation Resources International
8000 H Forbes Pl.
Springfield, VA 22151
703-321-0582
Archival materials.

Craftsman Wood Service Company
1735 West Cortland Ct.
Addison, IL 60101
708-629-3100
Wood finishing supplies.

D.A. Culpepper Mother of Pearl Company
P.O. Box 445
Franklin, NC 28734
704-524-6842
Mother-of-pearl, abalone, bone, and horn supplies.

Daly's Wood Finishing Products
3525 Stone Way N.
Seattle, WA 98103
1-800-735-7019
Wood finishing supplies.

Darworth Company
P.O. Box 639
3 Mill Pond Ln.
Simsbury, CT 06070
1-800-624-7767
Wood-patch and putty stick compounds.

DEMCO, Inc.
P.O. Box 7488
Madison, WI 53707-7488
1-800-356-1200
Acid-free paper, adhesives, and restoration supplies.

Easy Time Wood Refinishing Products Corp.
1208 Lisle Pl.
Lisle, IL 60532
708-515-1160
Wood refinishing products.

Environsafe Cleaning Products
P.O. Box 620356
Woodside, CA 94062
1-800-227-9744
A wide variety of environmentally safe wood, metal, and glass cleaning products.

Epoxy Technology, Inc.
14 Fortune Dr.
Billerica, MA 01821
1-800-227-2201
Epoxy supplies.

Exposures
41 S. Main St.
Norwalk, CT 06854
1-800-222-4947
Archival photographic supplies.

Finishing Products
8165 Big Bend
St. Louis, MO 63119
314-962-7575
Wood finishing and painting supplies.

Floyd J. Rosini
Rt. 22 North
Millerton, NY 12546
518-789-3582
Rosini brand wood refinishing products.

Fox River Paper Co.
200 E. Washington St., Suite 300
Appleton, WI 54913
414-733-7341
Archival supplies.

G. Schoepfer, Inc.
138 W. 31st St.
New York, NY 10001
203-250-7794
Glass and plastic replacement eyes for dolls and toys.

Garrett Wade Company
161 Avenue of the Americas
New York, NY 10013
212-807-1155
Woodworking tools and supplies.

Gaylord Brothers
Box 4901
Syracuse, NY 13221
1-800-448-6160
Archival storage supplies.

George Basch Company, Inc.
P.O. Box 188
Freeport, NY 11520
516-378-8100
Cotton wadding and polishing cloths.

H.F. Staples and Co., Inc.
Webb Dr., Box 956
Merrimack, NH 03054
603-889-8600
Staples brand wax and wood care supplies.

Hollinger Corporation
P.O. Box 8360
Fredericksburg, VA 22404
1-800-634-0491
Archival photographic supplies.

Homestead Paint and Finishes
P.O. Box 1668
111 Mulpus Rd.
Lunenburg, MA 01462
508-582-6426
Paint and finishing supplies.

Hope Co., Inc.
P.O. Box 749
12777 Pennridge Dr.
Bridgeton, MO 63044
314-739-7254
Wood refinishing supplies.

Howard Products, Inc.
411 W. Maple Ave.
Monrovia, CA 91016
818-357-9545
Existing finish restorer products.

I.P.G.R., Inc.
P.O. Box 205
Kulpsville, PA 19443
1-800-869-5633
Glass, porcelain, jade, metal, and ceramic restoration products.

Liberon/Star Supplies
P.O. Box 86
Mendocino, CA 95460
707-937-0375
Wood finishing supplies.

M. Swift and Sons, Inc.
10 Love Ln.
P.O. Box 150
Hartford, CT 06141
1-800-828-9629
Gold-leaf and metal-leaf products and supplies.

Marshall Imports
816 N. Seltzer St.
Crestline, OH 44827
1-800-992-1503
Antiquax waxes and polishes.

Masters Magic Products, Inc.
P.O. Box 31
Perry, TX 76677
1-800-548-6583
Wood refinishing supplies.

Mini-Magic
3675 Reed Rd.
Columbus, OH 43220
614-457-3687
Acid free papers, museum washing paste, oxygen bleach, and other textile repair products.

Mylan Enterprises, Inc.
P.O. Box 194, Dept. R
Morris Plains, NJ 07950
201-538-6154
Packing materials.

Nielson and Bainbridge
40 Eisenhower Dr.
Paramus, NJ 07653
201-368-9191
Alphamat conservation mat board.

Origina Luster
Box 2092, Dept. K
Wilkes-Barre, PA 18703
717-693-3624
Compounds to restore sick glass and black-light kits.

Paper Technologies, Inc.
929 Calle Negocio, #D
San Clemente, CA 92673
714-366-8799
Archival paper products.

Paxton Hardware Ltd.
P.O. Box 256
7818 Bradshaw Rd.
Upper Falls, MD 21156
410-592-8505
Period brass hardware and restoration cleaning supplies.

Q.R.B. Industries
3139 US 31 North
Niles, MI 49120
616-683-7903
Paint removers and refinishing supplies.

QH&F
Box 23927
Cola, SC 29224
1-800-421-7961
Gold-leaf and faux finishing products.

Restoration Technology
319 N. Tampa Ave.
Orlando, FL 32805
407-423-5480
A complete line of restoration supplies.

Solar Screen
53-11 105th St.
Corona, NY 11368
718-592-8222
Ultraviolet UV screens.

Strobelite Co., Inc.
430 W. 14th St., #500
New York, NY 10014
212-929-3778
Blacklight kits.

Talas
213 W. 35th St.
New York, NY 10001
212-736-7744
Archival storage supplies.

University Products, Inc.
517 Main St.
Holyoke, MA 01040
1-800-628-1912
Archival storage supplies.

Van Dyke's
P.O. Box 278
Woonsocket, SD 57385
1-800-843-3320
Lamp replacement parts and a complete line of replacement hardware.

Wei T'o Associates, Inc.
21750 Main St., #27
Matteson, IL 60443
708-747-6660
Deacidification sprays and application equipment.

William Zinsser and Co.
39 Belmont Dr.
Somerset, NJ 08875
908-469-8100
Paint and refinishing supplies.

Inventory management software

BDL Homeware
2509 N. Campbell Ave., #328
Tucson, AZ 85719
1-800-BDL-4-BDL

Collector's Marketplace
RR 1, Box 213B
Montrose, PA 18801
1-800-755-3123

InfoVision Technologies, Inc.
18 Liman St., Suite I
Westborough, MA 01581
1-800-277-9600

MSdataBase Solutions
614 Warrenton Terrace NE
Leesburg, VA 22075
1-800-407-4147
703-777-5440 (fax)

PSG-HomeCraft Software
P.O. Box 974
Tualatin, OR 97062
503-692-3732
503-692-0382 (fax)

Further Reading

Magazines

Antiques & Collecting
1006 South Michigan Ave.
Chicago, IL 60605

Art & Antiques
2100 Powers Ferry Rd.
Atlanta, GA 30339

Art & Auction
P.O. Box 11344
Des Moines, IA 50340

Colonial Homes
P.O. Box 7142
Red Oak, IA 51591

The Magazine ANTIQUES
P.O. Box 10547
Des Moines, IA 50340

Smithsonian
Smithsonian Institution
P.O. Box 55593
Boulder, CO 80322-5593

Style 1900
333 N. Main St.
Lambertville, NJ 08530

Victorian Homes
P.O. Box 61
Millers Falls, MA 01349

Newspapers

Antiques and the Arts Weekly
P.O. Box 5503
Newton, CT 06470

Antiques & Collectibles
P.O. Box 1565
1000 Pioneer Way
El Cajon, CA 92022

Antiques & Collectible News
P.O. Box 529
Anna, IL 62906

Antiques and Collector's Guide
8510 Frazier Dr.
Beaumont, TX 77077

The Antique Finder Magazine
P.O. Box 16433
Panama City, FL 32406

Antique Gazette
6949 Charlotte Pike, #106
Nashville, TN 37209

Antique Press
12403 N. Florida Ave.
Tampa, FL 33612

Antique Review
P.O. Box 538
Worthington, OH 43085

Antique Shoppe
P.O. Box 2175
Keystone Heights, FL 32656

The Antique Trader Weekly
P.O. Box 1050
Dubuque, IA 52004

Antique Traveler
P.O. Box 656
115 S. Johnson
Mineola, TX 75773

Antiques & Auction News
P.O. Box 500
Mount Joy, PA 17552

Antiques & Collectibles Magazine
P.O. Box 33
Westbury, NY 11590

Antiques Today
977 Lehigh Circle
Carson City, NV 89705

Antique Week
27 N. Jefferson St.
Knightstown, IN 46148

Antiques West
3315 Sacramento St., #618
San Francisco, CA 94118

AntiqueWeek
P.O. Box 90
Knightstown, IN 46148

Auction World
417 W. Stanton
Fergus Falls, MN 56538

Indiana Antique Buyers News
P.O. Box 213
Silver Lake, IN 46982

Keystone Country Peddler
P.O. Box 467
Richmond, IL 60071

Maine Antiques Digest
911 Main St.
Waldoboro, ME 04572

MassBay Antiques
P.O. Box 192
Ipswich, MA 01938

Michigan Antiques Trading Post
132 S. Putnam
Williamston, MI 48895

MidAtlantic Antiques
P.O. Box 908
Henderson, NC 27536

New England Antiques Journal
P.O. Box 120
4 Church St.
Ware, MA 01082

New Hampshire Antiques Monthly
P.O. Box 546
Farmington, NH 03835

New York Antique Almanac
P.O. Box 335
Lawrence, NY 11559

New York City's Antique News
P.O. Box 2054
New York, NY 10159

Northeast Journal of Arts and Antiques
364 Warren St.
Hudson, NY 12534

Old Stuff
P.O. Box 1084
McMinnville, OR 97128

Old News is Good News Antiques Gazette
P.O. Box 65292
Baton Rouge, LA 70896

Renninger's Antiques Guide
P.O. Box 495
Lafayette Hill, PA 19444

Southeastern Antiques and Collectibles Monthly
Rt. 1, Box 8
Macon, GA 31210

Southern Antiques
P.O. Drawer 1107
Decatur, GA 30031

Unravel the Gavel
9 Hurricane Rd., #1
Belmont, NH 03220

Warman's Today's Collector
Krause Publications
700 E. State St.
Iola, WI 54990

Newsletters

American Bungalow News
P.O. Box 756
Sierra Madre, CA 91025

Antiques & Collectors Reproduction Newsletter
P.O. Box 71174
Des Moines, IA 50325

Farm Antique News
812 N. Third St.
Tarkio, MO 64491

Kovels' on Antiques and Collectibles
P.O. Box 420347
Palm Coast, FL 32142

Orientalia Journal
P.O. Box 94
Little Neck, NY 11363

Books

Andrews, John. *Antique Furniture: Starting to Collect.* Wappinger Falls: Antique Collectors Club, 1998.

Blade, Timothy Trent. *Antique Collecting.* Ames: Iowa State University Press, 1989.

Butler, Joseph T. *Field Guide to American Antique Furniture: A Visual System for Identifying the Style of Virtually Any Piece of American Antique Furniture.* New York: Facts On File Publications, 1985.

Carter, Mary Randolph. *American Junk: How to Hunt for, Haggle Over, Rescue and Transform America's Forgotten Treasure.* New York: Penguin USA, 1997.

Emmerling, Mary. *Mary Emmerling's New Country Collecting.* New York: Clarkson Potter, 1996.

Fairbanks, Jonathan L.; and Bates, Elizabeth Bidwell. *American Furniture: 1620 to the Present.* New York: Richard Marek Publishers, Inc., 1981.

Hiesinger, Kathryn B. and George H. Marcus. *Antiquespeak: A Guide to the Styles, Techniques, and Materials of the Decorative Arts.* New York: Abbeville Press, 1997.

Jenkins, Emyl. *Emyl Jenskins' Guide to Buying and Collecting Early American Furniture.* New York: Crown Publishers, Inc., 1991.

Kovel, Ralph and Terry. *Kovels' Guide to Selling, Buying, and Fixing Antiques and Collectibles.* New York: Crown Trade Paperbacks.

Kovel, Ralph M. and Terry H. *Kovels' Antiques & Collectibles Price List.* New York: Three Rivers Press.

Loomis, Frank Farmer. *Is it Antique Yet?* Alexander: Alexander Books, 1998.

Marion, John L. *The Best of Everything.* New York: Simon and Schuster, 1989.

Miller, Judith. *Miller's Antiques Encyclopedia.* London: Mitchell Beazley, 1998.

Miller, Judith. *Miller's Understanding Antiques.* Wappinger Falls: Antique Collector Club, 1997.

Peake, Jacquelyn. *How to Start a Home-Based Antiques Business—2nd Edition.* Old Saybrook: The Globe Pequot Press, 1997.

Rinker, Harry L. *How to Make the Most of Your Investments in Antiques and Collectibles.* New York: Arbor House, 1988.

Stoddard, Alexandra. *Open Your Eyes: 1,000 Simple Ways to Bring Beauty into Your Home and Life Every Day.* New York: William Morrow and Company, Inc.

Vesely, Milan. *Antiques for Amateurs: Secrets to Successful Antiquing.* Iola: Krause Publications, 1999.

Major Auction Houses, Directories, Markets, and Shows

Auction houses

Alderfer Auction Company
501 Fairgrounds Rd.
Hatfield, PA 19440
215-393-3000
215-368-9055 (fax)

American Social History
4025 Saline St.
Pittsburgh, PA 15217
412-421-5230
412-421-0903 (fax)

American West Archives
P.O. Box 100
Cedar City, UT 84721
435-586-9497
435-586-6227 (fax)

Apple Tree Auction Center
1616 W. Church St.
Newark, OH 43055
740-344-9449
740-344-3673 (fax)

Baltimore Book Company
2114 N. Charles St.
Baltimore, MD 21218
410-659-0550

Barry S. Slosberg, Inc.
2501 E. Ontario St.
Philadelphia, PA 19106
215-425-7030

Michael Bennett Auctions
165 Locust St.
Dover, NH 03820
603-742-9955
603-742-2992 (fax)

Frank H. Boos Gallery
420 Enterprise Ct.
Bloomfield Hills, MI 48302
248-332-1500
248-332-6370 (fax)

Bowers and Merena
61 S. Main St.
Wolfeboro, NH 03894
603-569-5095
603-569-5319 (fax)

Butterfield & Butterfield
220 San Bruno Ave.
San Francisco, CA 94103
415-861-7500
415-861-8951 (fax)

Castner Auction and Appraisal Service
6 Wantage Ave.
Branchville, NJ 07826
973-948-3668
973-948-3919 (fax)

W.E. Channing and Co.
53 Old Santa Fe Trail
Santa Fe, NM 87501
505-988-1078
505-988-3879 (fax)

Christie's
502 Park Avenue
New York, NY 10022
212-546-1000
212-980-8163 (fax)
www.christies.com

David M. Cobb Auction Service
1909 Harrison Rd.
Johnstown, OH 43031
740-964-0444
740-927-7701 (fax)

Collector's Auction Service
RR2, Box 432 Oakwood Rd.
Oil City, PA 16301
814-677-6070
814-677-6166 (fax)

Collector's Sales and Service
575 E. Main
Middletown, RI 02842
401-849-5012
401-846-6156 (fax)
www.antiquechina.com

Samuel Cottone Auctions
15 Genesee
Mt. Morris, NY 14510
716-658-3180
716-658-3152 (fax)

Copake Country Auction
Old Rt. 22, Box H
Copake, NY 12516
518-329-1142

Dawson's
128 American Rd.
Morris Plains, NJ 07950
973-984-6900
973-984-6956 (fax)
www.idt.net/~dawson1

Jim Depew Galleries
1860 Piedmont Rd. NE
Atlanta, GA 30324
404-874-2286

William Doyle Galleries
175 East 87th St.
New York, NY 10128
212-427-2730
212-369-0892 (fax)
www.doylegalleries.com

DuMouchelle Art Gallery
409 E. Jefferson Ave.
Detroit, MI 48226
313-963-6255

Dunbars Gallery
76 Haven St.
Milford, MA 01757
508-634-8697
508-634-8698 (fax)

Dunnings Auction Service
755 Church Rd.
Elgin, IL 60123
847-741-3483
www.dunnings.com

Early Auction Company
123 Main St.
Milford, OH 45150
513-831-4833
513-831-1441 (fax)

Robert C. Eldred Co., Inc.
P.O. Box 796
1483 Rt. 6A
East Dennis, MA 03641
508-385-3116
508-385-7201 (fax)

F.O. Bailey Co.
141 Middle St.
Portland, ME 04141
207-774-1479
207-774-7914 (fax)

Ken Farmer Auctions and Estates LLC
105A Harrison St.
Radford, VA 24141
540-639-0939
540-639-1759 (fax)
www.kenfarmer.com

Fink's Off the Wall Auction
108 East 7th St.
Lansdale, PA 19446
215-855-9732
www.finksauction.com

Frasher's Doll Auctions
Rt. 1, Box 142
Oak Grove, MO 64075
816-625-3786
816-625-6079 (fax)

Freeman Fine Arts of Philadelphia
1808 Chestnut St.
Philadelphia, PA 19103
215-563-9275
215-563-8236 (fax)

Garth's
2690 Stratford Rd.
Delaware, OH 43015
614-362-4771
614-363-0164 (fax)

Glass Works Auctions
P.O. Box 180
East Greenville, PA 18041
215-679-5849
215-679-3068 (fax)

Great Gatsby's
5070 Peachtree Industrial Blvd.
Atlanta, GA 30341
1-800-428-7297
404-457-7250 (fax)

Greenberg Auctions
7566 Main St.
Sykesville, MD 21784
401-795-7447

Green Valley Auctions, Inc.
Rt. 2, Box 320
Mt. Crawford, VA 22841
703-434-4260
703-434-0309 (fax)

Harris Auction Galleries, Inc.
875 N. Howard St.
Baltimore, MD 21201
410-728-7040
410-728-0449 (fax)

Gene Harris Family Antique Auction Center
203 S. 18th Ave.
Marshalltown, IA 50158
515-752-0600

Hart Galleries
2301 S. Voss Rd.
Houston, TX 77057
713-266-3500

Hakes' Americana and Collectibles
P.O. Box 1444
York, PA 17405
717-848-1333
717-852-0344 (fax)

H.R. Harmer Inc.
3 W. 28th St.
New York, NY 10016
212-532-3700
212-447-5625 (fax)

Willis Henry Associates
22 Main St.
Marshfield, MA 02050
781-834-7774
781-826-3520 (fax)

Jackson Auction Co.
2229 Lincoln St.
Cedar Falls, IA 50613
319-277-2256
319-277-1252 (fax)
www.jacksonsauction.com

James D. Julia, Inc.
Route 201, Skowhegan Rd.
Fairfield, ME 04937
207-453-7125
207-453-2502 (fax)

William J. Jenack Auctioneers and Appraisers
37 Elkay Dr.
Chester, NY 10918
914-469-9095
914-469-7129 (fax)

Joy Luke Fine Arts Brokers
300 E. Grove St.
Bloomington, IL 61701
309-828-5533
309-829-2266 (fax)

Charles E. Kirtley
P.O. Box 2273
Elizabeth City, NC 27906
252-335-1262
252-335-4441 (fax)

L.A. Landry Antiques
164 Main St.
Essex, MA 01929
978-768-6233

Lincoln Galleries
225 Scotland Rd.
Orange, NJ 07050
973-677-2000

Los Angeles Modern Auctions
P.O. Box 462006
Los Angeles, CA 90046
323-845-9456
323-845-9601 (fax)
www.lamodern.com

Majolica Auctions
200 N. Main
Wolcottville, IN 46795
219-854-2859
219-854-3979 (fax)

Manion's Militaria and Antiques
P.O. Box 12214
Kansas City, KS 66112
913-299-6692
913-299-6792 (fax)

Mark Vail Auction Co.
Kelly Ave., P.O. Box 956
Pine Brush, NY 12566
914-744-2120
914-744-2450 (fax)

Martin Auction Co., Inc.
383 U.S. Highway 51 S.
Clinton, IL 61727
217-935-8211
217-768-7714 (fax)

Morton M. Goldberg Auction Galleries
547 Baronne St.
New Orleans, LA 70113
504-282-7611
504-592-2311 (fax)

Neal Auction Company
4038 Magazine St.
New Orleans, LA 70115
504-899-5329
504-897-3808 (fax)

Nutmeg Auction Service
661 Washington St.
Woodbury, CT 06798
203-263-5599
203-264-6160 (fax)

Norton Auctioneers of Michigan, Inc.
Pearl at Monroe
Coldwater, MI 49036
517-279-9191
517-279-9063 (fax)

O'Gallerie, Inc.
228 NE 7th St.
Portland, OR 97232
503-238-0202
503-236-8211 (fax)

Richard Opfer Auctioneering, Inc.
1919 Greenspring Dr.
Lutherville Timonium, MD 21093
410-252-5035
410-252-5863 (fax)

Pettigrew's
1645 S. Tejon St.
Colorado Springs, CO 80906
719-633-7963
719-633-5035 (fax)

Phillips Sons & Neale, Inc.
406 E. 79th St.
New York, NY 10021
212-570-2207

Slater's Americana
5335 North Tacoma Ave., #24
Indianapolis, IN 46220
317-257-0863
317-254-9167 (fax)

Skinner, Inc.
The Heritage on the Garden
63 Park Plaza
Boston, MA 02116
617-350-5400

R.M. Smythe and Co., Inc.
26 Broadway, #271
New York, NY 10004
212-943-1880
212-908-4047 (fax)

Swann Galleries
104 E. 25th St.
New York, NY 10010
212-254-4710
212-979-1017 (fax)

Sotheby's
1334 York Ave.
New York, NY 10021
212-606-7000
www.sothebys.com

Superior Stamp and Coin
9478 West Olympic Blvd.
Beverly Hills, CA 90212
1-800-421-0754
213-203-0496 (fax)

Treadway Gallery
2029 Madison Rd.
Cincinnati, OH 45208
513-321-6742
513-871-7722 (fax)

Waverly Auctions, Inc.
4931 Cordell Ave.
Bethesda, MD 20814
301-951-8883
301-718-8375 (fax)

Weschler's
909 E. Street NW
Washington, DC 20004
202-628-1281
202-628-2366 (fax)

Winter Associates
21 Cooke St.
Plainville, CT 06062
860-793-0288
860-793-8288 (fax)

York Town Auctions, Inc.
1625 Haviland Rd.
York, PA 17404
717-751-0211
717-767-7729 (fax)

Young Fine Art, Inc.
P.O. Box 313
North Berwick, ME 03906
207-676-3104
207-676-3105 (fax)

Directories

Clark's Flea Market U.S.A.
419 Garcon Point Rd.
Milton, FL 32580
904-623-0794

A national directory of flea markets and swap
meets, $8.50 per issue or $30 per year (four issues)

The Official Directory to U.S. Flea Markets
House of Collectibles
201 E. 50th St.
New York, NY 10022
212-751-2600

A directory that provides essential information
about flea markets nationwide, $6.99

Markets

A–Z Swap
1697 Clearwater Largo Rd., Clearwater, Fla.
813-586-4467

Monday–Friday, 10 A.M.–5 P.M.,
Saturday, 10 A.M.–4 P.M.

Ann Arbor Antiques Market
5055 Ann Arbor Saline Rd., Ann Arbor, Mich.
850-984-0122
Third Sunday April through October

Georgetown Flea Market
Wisconsin Street between S and T Streets,
Washington, D.C.
202-223-0289
Sundays from March through Dec. 25,
9 A.M. to 5 P.M.

Long Beach Outdoor Antiques and
Collectibles Market
Veterans Memorial Stadium on Conant Street
between Lakewood and Clark Boulevards, Long
Beach, Calif.
213-655-5703
Third Sunday of every month, 6:30 A.M.–3 P.M.

Mile Hi Flea Market
7007 E. 88th Ave., Henderson, Colo.
Every Wed., Sat., Sun.

Pasadena City College Flea Market
1570 E. Colorado Ave., Pasadena, Calif.
818-585-7906
First Sunday of every month, 8 A.M.–3 P.M.

Rose Bowl Flea Market
100 Rose Bowl Dr., Pasadena, Calif.
213-587-5100/213-588-4411
Second Sunday of every month, 9 A.M.–3 P.M.

Santa Monica Outdoor Antique and
Collectible Market
South side of the Santa Monica Airport on Airport
Avenue off Bundy Avenue, Santa Monica, Calif.
213-933-2511
Fourth Sunday of every month, 6 A.M.–3 P.M.

Shows

January

Americana at the Piers
New York, N.Y.
212-255-0002

Antiques at the Other Armory
New York, N.Y.
212-255-0002

Coconut Grove Antiques Show
Miami, Fla.
703-780-9200

Mancuso Antiques Show
Wilmington, Del.
215-862-5828

New York Ceramics Fair
New York, N.Y.
301-924-5002

New York Winter Show
New York, N.Y.
718-292-7392

Sarasota Antiques Show and Market
Sarasota, Fla.
954-563-6747

The Pride of Dixie Show
Atlanta, Ga.
770-279-9853

West Palm Beach Antique Show
West Palm Beach, Fla.
561-483-4047

February

Antiques and Garden Show of Nashville
Nashville, Tenn.
615-254-6785

Gramercy Garden Antiques Show
New York, N.Y.
212-255-0002

Mancuso's Willamsburg Show
Williamsburg, Va.
215-862-5828

Martinsville Antiques Show
Martinsville, N.J.
215-862-5828

Nashville Winter Antiques Week
Nashville, Tenn.
615-297-1029

New England Antiques Show
Wilmington, Mass.
207-563-1013

North Palm Beach Antiques Show
North Palm Beach, Fla.
954-943-2533

March

D.C. Spring Antiques Show
Washington, D.C.
301-924-5002

Indianapolis Art and Antiques Show
Indianapolis, Ind.
301-924-5002

Mid-Atlantic Scientific Associates Show
Somerset, N.J.
301-384-1394

New England Antiques Show
Hartford, Conn.
207-563-1013

Triple Pier Expo
New York, N.Y.
212-255-0002

April
Atlantique City
Atlantic City, N.J.
1-800-526-2724

Bustamante Antiques Show
San Francisco, Calif.
209-358-3134

Chicago Toy Show
Kane County Fairgrounds
St. Charles, Ill.
847-526-1645

Melbourne Antiques Show
Melbourne, Fla.
561-483-4047

Mid-West Antiques Show
Cedar Rapids, Iowa
319-643-2065

Philadelphia Antiques Show
Philadelphia, Penn.
215-387-3500

Portsmouth Antiques Show
Portsmouth, N.H.
207-625-3577

Round Top Texas Antiques Show
Round Top, Tex.
281-493-5501

May

Brimfield's Heart-of-the-Mart Show
Baimfield, Mass.
413-245-9556

Country Heritage Antiques Show
Greenwood, Mo.
816-537-7822

Heritage Antiques Show
Fishersville, Va.
804-846-7452

Morristown Antiques Show and Sale
Morristown, N.J.
212-255-0002

Savannah Antiques Show
Savannah, Ga.
561-483-4047

Springfield Antiques Market and Show
Springfield, Ohio
937-325-0053

Town and Country Show
Rockville, Md.
703-780-9200

June

Drummer Boys Antiques Show
Topsfield, Mass.
978-532-5266

Lake Forest Academy Antiques Show
Lake Forest, Ill.
847-234-3210

Liberty Super Collectibles Expo
Liberty State Park, N.Y.
212-255-0002

July
Antiques in the Churchyard
Vista, N.Y.
914-273-4667

Brimfield Market
Brimfield, Mass.
413-245-7479

Cape May Antiques Fair
Cape May, N.J.
212-255-0002

Maine Antiques Dealers Association Antiques Show
Portland, Maine
207-563-3897

Pappabello Antiques Show and Sale
Cleveland, Ohio
301-924-5002

The Pride of Dixie Show
Atlanta, Ga.
770-279-9853

August
Antiques Weekend in Sommerset
Somerset, N.Y.
212-255-0020

Baltimore Summer Antiques Fair
Baltimore, Md.
301-924-5002

Lee District Summer Antiques Show and Sale
Alexandria, Va.
301-924-5002

Madison-Bouckville Antiques Show
Madison, N.Y.
315-824-2462

September
Antiques Extravaganza
Greenville, S.C.
336-924-4359

Armacost Antiques Show
Chevy Chase, Md.
410-435-2292

Chevy Chase Antiques Show
Chevy Chase, Md.
410-652-8480

Delaware Coast Antiques Show
Rehoboth Beach, Del.
302-875-5326

Great American Country Fair
Mahwah, N.J.
212-255-0002

Great Plains Antiques Show
Wichita, Kans.
316-942-3499

Southern Oregon Antiques Show
Medford, Ore.
541-535-1231

Theta Charity Antiques Show
Houston, Tex.
713-942-8699

Renningers Antiques Show
Kutztown, Penn.
570-385-0104

Waterloo Antiques Fair
Stanhope, N.J.
212-255-0002

York Antiques Show
York, Penn.
1-888-878-9675

October
Cleveland Fall Papabello Show
Cleveland, Ohio
301-924-5002

Dulles International Fall Antiques Show and Sale
Chantilly, Va.
301-924-5002

Gramercy Park Modern Show
New York, N.Y.
212-255-0020

Gramercy Park Antiques and Textile Show
New York, N.Y.
212-255-0002

Round Top Antiques Show
Round Top, Tex.
1-800-947-5799

Forbes and Turner Antiques Show
Hartford, Conn.
207-767-3967

Washington Antiques Show
Washington, D.C.
301-924-5002

November
Allentown Antique Toy Show and Sale
Allentown, Penn.
610-821-7730

Hart Antiques Show
Cincinnati, Ohio
513-281-0022

Old Lace and Linen Fair
Marietta, Ga.
954-742-4796

Pompano Antiques Show
Pompano Beach, Fla.
954-943-2533

Towson Thanksgiving Antiques Fair
Towson, Md.
301-924-5002

Triple Pier Expo
New York, N.Y.
212-255-0002

December

D.C. Armory Winter Antiques Fair
Washington, D.C.
301-924-5002

Hart Antiques Show
Cincinnati, Ohio
513-281-0022

New England Antiques Show
Hartford, Conn.
207-563-1013

Scott Antique Markets
Columbus, Ohio
740-569-4112

Vero Beach Antiques Show
Vero Beach, Fla.
954-943-2533

Internet Resources

Directories and clearinghouses

www.antiqibles.com

A directory of dealers, malls, flea markets, and online auctions with active links to businesses listed.

www.antiques-n-auctions.com

A directory of dealers, shows, flea markets, and antiques malls.

www.antiqnet.com

A popular directory with news about upcoming events, national shows promoters, dealers, and appraisers. Features links to businesses and associations.

www.antiqueresources.com

A clearinghouse of information about dealers, shows, flea markets, and antiques malls.

www.antiqueweb.com

A directory featuring news articles and press releases from the antiques and collectibles marketplace. Also provides good links to malls, dealers, and no-fee online auctions.

www.antiquesworld.com
Links to the antiques and collectibles marketplace, bookstores, news lists, news stories, and classified advertising.

www.classifieds2000.com
Classified ad listings.

www.collectoronline.com
A good online source for information on collectors' clubs online.

www.collectors.org
The official Web site of the National Association of Collectors, with information on shows, clubs, flea markets and other areas of interest to collectors.

www.CollectorsWeb.com
A collecting Web site that also features a message board where collectors can chat.

www.curioscape.com
A directory of dealers, shops, and miscellaneous antiques resources.

www.switchboard.com
White and yellow pages.

www.TIAS.com
A popular directory with links to dealers, malls, resources (including the Kovels' online price guide), and an extensive calendar of upcoming events.

General resources

http://aic.standord.edu
The Web site for the American Institute for Conservation of Historic and Artistic Works.

www.amnumsoc.org
The Web site for the American Numismatic Society.

www.appraisers.org
The Web site for the American Society of Appraisers.

www.artdealers.org
The Web site for the Art Dealers Association of America

www.copernic.com
The Web site for Copernic 99, a metasearch agent that speeds up Internet searches by compiling information from several search engines at the same time.

www.fraud.org
The Web site for the National Fraud Information Center, an arm of the National Consumer's League.

www.kovels.com
The online price guide operated by antiques and collectibles experts Ralph and Terry Kovel. Requires payment of a fee after a free trial period.

www.askjeeves.com
The Web site for AskJeeves, another metasearch engine that can speed up an Internet search by compiling information from several search engines at the same time.

www.isa-appraisers.org
The homepage for the International Society of Appraisers. This site can help you find member appraisers and provides other useful information.

www.silversmithing.com
The Web site for the Society of American Silversmiths. Contains thorough information on sterling silver care.

http://palimpsest.stanford.edu/icom/vlmp
Known as the Virtual Library Museum page.
Provides links to some of the world's best museums
and information about exhibitions.

Newspapers and trade periodicals

www.maineantiquedigest.com
Maine Antique Digest's online version, with an extensive calendar of shows and auctions, industry information, various stories on the industry, and links to
advertisers. Includes a price guide for popular collecting categories.

www.thebee.com
The online version of *Antiques and the Arts Weekly* is
available at this site. Contents include information
on art galleries, antiques, auction results, a calendar
of upcoming shows and auctions, and links to eBay,
eHammer, and OnlinePriceGuide.com.

www.the-forum.com
Advertiser-sponsored links to information about arts
and collectibles. This site also has a classified ad section, a museum locator, dealer locator, and a link to
the Web site for *Unravel the Gavel*, the popular New
England area newspaper that tracks the auction
business in the Northeast.

Online auctions

www.amazon.com
Began as a bookseller, but has expanded its business
to online auctions of collectibles, personal property,
and antiques.

www.sothebys.amazon.com
The joint venture for the sale of fine arts, col-
lectibles, and antiques established in 1999 between
Sotheby's and Amazon.com.

www.ebay.com
The preeminent place on the World Wide Web for auctions of all kinds, including collectibles and antiques.

www.butterfields.com
The home Web site for Butterfield & Butterfield, the distinguished San Francisco auction house specializing in fine arts and antiques.

www.christies.com
The homepage for Christie's, the international auction house. A source for information about upcoming auctions, auction results, current and archived catalogues, and other services.

www.doylegalleries.com
The home page for William Doyle Galleries. Provides access to auction calendars, catalogs, and other services offered by this internationally recognized firm.

www.ehammer.com
One of the original online auction companies; organized much like eBay or Amazon.com, but with a focus on American, British, and European antiques.

www.hometown.aol.com/skinnauct
A Web site offered through America Online that allows entry into Skinner Inc.'s auction house in Boston, Mass. Skinner's is considered to be one of the leading auctioneers of fine art in the United States.

www.icollector.com
The premier international antiques market Web site, with links to dealers across the U.K., Australia, Canada, and Europe. An excellent source for online auctions of fine antiques, auction results, catalogues, antiques publications, and news.

www.livebid.com

The auction facilitator that allows users to participate in live estate auctions conducted by such firms as Noel Barrett Auctions, David Rago Arts, T.W. Conroy, and many others.

www.sothebys.com

The primary source for information about upcoming auctions, auction results, access to current and archived catalogues, and other services offered by Sotheby's.

www.uTrade.com

An online auction featuring a wide variety of collectibles and antiques.

Online escrow services

The firms listed below all facilitate e-commerce transactions between buyers and sellers.

    www.iescrow.com

    www.trade-direct.com

    www.tradesafe.com

New information is also constantly being added to the Internet. If you can't find what you're looking for with one search service, try your search using another one, or use a meta search service, such as Metacrawler (www.metacrawler.com), Dogpile (www.dogpile.com), AskJeeves (www.askjeeves.com), or Copernic 99 (www.copernic.com).

It's also possible to find online collecting communities by searching other antiques-related sites, and it's a good idea to keep checking sites that you like because content is constantly being added to the Internet. For example, one of my recent searches turned up a community center, expert chat, and bulletin boards at David Rago's Web site (www.ragoarts.com.)—all of them added since my last visit there.

Major price guides available online include the one maintained by the *Maine Antique Digest* (www.maineantiquedigest.com). The Kovels also have a free online guide (www.kovels.com) that includes listings for more than 200,000 items. Specialty price guides are coming online as well; the Slawinski Auction Company (www.slawinski.com) recently launched one dedicated solely to Victorian furniture and accessories. Every article listed is illustrated by professional photographs that allow the buyer to compare the condition as well as the price of similar objects.

Museums also are mounting efforts to make their information and services more accessible to the public. The American Association of Museums (aam-us.org), for example, is the sponsor of the Museum Digital Library Collection (http://museumlicensing.org), which was formed to make the information resources of museums available to a wider public through digitized collections. It's also where you can find links to hundreds of other museums with Internet presences.

Usenet Newsgroups
Rec.antiques
A general discussion area.

Rec.antiques.marketplace.
For buying and selling antiques and collectibles.

A

The *Unofficial Guide*™ Reader Questionnaire

If you would like to express your opinion about collecting antiques or this guide, please complete this questionnaire and mail it to:

The *Unofficial Guide*™ Reader Questionnaire
Macmillan Lifestyle Group
1633 Broadway, floor 7
New York, NY 10019-6785

Gender: ___ M   ___ F

Age: ___ Under 30   ___ 31–40   ___ 41–50
___ Over 50

Education: ___ High school   ___ College
___ Graduate/Professional

What is your occupation?

_____

How did you hear about this guide?
___ Friend or relative
___ Newspaper, magazine, or Internet
___ Radio or TV
___ Recommended at bookstore
___ Recommended by librarian
___ Picked it up on my own
___ Familiar with the *Unofficial Guide*™ travel series

Did you go to the bookstore specifically for a book on collecting antiques? Yes ___   No ___

Have you used any other Unofficial Guides™?
Yes ___   No ___

If Yes, which ones?

_____
_____
_____

What other book(s) on collecting antiques have you purchased? _____
_____
_____

Was this book:
____ more helpful than other(s)
____ less helpful than other(s)

Do you think this book was worth its price?
Yes ____   No ____

Did this book cover all topics related to collecting antiques adequately?
Yes ____   No ____

Please explain your answer:
_____
_____
_____

Were there any specific sections in this book that were of particular help to you?   Yes ____   No ____

Please explain your answer:
_____
_____
_____

On a scale of 1 to 10, with 10 being the best rating, how would you rate this guide? ____

What other titles would you like to see published in the *Unofficial Guide*™ series?
_____
_____

Are Unofficial Guides™ **readily available in your area?**   Yes ____   No ____

Other comments:
_____
_____
_____
_____

Get the inside scoop...with the *Unofficial Guides*™!

Health and Fitness

The Unofficial Guide to Alternative Medicine
ISBN: 0-02-862526-9 Price: $15.95

The Unofficial Guide to Conquering Impotence
ISBN: 0-02-862870-5 Price: $15.95

The Unofficial Guide to Coping with Menopause
ISBN: 0-02-862694-x Price: $15.95

The Unofficial Guide to Cosmetic Surgery
ISBN: 0-02-862522-6 Price: $15.95

The Unofficial Guide to Dieting Safely
ISBN: 0-02-862521-8 Price: $15.95

The Unofficial Guide to Having a Baby
ISBN: 0-02-862695-8 Price: $15.95

The Unofficial Guide to Living with Diabetes
ISBN: 0-02-862919-1 Price: $15.95

The Unofficial Guide to Overcoming Arthritis
ISBN: 0-02-862714-8 Price: $15.95

The Unofficial Guide to Overcoming Infertility
ISBN: 0-02-862916-7 Price: $15.95

Career Planning

The Unofficial Guide to Acing the Interview
ISBN: 0-02-862924-8 Price: $15.95

The Unofficial Guide to Earning What You Deserve
ISBN: 0-02-862523-4 Price: $15.95

The Unofficial Guide to Hiring and Firing People
ISBN: 0-02-862523-4 Price: $15.95

Business and Personal Finance

The Unofficial Guide to Investing
ISBN: 0-02-862458-0 Price: $15.95

The Unofficial Guide to Investing in Mutual Funds
ISBN: 0-02-862920-5 Price: $15.95

The Unofficial Guide to Managing Your Personal Finances
ISBN: 0-02-862921-3 Price: $15.95

The Unofficial Guide to Starting a Small Business
ISBN: 0-02-862525-0 Price: $15.95

Home and Automotive

The Unofficial Guide to Buying a Home
ISBN: 0-02-862461-0 Price: $15.95

The Unofficial Guide to Buying or Leasing a Car
ISBN: 0-02-862524-2 Price: $15.95

The Unofficial Guide to Hiring Contractors
ISBN: 0-02-862460-2 Price: $15.95

Family and Relationships

The Unofficial Guide to Childcare
ISBN: 0-02-862457-2 Price: $15.95

The Unofficial Guide to Dating Again
ISBN: 0-02-862454-8 Price: $15.95

The Unofficial Guide to Divorce
ISBN: 0-02-862455-6 Price: $15.95

The Unofficial Guide to Eldercare
ISBN: 0-02-862456-4 Price: $15.95

The Unofficial Guide to Planning Your Wedding
ISBN: 0-02-862459-9 Price: $15.95

Hobbies and Recreation

The Unofficial Guide to Finding Rare Antiques
ISBN: 0-02-862922-1 Price: $15.95

The Unofficial Guide to Casino Gambling
ISBN: 0-02-862917-5 Price: $15.95

All books in the *Unofficial Guide*™ series are available at your local bookseller, or by calling 1-800-428-5331.